D1617594

LINCOLN
APOSTATE

LINCOLN APOSTATE

THE MATSON SLAVE TRIAL

CHARLES R. McKIRDY

UNIVERSITY PRESS OF MISSISSIPPI / JACKSON

www.upress.state.ms.us

The University Press of Mississippi is a member of the Association of
American University Presses.

Copyright © 2011 by Charles R. McKirdy
All rights reserved
Manufactured in the United States of America

First printing 2011

∞

Library of Congress Cataloging-in-Publication Data

McKirdy, Charles Robert, 1943–
Lincoln apostate : the Matson slave case / Charles R. McKirdy.
p. cm.
Includes bibliographical references and index.
ISBN 978-1-60473-985-5 (cloth : alk. paper) — ISBN 978-1-60473-987-9
(ebook : alk. paper) 1. Bryant, Jane—Trials, litigation, etc. 2. Matson,
Robert. 1796–1859—Trials, litigation, etc. 3. Slavery—Illinois—
Coles County—Legal status of slaves in free states—Cases. 4.
Habeas corpus—Illinois—Coles County—Cases. 5. Lincoln, Abraham,
1809–1865—Career in law. I. Title.
KF228.B778M38 2011
306.3'620977372—dc22   2010038782

British Library Cataloging-in-Publication Data available

To my wife, Kathie,
for forty wonderful reasons and still counting

CONTENTS

ACKNOWLEDGMENTS

WRITING A BOOK IS BY NATURE A SOLITARY PURSUIT, BUT ONE THAT I would have found impossible to do without "a little help from my friends." I was lucky to have many. I start with the late Clarence Ver Steeg of Northwestern University, a truly remarkable man, who never stopped teaching me things worth learning. Then there is my sister, Agnes Greenhall, who took time off from her editorial duties at the *New York Times* to offer gentle suggestions, and Professor Gordon McKinney, who critiqued an early version of the book to the great benefit of the final product. I cannot say enough good things about Daniel R. Coquillette, professor of law at Boston College Law School and scholar extraordinaire, whose gracious encouragement made anything seem possible.

Like all who write about the past, I owe a debt to people whom I have never met—those historians who came before me and lit a path to guide my way. That indebtedness extends as well to the librarians of the Library of Congress, the Abraham Lincoln Presidential Library, the Chicago Historical Society, Northwestern University, the University of San Diego Law School, the University of California at San Diego, and the Rancho Bernardo branch of the San Diego Public Library. So too to those enthusiastic yet careful part-time local and family historians, epitomized by Dorothy Burditt, Linda Kern Moore, Carol Doward, and Kit Zinser, whose research about ordinary people often gives context and dimension to the study of the lives of extraordinary ones.

Patient, professional, and good-humored, Craig W. Gill, editor-in-chief of the University Press of Mississippi, along with his staff, deftly guided me through the editorial process. Finally, I must thank my family and friends who lived with this project for a long time and, although doubtlessly weary of it, never let on, not even once.

LINCOLN
APOSTATE

INTRODUCTION

ABRAHAM LINCOLN WAS DEAD. HE HAD BEEN DEAD FOR MANY YEARS. The deification process had begun long ago. The old man did not care. He could not forgive. To his dying day, he maintained that "Lincoln arrived at the trial with chains to be used to take the slaves back to captivity."[1] He could not forget. "[J]ustice demands," he insisted, "that it be said that neither [Lincoln's] speeches nor his conduct at or during the litigation was worthy of his name and subsequent fame."[2]

The old man was Dr. Hiram Rutherford. He died in 1900 after sixty years as a physician in Coles County, Illinois. The "litigation" in question was a trial in the Coles County Circuit Court in 1847. In that trial, Abraham Lincoln represented a slave owner named Robert Matson in his efforts to recover five slaves—a mother and her four children—who had escaped from slavery on Matson's Illinois farm and taken refuge with Dr. Rutherford. The physician had known Abraham Lincoln back then—known him and liked him. He was angry and dumbfounded when Lincoln chose to take Matson's side and argue that the fugitives be returned to slavery.

Historians differ in their reactions to Lincoln's role in the so-called "Matson Slave Case." Some share Rutherford's bewilderment. To some, Lincoln's actions seem a profound aberration in the life of the "Great Emancipator." One of his earliest biographers, his fellow lawyer Henry Clay Whitney, described the incident as "one of the strangest episodes in Lincoln's career at the bar."[3] Writing about a century later, legal historian John J. Duff agreed. He called Lincoln's representation of Matson "one of the oddest anomalies in the life of this man of paradox."[4] Some found Lincoln's action very disturbing. In his often insightful *Lincoln and the Negro*, Benjamin Quarles mourned the episode as Lincoln's "one fall from grace" and, more recently, in a book directed at young readers, author Peter Burchard characterized it as an "inexplicable mistake."[5]

3

Historians do not like the word "inexplicable." After all, attempting to explain the past is a part of the essence of their profession, and Lincoln's representation of Robert Matson is a task certainly worthy of the attempt. Their general consensus seems to be that, when all is said and done about Lincoln and Matson, it comes down to this: "business is business." Abraham Lincoln was a lawyer, Robert Matson was a client in need of a lawyer, and everything else, in particular Lincoln's feelings about slavery, was irrelevant.

In his 1952 biography, Benjamin Thomas put it this way: Lincoln "took slave cases, like other business, as they came."[6] The great Lincoln historian David Donald agrees: "Like most other attorneys, Lincoln . . . took on whatever clients came [his] way. . . . [H]is business was law, not morality."[7] Quite recently, Brian Dirck's *Lincoln the Lawyer* reiterates this explanation: "The Matson case . . . may have given Lincoln a moment of pause before he sighed and got on with his job; but got on with his job he did. Lincoln always drew a line between the moral and legal aspects of slavery. . . ."[8]

This "line" has become a particular focus of attention—how was Lincoln able to draw such a line "between the moral and legal aspects of slavery," especially when the distinction moved from the theoretical to the actual as it did in the Matson case? In his *An Honest Calling: The Legal Practice of Abraham Lincoln*, Mark Steiner looks to find an answer in what he sees as Lincoln's Whiggish view of the legal system. Steiner argues that Lincoln viewed the legal system as a neutral means to resolve disputes and maintain order in which the lawyer's role was to effectively represent clients and not to make moral judgments about their clients' causes.[9]

Others have been less kind. They maintain that there was no "line." They contend that Lincoln's representation of Matson demonstrates that he had little or no genuine antipathy for slavery and no real empathy for its victims. Allen C. Guelzo is representative of this school of thought. In *Abraham Lincoln: Redeemer President*, Guelzo argues that Lincoln's advocacy on Matson's behalf merely underscored "his indifference to slavery as injustice to blacks."[10]

With all due respect, it is not that simple. Lincoln's actions in the Matson case defy easy explanation because not only do they seem inconsistent with many actions and statements that he made earlier and later in his career, they also seem inconsistent with one another. Lincoln did not simply opt to represent Robert Matson. That was only the beginning. After he met with Dr. Rutherford, who asked him to represent Jane and her children, Lincoln attempted to switch sides. Then, when Rutherford rejected his belated offer of assistance, Lincoln returned to Matson's corner.

Obviously, there were conflicting forces at work here. Lincoln's still inchoate attempt to reconcile slavery, morality, and law was an important factor. So too were less ideological concerns. Ambition and loyalty may have played a role. The trial took place center stage and Lincoln was not one to avoid the spotlight. Moreover, the case involved a cast of intriguing and powerful personalities. Not the least of these was an attorney named Usher Linder. A racist, a demagogue, and a drunkard, Linder was a friend of Lincoln's and his influence may have been a determining factor in Lincoln's decision to represent Matson.

The situation is further complicated by the fact that although the case involved runaway slaves, it was not a *fugitive* slave case as that term generally is understood, i.e., slaves fleeing from a slave state into a free state, and it involved law that still was in the formative stage in Illinois. Finally, the Matson trial did not take place in a vacuum. It played out against the backdrop of the race hatred, shrill arguments about slavery and morality, and deadly mob violence found in Illinois in 1847. If we are to understand what happened in Coles County in the autumn of that year and why Lincoln did what he did there, that backdrop is the best place to start.

CHAPTER 1

A DARK CANVAS

In 1847, the year that Abraham Lincoln tried the Matson case, Illinois purportedly was a "free" state. That status dated back to 1787 when the Congress of the United States adopted the Northwest Ordinance. This far-sighted legislation mandated a system for creating states out of the territory northwest of the Ohio River. Article VI of the ordinance provided that "[t]here shall be neither slavery nor involuntary servitude in the said territory, otherwise than in the punishment of crimes whereof the party shall have been duly convicted. . . ." The ordinance made it clear that Article VI was one "of compact between the original States and the people and States in the said territory," and that it would "forever remain unalterable, unless by common consent."[1] Illinois was one of the states formed out of the Northwest Territory in which slavery and involuntary servitude seemingly were forbidden.

How then to explain the last will and testament of William R. Adams of Pope County, Illinois? In his will, Mr. Adams freed Lucinda and her eight children from slavery. The will is dated December 28, 1846—almost sixty years after Article VI of the Northwest Ordinance became the law of the land.[2] Congressional edicts aside, slavery was a fact in the life of William R. Adams and in the lives of Lucinda and her eight children as it had been a fact of life in Illinois for about 150 years.

The anomaly of slavery in "free" mid-nineteenth-century Illinois stemmed from the state's location, size, configuration, and history. Although Illinois usually is considered a northern state (its soldiers wore Yankee blue in the Civil War), geographically and politically that description is not wholly accurate. Illinois is a vertical state, running north-south, and is considerably longer (about 375 miles) than it is wide (about 175 miles). This means that while northern Illinois borders on Wisconsin and the shores of Lake Michigan, southern Illinois touches Missouri and Kentucky. Cairo (pronounced "Kayro") in the state's southern tip is more than 100 miles south of Richmond, Virginia, the capital of the Confederacy. In fact, Cairo is closer to Birmingham, Alabama, than it is to Chicago, and almost one-half of Illinois, including Coles County where Lincoln argued the Matson case, is south of the Mason-Dixon Line.[3]

Slavery in Illinois can be traced back to 1719 when the "Illinois Country" belonged to the French as part of the colony La Louisiane which, anchored by New Orleans at the mouth of the Mississippi River, stretched all the way north to the Great Lakes. In that year, five hundred slaves from Santo Domingo were sold to French settlers in Illinois on the east bank of the Mississippi River.[4]

When Illinois passed to Great Britain in 1763 as a result of its victory in the French and Indian War, the slave population in Illinois increased as settlers, primarily from the southern colonies, moved into southern Illinois. Because the British government did not prohibit slavery there, these settlers brought their slaves with them. Twenty years later, when the treaty ending the American Revolution granted the United States all lands east of the Mississippi River from Spanish Florida to Canada, the state of Virginia, among others, asserted a right to thousands of square miles of this territory including what is now Illinois.[5]

In 1784, Virginia was prevailed upon to surrender its claims to the area north of the Ohio River, but it did so with several caveats. One of these was that the French, Canadian, and other inhabitants of Illinois "shall have their possessions and titles confirmed to them and be protected in the enjoyment of their rights and liberties."[6] They could keep their slaves. Arguably, there was language in the ordinance of 1787 reaffirming this promise, but, of course, it also included Article VI's prohibition of slavery in the territory.[7]

Convinced that Article VI was inimical to the growth of Illinois because it inhibited immigration from slave states, which, in the early nineteenth century were its natural sources for new settlers, some of the territory's leading citizens repeatedly petitioned Congress to repeal the provision. All of these efforts failed, but innovation is said to be the hallmark of the frontier.[8]

In 1805, the territorial government of the Indiana Territory (which then included Illinois) promulgated an indenture law that was revised and reenacted in 1809. Under the terms of these acts, a slave over the age of fifteen years could be brought into and kept in the territory if, within thirty days, he or she entered into a formal written agreement (an indenture) to serve as an indentured servant for a specified number of years. If no agreement could be reached, the master had sixty days to remove the slave from the territory. Under the law, a female indentured servant's male children were required to serve their mother's master until they were thirty, female children to age twenty-eight. Slaves under age fifteen might be brought into the territory and simply registered to serve—males to age thirty-five, females to age thirty-two.[9]

When Illinois became a territory in its own right in 1809, it adopted Indiana's indentured servant law as its own. Despite attempts to give them the trappings of arms-length transactions, by any legal definition the indentures were unconscionable. The agreement between John Beaird and "Harry, a negro boy, aged near upon sixteen" was not unusual:

> *Be it remembered that on the 17th day of October of the year 1814, personally came before me the subscriber, clerk of the court of common pleas . . . , John Beaird . . . and Harry, a negro boy, <u>aged near upon sixteen</u>, and who <u>of his own free will and accord</u>, did in my presence, agree, determine, and promise, to serve the said John Beaird, for the full space of time, and term of <u>eighty years</u> from this date. And the said John Beaird, in consideration thereof, promises to pay him, said Harry, the sum of <u>fifty dollars, at the expiration of his said service.</u>[10]*

With terms of service that often exceeded the life expectancies of the servants, Illinois's Negro indenture system was virtually identical with slavery.[11] The status was inheritable. Indentured servants were taxable property. They were used as consideration to satisfy contracts and as security for notes. They were rented out and sold with the price based on the time of service remaining on the term of indenture.[12]

Its indenture system and remaining vestiges of actual slavery were a problem in 1818 when Illinois applied for statehood and was confronted with the task of drafting a state constitution which did not run afoul of Article VI. By then, Illinois had become a territory divided on the question of involuntary servitude. While the territory's southern counties still were overwhelmingly proslavery, northern Illinois was filling up with settlers from northern states, many of whom brought with them strong antislavery sentiments.[13] This hostility focused on the indenture system especially after neighboring Indiana repealed its indenture laws.[14] The dichotomy over indentures was reflected in the membership of the territory's constitutional convention and resulted in a compromise that protected servitude as it then existed in Illinois.

The Illinois Constitution of 1818 prohibited only the *future* introduction of slavery or involuntary servitude into the state.[15] With regard to Negro indentures, the new constitution prohibited males over the age of twenty-one and females over age eighteen from being held as a servant by any indenture "hereinafter made," unless that person entered into the indenture "while in a state of perfect freedom" in return for "bona fide consideration."[16] The constitution also invalidated subsequent indentures of blacks that had been entered into out of state or which had a duration of more than one year.[17]

Again, this provision applied only to future indentures. Lest there be any confusion on the subject, the new constitution made it clear that it did not reach existing indentures and stated that "those bound to serve by contract or indenture" under existing law "shall be held to specific performance of their contracts and indentures; and such negroes and mulattoes as have been registered in conformance with the aforesaid laws, shall serve out the time appointed by said laws."[18]

Thus, the Illinois Constitution of 1818 confirmed, with minor modifications, the system of involuntary servitude then in place in Illinois. The few limitations that had been tacked on were more apparent than real. For example, the constitution stated that those who indentured themselves were entitled to "bona fide consideration" (i.e., meaningful compensation), but, in practice, this could be merely a promise of room and board, the only "consideration" most slaves could expect to receive anyway.[19] The one-year limit on new indentures quickly led to a system of yearly renewals.[20] The constitution did nothing to shorten the length of existing indentures or to alter the status of those enslaved in Illinois. In fact, it confirmed their status, incorporating it into the fundamental law of the state. Nevertheless, the new constitution passed muster with Congress. Illinois became a state. The advocates of slavery were emboldened.[21]

In 1819, the Illinois legislature passed "An Act respecting Free Negroes, Mulattos, Servants, and Slaves," which, as its name implies, regulated the activities of blacks and servants in the state and mandated punishment for those who disobeyed.[22] It represented a definite and unmistakable proslavery statement. As legal historian Paul Finkelman astutely points out: "While not explicitly declaring that slavery was still legal in Illinois, the statute recognized the existence of slaves in the state, and implied that there was nothing improper about this. Indeed, the statute underscored the presumption that the 1818 constitution was not meant to free all slaves in Illinois."[23]

The act of 1819 represented the high-water mark for the proslavery forces in Illinois. Their efforts to promulgate a new state constitution explicitly legalizing slavery in the state failed in 1824 when, voting primarily along regional lines, 57 percent of the voters cast their ballots against calling a constitutional convention.[24] Then the Illinois Supreme Court began to chip away at the varieties of servitude in the state.

At first, the court was somewhat circumspect. In a series of decisions in the 1820s, it upheld the system of black indentures, but the justices did not wear blinders.[25] A majority of the court recognized that "nothing can be further from the truth, than the idea that there could be a voluntary contract between the negro and his master."[26] The court clearly understood that the services of indentured servants "were held in the same manner that the services of absolute slaves are held."[27]

This, of course, would seem to violate the antislavery provisions of the Northwest Ordinance, but the Illinois Supreme Court ruled otherwise. The ordinance provided that its articles "shall remain unalterable unless by common consent."[28] The court held that "common consent" had been obtained with regard to black indentured servitude in Illinois when its preservation was included in the Illinois Constitution of 1818, and Congress approved that constitution by admitting Illinois into the union as a state.[29]

While the court recognized the legality and constitutionality of the state's indenture system, it was quick to use technical grounds to strike down claims in particular instances. In 1825, the court voided an indenture that had not been signed by the master.[30] In 1828, it rejected a claim to a servant by the heir of her master as being inconsistent with the state's inheritance laws.[31] In 1836, the court invalidated an indenture that was not entered into within the required time frame[32] and, in the case of *Boon v. Juliet* (1836), declared that "the children of registered [indentured] negroes and mulattoes . . . are unquestionably free."[33]

Five years later, in 1841, the court established an important precedent with regard to whether or not blacks in Illinois were presumed at law to be slave or free. The case was *Kinney v. Cook*.[34] Thomas Cook, a Negro, had sued William Kinney to recover for services that he had rendered Kinney during a period in which Kinney had "pretended to hold such plaintiff as a slave."[35] There was no evidence that Cook ever, in fact, was a slave. Kinney argued that the suit should have been dismissed because, as a black man, Cook had the burden of proving that he was *not* a slave and had failed to do so.[36]

The supreme court disagreed. In a short but surprisingly eloquent opinion, Justice Theophilus Smith declared that, unlike the rule in the southern states, Illinois law presumed that all men and women, black or white, were free:

> *With us the presumption is in favor of liberty, and the mere claim of the defendant to hold the plaintiff as a slave, and the fact of his having resided with the defendant during the time when the services were rendered, devolved no legal necessity on the plaintiff to prove his freedom. . . .*
>
> *The rule, in some or most of the slaveholding States, from consideration of public policy, is undoubtedly that the onus pro-bandi [burden of proof] in such cases, lies with the party asserting his freedom. This rule, however,*

it is conceived is founded in injustice. It is contrary to one of the fundamen-
tal principles upon which our Government is founded; and is repugnant to,
and subversive of natural right. . . .[37]

In 1845, the court abolished the last remnants of French slavery in Illinois.[38] But that was as far as it would go. Although weakened, Negro indentured servitude survived, the court reaffirming its legality in 1843.[39] Moreover, the court left the status of free blacks in Illinois untouched and unfortunate.

The simple fact was that while the white citizens of Illinois were divided over the propriety of slavery within the state, they generally were united in their antipathy toward blacks, slave or free. Furthermore, like their contemporaries in other northern states, whites in Illinois had institutionalized their antipathy into law. Beginning in the year after it had achieved statehood, Illinois enacted one law after another that restricted the rights of blacks and ignored their humanity.

In essence, the Illinois "Black Code" presumed that all Negroes and mulattos should be slaves and were to be treated as such unless they could prove otherwise.[40] The law of Illinois held that before they could settle in the state, Negroes and mulattos had to come up with a "duly authenticated" certificate of freedom from a court of record and endorsed by the clerk of the Illinois county in which they wished to reside. The law also required immigrant blacks to post a one-thousand-dollar bond for good behavior.[41] It was illegal to bring a slave into Illinois for the purpose of freeing him. Anyone who did so, if convicted, was subject to a one-hundred-dollar fine.[42]

Resident free Negroes and mulattos in Illinois were treated no better. They, too, had to file evidence of their free status with the county clerk.[43] Anyone who hired a Negro who failed to have a certificate of freedom was subject to a five-hundred-dollar fine.[44] The state constitution prohibited blacks from serving in the state militia.[45] Laws banned them from voting.[46] In judicial proceedings, blacks could not be witnesses in favor of or against whites.[47] Miscegenation was prohibited.[48] By law, custom, or practice, virtually all schools, academies, and colleges were closed to blacks (although they were required to pay school taxes).[49]

Illinois law presumed that any Negro or mulatto without a certificate of freedom was a runaway slave subject to arrest and imprisonment. "Any inhabitant" of the state was empowered to haul a person of color before a justice of the peace who had the "duty" to commit the suspect to the local sheriff's custody if the suspect could not produce a certificate of freedom. The accused then faced a year of imprisonment during which time the sheriff was to advertise "such black person or mulatto, stating a description of the most remarkable features of the supposed runaway" and to hire him or her out "for the best price he can get . . . from month to month."[50]

If a year passed and no one appeared with a verifiable claim to the prisoner, "The sheriff shall give a certificate to such black or mulatto person, who, on producing the same to the next circuit court of the county, stating the facts, and the person shall be deemed a free person, unless he shall be lawfully claimed by his proper owner or owners thereafter."[51]

Those who informed against runaway slaves were entitled to a reward.[52] Anyone who harbored a Negro or mulatto who did not have a certificate of freedom, or hired, or "in anywise [gave] sustenance" to one was subject to a five-hundred-dollar fine.[53]

With such laws in place, free blacks always were at risk. Joseph Warman found this out when he attempted to make his way from southern Illinois north to Chicago. He got as far as the town of Petersburg in Menard County in the central part of the state.[54] There, he was "arrested with force of arms," dragged before a local justice of the peace, "condemned as being a runaway slave without evidence," and "committed to the common jail."[55]

Perhaps no single episode more clearly epitomizes the attitudes of most of the people of Illinois with regard to blacks in the year of the Matson trial than the Illinois constitutional convention of 1847. The convention had not been called to discuss race issues, but given the existing constitution's provisions dealing with involuntary servitude, the state supreme court's decisions on the subject, and the climate of the times, the subject of race was bound to come up and it did.[56]

At first there was just minor skirmishing. Virtually all of the delegates agreed that the language of the 1818 constitution prohibiting slavery and involuntary servitude had to be brought in line with subsequent court decisions.[57] They quickly rejected, however, a resolution that the constitution's prohibition against slavery include language forbidding any person from being "deprived of liberty on account of color."[58]

The same swift fate met a petition from antislavery elements in Perry County "praying equal rights and privileges to all persons without distinction of color."[59] Similarly, a motion to strike the word "white" from the definition of those qualified to vote "was decided in the negative—yeas 7, nays 137."[60]

On the other side, while a sizable minority supported provisions which would have forever banned the extension of suffrage to Negroes and mulattos, prohibited them from holding public office, and made it a crime for blacks and whites to marry, these proposals died in committee.[61] Their death, however, was not due to liberal opposition, but to the fear that their inclusion was an "implied admission" that people of color enjoyed such rights as citizens of Illinois and the United States.[62]

Everything heated up considerably when Benjamin Bond, a lawyer from Clinton County, proposed a resolution that the convention's Committee on Rights be instructed "to report a provision prohibiting free Negroes from emigrating into this State, and that no person shall bring slaves into this State from other States and set them free, and that sufficient penalties be provided to effect the object in view."[63] His proposal ignited two days of sometimes acrimonious debate. This debate provides a snapshot of how, just a few months before Lincoln's involvement in the Matson trial, what one convention member described as "the best body of men ever assembled in the state" viewed African Americans in general and those who might enter the state in particular.[64] It is not an attractive picture.

Arguments in support of Bond's measure often began with a declaration of paternalistic concern for Negro welfare which, somehow, lacked the ring of true sincerity. Bond, himself, declared that "[t]here was no one who had greater desire to do justice to that class of unfortunate individuals."[65] James Washington Singleton, an exclusion advocate, talked about his "deep sympathy for slaves," while his cohort, Thomas Geddes, piously maintained that he "felt deeply for the unfortunate negro."[66] Nevertheless, despite all their professed concern, the prohibition's supporters maintained that exclusion was necessary as a matter of "self preservation."[67]

The reasons advanced in support of this need for "self preservation" differed, but all of them shared the same racist root. One professed concern was that, in Illinois, "large numbers" of free blacks "do nothing, idle away their time, and are as trifling, worthless, filthy, and degraded as in any part of the Union."[68] This charge was repeated, almost ritually, again and again—free blacks were "all idle and lazy," they were "good-for-nothing," they were "mostly, idle and worthless persons."[69]

Sometimes these assertions were coupled with accusations that it was "the custom" for southern slave owners to dump "their old and worn out negroes and those whom they emancipated" into Illinois and that settlements of free Negroes (presumably those not "old and worn out") were hotbeds of potential violence.[70] Bond claimed that "[i]n his part of the State he had seen little settlements of these free negroes spring up, and their object was to aid slaves from the south to escape their masters."[71]

Despite the Black Laws on the books, supporters of the exclusionary provision cynically argued that if free blacks were permitted to enter Illinois, they would have to be granted the same political and social rights as whites. This argument conjured up an unwelcome prospect. For example, Bond contended that "he wanted no persons to come into this State, unless they came with the right to be our equal in all things," and that he was unwilling to do this "in favor of these people."[72] James Brockman, a physician from Mt. Sterling in western Brown County, asserted that granting equal rights could not be done because "the distinction between the two races is so great as to preclude the possibility of them living together on equal terms."[73]

These were some of the more restrained comments on the subject. It got uglier. Montgomery County's James M. Davis declared that if he should ever "advocate that negroes are entitled to all the privileges of citizenship—social and political—I hope the tongue which now speaks may cleave to the roof of my mouth."[74] Singleton, the man who claimed a "deep sympathy for slaves," sarcastically advised those who opposed excluding blacks, those "so extraordinarily anxious to associate with negroes," to leave Illinois with "their favorites." In "this State," the Virginia-born delegate continued, "there are men who prefer the society of white men, and who have come here to get rid of an intolerable nuisance."[75]

Now warming to the subject, Dr. Brockman asked his colleagues whether they would "like to see their posterity sitting in a legislative assembly with a mixed delegation."[76] And, of course, there was the trusty old blunderbuss of racists everywhere. William C. Kinney, a Belleville Democrat, dragged it out and blasted away: "If we would allow the negroes any kind of equality we must admit them to our social hearth. It was then that equality commenced. We must live with them and permit them to mingle with us in our social affairs, and, also, if they desired it must not object to proposals to marry our daughters."[77]

The racism became even more blatant when George Lemon, a farmer from DeWitt County, invoked his "wit" (or at least half of it) in support of the resolution. Apparently, his remarks evoked such an uproariously sympathetic response that the convention's reporter felt compelled to make note of the fact: "In conclusion, [Lemon] said, that he did not believe [African-Americans] were altogether human beings. If any gentleman thought they were, he would ask them to look at the negro's foot (Laughter.) What was his leg doing in the middle of it? If that was not sufficient, let them go and examine their nose, (roars of laughter) then look at their lips. Why their sculls [sic] were three inches thicker than white peoples."[78]

As noted, Bond's proposal was not unopposed. A few delegates were against it for humanitarian reasons. None was more eloquent than Daniel J. Pinkney, a young preacher from Ogle County, whose words still resonate today:

The gentleman has an object in view in moving these resolutions—he would show by making them a part of our constitution—by keeping negroes out of our State under a heavy penalty, that we are determined to protect the rights of our sister states. Rights! What rights? The right to chase an oppressed and unfortunate fellow being through our territory; to drag him to prison; to beat him, and at the same time prohibit me, or any man on this floor from giving him a morsal of bread or meat, though he be starving? A right to compel us to force a perishing woman from our door; and drive her forth into the pitiless peltings of the midnight storm! Are these their rights? I can not admit them; they conflict with higher authority. They fly in the face of Jehovah. His law calls upon me to feed the hungry and succor the distressed. This with me settles all; and I shall endeavor to obey it, notwithstanding these rights.[79]

A few delegates from other northern counties followed Pinkney's lead and condemned the proposed resolution on moral or humanitarian grounds, but most were unwilling to go that far. Most arguments against the resolution were based on legal or pragmatic considerations.

Several of the resolution's foes argued that the resolution violated the Declaration of Independence and the federal constitution's requirement "that citizens of one State shall be entitled to all the privileges and immunities of the several States."[80] The majority of those who opposed the resolution took a more practical position. They contended that the inclusion of the exclusionary provision would divide the state and threaten ratification of the new constitution.[81]

Many who took this tack professed no sympathy whatsoever for free Negroes, but viewed the constitution's ratification as paramount. James M. Davis, who made it clear that he "was opposed to allowing people of color the right to vote," probably articulated the prevailing sentiment of the majority when he declared that "he was in favor of leaving the matter stand as it does in our present constitution. He had no desire to engraft anything in that constitution which would offend the people of any portion of the State."[82]

Bond's resolution was tabled for two months until a compromise could be hammered out. On August 23, 1847, he proposed a provision which would have required the legislature, at its first session, to pass legislation prohibiting Negro immigration into Illinois.[83] The provision was to be voted on separately from the rest of the constitution and only would become part of the constitution if it received a majority vote.[84] The delegates adopted the proposal with little debate and a year later, when it was submitted to the electorate, the measure was overwhelmingly approved.[85]

There was only one abolitionist at the Illinois constitutional convention in 1847.[86] This was not surprising. Although the movement for the national abolition of slavery had reached the state about ten years before and had some limited success in the northern counties, it had failed to gain much traction in Illinois.

Like most northern whites, most of those in Illinois in 1847 opposed abolitionism. The reasons for this hostility varied. For some, perhaps many in southern Illinois, southern roots and sympathies were strong factors.[87] Some working men opposed abolitionism because they feared black competition for jobs, and many northern businessmen were concerned that antislavery agitation would interfere with their commerce with the South.[88]

The abolitionist attack on established churches as "the refuge and the hiding place of the slavery Monster" disturbed many.[89] Others feared that abolitionism must inevitably lead to the breakup of the union.[90] But the fear went much deeper than this. As noted earlier, like most of the rest of the North, Illinois was permeated with racial prejudice.[91] The *National Slavery Standard* had it right when it attributed antiabolitionist sentiment to those who "are unwilling that the negroes should be turned loose to remain among us, in the full enjoyment of equal rights, in civil and religious society.[92]

Given this reality, those with political aspirations in Illinois distanced themselves from abolitionists and the abolition movement. For example, Daniel Pinkney, who, in the constitutional convention, spoke out so eloquently against the proposal that would bar free blacks from entering Illinois, made it clear that he had no use for "political abolitionists," and condemned it as a "disgrace" for any man to assist slaves to escape from their masters.[93] In the words of one astute contemporary observer, abolitionists were "equally held in disesteem by both political parties, for the simple reason that to have done otherwise would have amounted to political suicide."[94]

There also was a more ominous aspect to the question. Abolition was an emotionally charged issue in Illinois. While its proponents thundered that slavery was "an awful sin . . . in direct violation of the laws of God" and pledged "to endeavor by all means sanctioned by Law, Humanity and Religion to effect the entire Abolition of Slavery in these United States," their opponents chastised them as "dark and damnable demons of the lower regions."[95]

The antiabolitionists' vehemence went beyond rhetoric. Antiabolitionist mobs threatened abolitionists and disrupted their meetings.[96] In Peoria, a newspaper editor was run out of town when he failed to heed a citizen committee's warning not to publish anything about slavery, as it was "contrary to our interests and honor."[97] A "stranger" who circulated an abolitionist petition in

Pike County was hunted down, whipped, and ordered out of the state.[98] Elijah Lovejoy, an abolitionist newspaper editor in Alton, Illinois, was shot down by a mob that was besieging the warehouse where Lovejoy's press was stored.[99] The mob's intent was clear. During the siege, those defending the warehouse heard "[s]avage yells" threatening to "fire the building and shoot every d[amned] Abolitionist."[100]

Lovejoy was murdered in 1837. In the ten years that followed, while there were numerous assaults on abolitionists, none were killed. Nevertheless, there was a very real and readily apparent potential for a bloodbath over the issue. This was because by 1847, the year of the Matson trial, more and more people in Illinois were seeking to deal with social problems and settle their differences through recourse to extralegal remedies. Mob violence on an unprecedented scale had become endemic in Illinois and the trajectory was rising.[101] In many areas of the state, the civil authorities were helpless, anarchy reigned, and the rule of law was a chimera.

In 1841, frustrated with local law enforcement's inability to deal with outlaw gangs that had terrorized the Rock River Valley for almost a decade, local citizens in northwestern Illinois organized "Regulator" companies to deal with the problem. Taken together, the membership of these paramilitary units may have totaled a thousand, making the northwestern Illinois Regulator movement the largest vigilante movement in America since colonial times.[102]

The Regulators operated without official imprimatur. Their approach to dealing with criminal activity was simple—eliminate due process of law. If, after an examination by some Regulators, supposedly "conducted with the utmost fairness and regularity . . . it appears that the accused is one of the gang," he "is notified that he must leave this section of the country within a given number of days with an assurance that if he shall be found here, after the time fixed, he will be immediately proceeded against by the infliction of such number of lashes upon the bare back, as the committee of the society shall Order."[103]

While suspected gang members were the Regulators' prime target, they were not the only target. The Regulators also went after the outlaws' business patrons and associates.[104] The legally constituted authorities did nothing to interfere with them.[105]

Apparently, the Regulators had the support of the community. The *Galena Gazette*, for example, condoned the vigilantes' action in hanging two alleged murderers with the comment that while "[t]he violation of the law should always be condemned . . . [i]f forced to choose between <u>professed villains</u> and <u>professed honest</u> men, we shall not hesitate to be found on the side of the latter."[106] On the other hand, a few days after it had pointedly editorialized about the evils of vigilantism, the *Rockford Star's* offices were destroyed.[107]

The vigilantism in the Rock River Valley found more extreme expression hundreds of miles away in the southern tip of Illinois. In that part of the state, which is bounded on the east by the Ohio River, Hardin, Pope, and Massac counties became the battleground for the so-called "little rebellion" between another group of Regulators and the "Flatheads."[108]

Formed in 1846 to deal with the lawless element in the community, these Regulators soon alienated many law-abiding citizens who viewed the vigilantes as high-handed and dangerous. In time, as criticism of them continued to grow, the Regulators came to view all of their opponents and detractors in monolithic terms, considering them all, good men and bad, as their enemies. For whatever reason, these enemies were stuck with the unflattering sobriquet "Flatheads."[109]

According to one student of the situation, "[A] state approximating civil war between the two parties, and in time, complicated by family quarrels and political differences, degenerated into something like a general feud."[110] Local and state authorities could do little to quell the violence. When an opposition candidate was elected sheriff of Massac County, the Regulators hounded him out of the county. When some of their number were indicted, hundreds of heavily armed Regulators freed them from jail, drove off the sheriff, and drowned some members of his posse in the Ohio River. When the governor called on the state militia of Union and other nearby counties to enforce the peace, the militiamen stayed home.[111]

Finally, on February 26, 1847, the Illinois state legislature took direct aim at the Regulators, passing "An Act to Suppress Riot and regulating Companies, and maintain the Supremacy of the Laws."[112] Among other things, the statute made it a crime to coerce a confession, to forcibly compel a person to leave the state or county, to assault a witness, juror, or member of a posse, or to "try another for any real or pretended offense . . . without any authority of law . . . to do so."[113]

The legislation also established a special court to deal with the situation, and the governor dispatched a state supreme court justice to Franklin County to try those accused of assisting the Regulators.[114] After nine days of wrangling over its jurisdiction, the court adjourned and, apparently, never convened again.[115] The violence continued, only burning itself out at the end of the decade, leaving an estimated twenty people dead.[116]

Meanwhile, on the other side of the state, on the eastern bank of the Mississippi River, Hancock County was ablaze.

The causes and course of what became known as the Mormon War (1844–1846) need not concern us here. For our purposes what is important about this struggle is that as a result of two years of conflict between Mormons and anti-Mormons, Hancock County witnessed a series of shootings, burnings, and reckless violence on both sides. Joseph Smith, the leader of the Mormons in Nauvoo, was assassinated, and thousands of Mormons were driven from the state.[117]

Moreover, throughout these violent years, as in the Rock River Valley and Massac County, the lawfully constituted authorities were totally ineffective at keeping the peace. After Joseph Smith voluntarily surrendered himself into state custody, the state could not protect him. He was killed by a mob that rushed the jail where he was being held. The governor appealed to both sides to "end mob violence" as it was threatening "anarchy and ruin . . . menacing our fair form of government . . . and destroying the confidence of the patriot in the institutions of his country."[118] His plea was met only with more lawlessness.[119] When he dispatched an officer to take charge of an anti-Mormon posse, the men refused to follow his orders.[120] When he called out the militia from nearby Adams County to restore order, the company "declined to act."[121]

The conflict ended only when an anti-Mormon force of about eight hundred men, acting without any state authorization but armed with state artillery supplied by local militia companies, moved on the Mormons still in Nauvoo.[122] A short but fierce firefight ensued in which, according to one participant, the "firing of small arms was kept up with spirit, by both parties, whilst artillery on both sides, was raining down solid and grape shot."[123] When it was over four men lay dead or dying and the Mormon defenders were left with no choice but to leave the state.[124]

Its legacy of slavery, deeply imbedded racism, strident and hated voices for abolition, and the ever-present specter of unbridled mob violence were important elements of the dark canvas that was Illinois in 1847 and against which the Matson trial would be played out. To varying degrees they influenced Lincoln's approach to the law, to the practice of law, and, in particular, to his decision to represent Robert Matson.

CHAPTER 2

THE INITIAL HEARING

MOST ACCOUNTS OF THE MATSON SLAVE CASE BEGIN WITH ROBERT
Matson—the man who owned the slaves.[1] Whether this reflects nineteenth century prejudices, convenience of style, or mere coincidence, it would seem more
appropriate to start with the slaves—Jane Bryant and her four children. After
all, they had much more at stake in the proceedings. Matson stood to lose some
valuable property; the Bryants stood to gain their freedom.

Jane Bryant was a slave. She belonged to Robert Matson. At the time of the
trial, Jane was in her late thirties or early forties.[2] According to one description,
her face was "slightly pockmarked."[3] Jane's complexion was so light that court
documents describe her as a "bright mulatto."[4] Most likely, her father was white.
Stories that have come down maintain that Jane's father may have been one of
Robert Matson's brothers. If true, this would have made Robert Matson Jane's
uncle and Jane, Robert Matson's niece.[5]

Jane was married to Anthony Bryant, a free black. Apparently, Anthony was
considerably older than Jane. He worked as a foreman or overseer for Matson.
Anthony had taught himself to read the Bible and was a licensed Methodist
"exhorter," or preacher.[6]

Jane Bryant had at least four children—three girls and a boy—Mary Catherine, Sally Ann, Mary Jane, and Robert Noah. They ranged in age from about
five years old to about fourteen. Mary Catherine was the eldest and Robert
Noah the youngest.[7] Like their mother, the Bryant children were described as
"bright mulattos."[8] One of the girls had blue eyes and long red hair.[9] It is likely
that at least some of the children had white fathers, perhaps the same father.
Again, one of Robert Matson's brothers has been mentioned as a possibility.[10]
The law took no notice. Because their mother was a slave, all of Jane's children
were slaves and all four, like their mother, belonged to Robert Matson.

Most published reports of the Matson slave case tell us very little of substance about Robert Matson. Many of the accounts verge on the romantic. He has been variously described as a "young, unmarried man of good family,"[11] "an unmarried Kentuckian of aristocratic background,"[12] and as "a more or less disreputable slave-owner."[13] The truth lies somewhere in the middle.

Robert Matson was, indeed, a Kentuckian. He was born in Bourbon County, Kentucky, in 1796.[14] So much for his reputed youth. When the trial took place in 1847, Matson was over fifty years old. Apparently, he was not without his good qualities. Hiram Rutherford, whom Matson was to sue for harboring his runaway slaves, had only kind words for his adversary. Rutherford maintained that throughout it all, he and Matson "were always on speaking terms," and during a break in the proceedings, the two "discussed our controversy in good humor."[15] In Rutherford's opinion, Matson "had the manners of a gentleman."[16]

Orlando Ficklin, the attorney who represented Rutherford, described Matson as a man "of stalwart and well developed physical proportions, gentlemanly bearing and pleasant feature, with intellect above the average . . . . The General kept the family bottle supplied with choice bourbon on his improvised board in compliance with the time honored custom of his 'Old Kentucky home.'"[17]

Robert Matson's family had a somewhat checkered past. His father, James Matson, was a Revolutionary War veteran who had moved to Kentucky after the war when Kentucky still was a dark and bloody battleground between settlers and Indians. James brought his wife, Mary "Molly" Peyton, with him to the frontier. She was ten years his junior. The move must have been something of a shock for Mary. She had married James in the heart of the old South—Prince William County, Virginia, where her father was the sheriff and the Peytons were a family of stature.[18]

A successful farmer and slaveholder, James Matson lived a long and full life. When he died in 1826 at the age of eighty, he was married to his third wife and left a relatively large estate, including at least ten slaves. Molly, who had died earlier, in 1804, apparently bore all of James's children of record—six sons.[19] It was an interesting brood. Family lore has it that all of the sons had fiery tempers when crossed and often were at each other's throats.[20] At least two of them met mysterious deaths.

Robert probably was the youngest. His older brother Richard, who was born in 1794, captained a company in the Kentucky militia in the War of 1812. He served as far north as Michigan (where he escaped after the Indian defeat of American troops at the Raisin River) and as far south as Louisiana.[21] After the war, in about 1816, Richard and two of the other Matson boys, Enoch and Peyton, struck out for Missouri. While Enoch settled down and made a good life for himself in Pike County, it did not go so well for his two brothers.[22] In 1819, Peyton was reported "lost in the woods." He never was seen again.[23]

Richard Matson lived another twenty years. They were somewhat turbulent years. In 1830, he was tried for being an accessory to the murder of a Mr. Rouse. He was acquitted.[24] Two years later, Richard rose to the rank of colonel in the Blackhawk War. There is a plaque in northern Missouri commemorating his construction of a fort there, which he modestly named Fort Matson. After the war, Richard did not stay in Missouri, but moved farther west to Texas. There, in 1839, near Washington, Texas, he was found lying dead under his wagon—murdered.[25]

Robert Matson's life had followed a more successful course. Like his older brother Richard, Robert had served in the Kentucky militia in the War of 1812. Commissioned a lieutenant at the age of sixteen, he served in Captain Washington Kennedy's company of the fourth Kentucky regiment commanded by Lieutenant Colonel Robert Pogue.[26] Robert Matson remained in Kentucky after the war. So did his older (by eighteen years) brother Thomas.[27] It probably would have been better for all concerned if one of them had left the state. The two did not get along and too often took their nasty family quarrels to court.

In 1823, Robert sued Thomas for slanderously saying that Robert and a woman named Nancy Mallory had killed her child and "buried it secretly & privately . . . In the night."[28] The case was settled. Thomas denied on the record that he ever made the statements attributed to him and declared that he did not believe that the statements were true.[29]

Three years later, the two were in court again. As executor of their father's will, Robert continued a suit for money and land that the elder Matson had brought against Thomas just before his death.[30] It got ugly. Thomas responded with a suit of his own in which he claimed that Robert had exerted improper influence over their father. Thomas did not mince words. He maintained that his brother "entertained . . . the most unnatural and demonic hate toward him," and that Robert, to gratify "the cravings of insatiable avarice and his infernal malignity[,] . . . insidiously" prevailed upon their mentally incompetent father to bring "so false and so foul" a proceeding against him.[31]

It went on. The next year, Robert brought suit alleging that Thomas had torn down a fence between their properties, entered on Robert's land, and destroyed his crops.[32] After that, the two dealt with whatever differences that they might have had out of court.

Thomas died in 1833.[33] By then, Robert was a man of considerable stature in Kentucky. Apparently, he had remained in the state militia, receiving successive promotions. According to the *Lexington Reporter,* "General Matson's staff"

took part in the 1834 "ceremonies in commemoration of the virtues and patrio-
tism of the great and good La Feyette [*sic*]," who had died that year.[34] Bourbon
County sent him to the state legislature in 1832 and again in 1834. In his politics,
Matson was a Whig, a so-called "Cotton" or "Clay" Whig, as proslavery Whigs
were called in the 1840s.[35]

Robert Matson owned slaves. It was a family tradition. Matson's father had
owned slaves and when he died in 1826, he left four of them to his son Robert—
"a man Isaac, a man Jefferson, and a mulatto woman named Jenny (or Jerry)
and her child."[36] At least some of Matson's slaves were not resigned to their lot.
In 1827, three of them, including a mother and child, together with two slaves
from neighboring owners, attempted "to make their escape to the Ohio."[37] Although two of the Matson slaves "had crossed the river," they were recaptured
and returned.[38]

Matson owned real property in Kentucky and in Illinois. He began purchas-
ing land in Illinois in 1835. In August 1842, he bought a large tract on the Bushy
Fork of the Embarras River near Newman in what is now Douglas County but
which then was the northeast corner of Coles County. He named the farm
Black Grove and, in 1843, built a house near the center of the grove.[39]

Matson's migration to Coles County, located about 150 miles south of Chicago and 25 miles east of the Indiana state line, was not unusual. In the mid-
1840s, most of the county's population of nine thousand traced their roots back
to Kentucky or Tennessee. Politically, Coles County was fairly evenly divided
between Whigs and Democrats, with an edge to the Whigs. In presidential
elections, the county regularly voted Whig.[40] By one account, there were about
thirty free blacks in the county and exactly thirty-three abolitionists, many of
them living in the vicinity of Independence in the northern part of the county.[41]
Twelve of these voted for James G. Birney of the antislavery Liberty Party in the
presidential election of 1844.[42] Most of the rest of the county's populace probably viewed free blacks as an anathema. In 1848, Coles County was to vote 921
to 50 in favor of a proposal prohibiting "free persons of color from immigrating
to and settling in this state."[43]

Perhaps it was this prevailing local attitude that convinced Robert Matson
that there would be no problem if he farmed his Illinois acreage with slaves
that he brought from his land holdings in Kentucky. Every spring, he brought
a coffle of slaves across the Ohio River to his farm in Illinois, and every autumn, when the harvest was in, the slaves returned to Kentucky.[44] Supposedly,
each time that he did this, Matson always had someone witness "his solemn
assertion that the slaves were [in Illinois] temporarily and [would] be returned
shortly to his plantation in Bourbon."[45]

Anthony Bryant, Jane's husband, remained in Illinois all year to manage Matson's farm there. In the spring of 1845, Matson brought Jane and the four children from Kentucky to Black Grove.[46] His reasons for doing this are not altogether clear. The most logical explanation is that he needed help on the farm, but in an affidavit that he filed later, Matson maintained that he had brought Jane Bryant to Illinois at her request.[47] While this declaration had no legal significance, Matson may have believed that it put his case in a better light. It is possible that Jane had, in fact, made such a request. She could have wanted to be reunited with her husband year-round on Matson's Illinois farm. There also is the possibility that she saw the trip to Illinois as a trip to possible freedom for her and her children.[48]

Be that as it may, Matson made a major mistake when he brought Jane and her children to Illinois. In the summer of 1847, trouble erupted between Jane and Matson's housekeeper, a twenty-nine-year-old white woman named Mary Corbin. As a result of their quarrel, so the story goes, Mary persuaded Matson to send Jane and her children back to Kentucky for eventual sale "way down South in the cotton fields."[49]

Subsequent accounts have labeled Mary Corbin "a vicious negro hater"[50] and have blamed her actions on an "ungovernable temper."[51] This may be unfair. Mary was not merely Matson's housekeeper. She also was Matson's mistress, or, as historian John J. Duff delicately puts it, Mary "was living in more or less respectable sin" with Matson.[52] Moreover, she probably was the mother of at least one of his children. United States census records for Fulton County, Kentucky, where Matson and Mary later moved, indicate that, in 1850, Robert Matson had four children—one three-month-old infant; a boy, twelve; a girl, fourteen; and a girl—Mildred—who was four years old. According to the census report, all of the children were born in Kentucky except little Mildred, who was born in Illinois in 1846.[53] While it is difficult to say who was the mother of Matson's two older children, it seems highly likely that Mary Corbin was Mildred Matson's mother.

It also seems probable that, given the Matson brothers' reputed propensity to bed down with their slaves, Mary, Matson's lover and the mother of at least one of his children, suspected him of a dalliance with Jane (who, of course, would have had no choice in the matter). This would explain the virulence of Mary's reaction and her desire to send Jane and her children as far away from her and from Matson as possible.

Reportedly, in a fit of anger, Mary told Jane Bryant's brother, a slave named Simuel "Sim" Wilmeth, of her intentions toward his sister and her children. Wilmeth warned Jane, who told her husband. Desperate to save his wife and the children, Anthony Bryant turned for help to the white community.[54] First, he sought assistance from some of his fellow members of the Methodist church. They wished him well but chose not to interfere.[55] The Reverend William Watson of Camargo, a town about two miles north of Charleston, had a similar reaction when Anthony came to him, but went a bit farther. After assuring the worried man that he would pray for him, Watson begged Anthony to tell no one that he had sought the clergyman's assistance.[56] At the time, the clergyman was running for reelection to the state legislature. Watson was concerned that if the voters learned of Bryant's visit with him, "the cry of abolitionist would be started. . . ."[57]

Now what? Where? In desperation, Anthony headed for Independence (now Oakland), Illinois, the town nearest Matson's farm at Black Grove.[58] It is not clear whether Anthony went there in search of a particular individual or simply because the town had something of a reputation as a stronghold of Presbyterian antislavery sentiment.[59] In any event (perhaps Reverend Watson's prayers were working), Anthony was fortunate enough to connect with Gideon M. Ashmore. This thirty-seven-year-old transplant from the Duck River region of central Tennessee had filed the plat for recording Independence in 1835 and owned a hotel there.[60] According to one of his contemporaries, "Matt" Ashmore was one of "the most thorough-faced abolitionists of that Day."[61]

After hearing Anthony's story, Ashmore brought in a thirty-two-year-old physician named Hiram Rutherford. Born in Paxtany, near Harrisburg, Pennsylvania, Rutherford had graduated from Jefferson Medical College in Philadelphia in 1838 and had arrived in Independence in 1840. He soon established a successful medical practice and, by 1847, was a well-respected man in the community.[62] One of his patients had been Robert Matson, whom he had treated in 1842 and 1843.[63]

Rutherford had grown up in a family of abolitionists and was true to his heritage. Politically, he was a Whig, but, like Ashmore, had voted for the abolitionist James G. Birney of the Liberty Party in the 1844 presidential election.[64] Rutherford had met Anthony Bryant once before while visiting Matson's house.[65] About forty years after the fact, Rutherford related what occurred when he met Jane's husband for the second time under very different circumstances:

We told the frightened old negro . . . to return to the Matson place and bring his family down to us, spiriting them away, if necessary, during the night. Realizing the danger of such a proceeding both to us and to the slaves, we quietly invoked the aid of a few discreet and fair minded friends. The time had now come for us to show our hands. We met at the home of

*Ashmore and had our forces within hailing distance by nine o'clock that
night. We waited till midnight, when the party, father, mother, and one
child, on horseback, the rest on foot, arrived, all excited and panting from
their hurried journey across the prairie.*[66]

Matson came after Jane and her children. For the next two or three days,
he tried persuasion, threats, and intimidation. Matson himself attempted to
convince the family to return from Independence to Black Grove. He left the
threats and intimidation to one of his "trusted friends,"[67] a man named Joe
Dean who often is depicted as the real villain of the piece. Dean has been described as "infamous," "poor white trash," and an "ignorant and worthless fellow."[68] Of course, all of these opinions were voiced by those on the opposite side
of the controversy. Still, Dean apparently was one intimidating individual. But
the Bryants' protectors were not intimidated. They held their ground. Jane and
her children remained in Independence.[69]

Frustrated, Matson turned to the law. He hired Usher F. Linder, a local attorney and former Illinois attorney general. On August 17, 1847, acting on Linder's
instructions, Matson went before William Gilman, a justice of the peace, and
swore out an affidavit against Jane and her children. In his sworn statement,
Matson declared that the fugitives had been slaves in Kentucky, that he had
brought them into Illinois "by the request of said negroes, or part thereof . . .
on a temporary sojourn with the intention of returning to Kentucky" but that
they now refused to "return to said lawful service in Kentucky."[70] That same
day, Judge Gilman ordered the sheriff "to bring the said named colored persons
before me or some other justice of Coles County . . . to be dealt with according
to law. . . ."[71]

When Ashmore was served with the writ, he delivered Jane and the children
to Sheriff Lewis R. Hutchason at the Coles County Jail in Charleston. They were
incarcerated to await trial a few days later.[72] According to Ashmore's cohort,
Rutherford, "[t]his was just what we wanted—the intervention of the law."[73]

Now that the dispute had entered the legal arena, Ashford and Rutherford
realized that the runaways needed a lawyer. They chose Orlando B. Ficklin, an
attorney known at least as much for his political stature—he represented Coles
County's district in Congress—as for his legal ability.[74]

Ficklin's initial task was to make sure that William Gilman, the justice
of the peace who had authorized the Bryants' arrest, did not act as the sole
judge when the matter came to hearing. Apparently, Gilman was known for
his proslavery sympathies. One early account describes him as "a mere tool
in [Linder's] hands."[75] Therefore, Ficklin demanded that a board of three

magistrates adjudicate the case. Here, Ficklin's public prestige may have played a role—his request was granted. Two additional justices of the peace, a Captain John M. Eastin and a Mr. Shepard, were selected to serve with Judge Gilman to try the matter. Ficklin achieved at least part of his objective. While Eastin was overtly proslavery, Shepard was thought to be sympathetic to the defendants.[76]

The trial before the three magistrates took almost two days. Apparently, Matson's henchman, Joe Dean, testified on Matson's behalf.[77] Although his affidavit may have been entered into evidence, Matson probably did not take the witness stand. His interest in the case prevented him from doing so. In 1847, Illinois still followed a rule taken from the English common law which prohibited parties and anyone else who had a financial interest in the outcome of a case from testifying in that case.[78]

Most likely the same rule barred Jane and her children from testifying. Their testimony also was probably was excluded because of the color of their skin. By statute, as noted earlier, "[n]o negro, mulatto or Indian [could] not be a witness in any court, or in any case, against a white person."[79]

According to a less than completely reliable account, at the hearing Linder maintained that Kentucky was the slaves' legal domicile, that the law of the domicile must govern, and that, under Kentucky law, Jane and her children were slaves.[80] Rutherford reportedly said of Linder's presentation, "I have heard him a hundred times, but never knew him to make so great an effort."[81]

At that stage in the proceedings, things looked very promising for Matson. Rutherford later recalled that, when the court adjourned for dinner, "Matson was elated."[82] But in the afternoon, Ficklin came on strong. He argued that Matson had freed his slaves by voluntarily bringing them into the free state of Illinois.[83] For what it was worth, one (probably second- or thirdhand) account claims that Ficklin's presentation "was not only able and convincing, but carried with it the most profound sympathy of the vast crowd who listened to it,—so much so, that a number of strong men were seen to weep like children."[84]

Whether strong men were weeping or not, emotions were running high in Charleston. The potential of mob violence that so often plagued the state began to percolate. Outside the courthouse, there was a good deal of loud and threatening talk. Guns were conspicuously in evidence. Hoping for a favorable verdict, Matson's "henchman," Joe Dean, had a wagon and horses in readiness to carry the Bryants as rapidly as possible back across the Ohio River into Kentucky.[85] He was prepared to tie up the slaves "in case they should resist or become unduly demonstrative."[86] Anticipating this move, Rutherford and Ashmore had detailed a squad of horsemen to ride down the wagon "the moment they drove beyond the limits of Charleston."[87]

The three justices of the peace, all elected officials, were not oblivious to what was going on in the streets outside. Gilman may have favored slavery, but he also "was an exceedingly deliberate individual."[88] The three magistrates concluded that they had no jurisdiction to decide whether or not Jane and her children were free, but because the five were blacks in Illinois without letters of freedom, they were in violation of the state's Black Laws.[89] An order dated August 20, 1847, and signed by Gilman remanded the five to the custody of Coles County sheriff Lewis R. Hutchason, who was to "keep them until discharged by a due course of law."[90]

The chronology of what happened after the hearing is not completely clear. Within a few days, Matson was arrested and convicted "on a charge of living in an open state of fornication with one Mary Corbin."[91] According to the warrant, the justice of the peace in the case was "Samuel C. Ashmore," who probably was Gideon Ashmore's older brother.[92] No doubt in retaliation, Matson brought actions against Gideon Ashmore and Rutherford under the Illinois Black Laws for assisting Jane and her children to escape. He sought a total of twenty-five hundred dollars from each of them, five hundred dollars for each fugitive.[93]

Ashmore filed two petitions on behalf of the prisoners. Ficklin drafted both of them. The shorter of the two was a rather bare-bones request for a writ of habeas corpus. It alleged that Jane and her children had been committed to Sheriff Hutchason's custody "as runaway slaves," but that "they are by virtue of the laws of the State of Illinois free persons owing services to no person or persons."[94] It sought a writ of habeas corpus commanding the sheriff to bring the prisoners before the court so that they could prove their right to be free. [95] If they succeeded in doing so, Jane and her children requested that the court "discharge from the oppressive confinement to which they are subjected and that they be declared free and a certificate thereof furnished them."[96]

The second petition, which bears the same date as the first (October 16, 1847), also sought a writ of habeas corpus but is more of a narrative detailing the events leading up to the incarceration of Jane and her children.[97] This petition makes it clear that the prisoners "were slaves" of Robert Matson, that he had "voluntarily" brought them from Kentucky to Illinois, that he had done so in August 1845, and that they had remained "within the jurisdiction of the laws and Constitution" of Illinois ever since.[98] It contended that under those laws and that constitution, Jane and her children "are free and as freemen" could not be delivered "into the custody of their former master the said Robert Matson."[99]

The habeas corpus petitions and Robert Matson's case for damages were scheduled to be heard in the court of Coles County when Chief Justice William Wilson, sitting as judge of the circuit court, arrived in Charleston for the

October session.[100] By now, the case had attracted wide attention, and excitement was building by the day. Then, so the standard story goes, Abraham Lincoln arrived on the scene, was convinced to assist in representing Matson, and, as a consequence, had to turn down Rutherford when the doctor subsequently asked Lincoln to defend him against Matson's claim for damages.[101]

There is some factual basis for this account. Lincoln often was retained in cases more or less on the fly. Arriving in town with the circuit court judge as he traveled from county seat to county seat, Lincoln (like his fellow circuit-riding lawyers) would be approached by litigants or local lawyers seeking his services.[102] This may have been how Lincoln came to represent Matson, but it appears more likely that Lincoln had been retained prior to his arrival in Charleston in October 1847.

One old account of the Matson matter claims that some time before the trial, Matson had been spotted on horseback heading west on the old Springfield Trace, toward the state's capitol. The same account maintains that when Matson returned from Springfield or wherever he had gone, "he stated that he did not know where this thing—meaning his effort to take the negroes back to Kentucky—would end; that he had been to Springfield to consult Abraham Lincoln; that he did not like the way he talked about slavery still as he wanted the best lawyer in the country he had retained him for any litigation he might get into."[103]

There is evidence to support the contention that Matson or someone acting on his behalf had been in touch with Lincoln about the case before Lincoln showed up in Charleston. In the records of the Circuit Court of Coles County, there is a bond for costs relating to Matson's case against Rutherford. The bond appears to be in Lincoln's handwriting and bears his signature.[104] The bond is dated September 27, 1847. On that date, Lincoln was not in Coles County. He probably was in Springfield.[105]

Matson was not the only one who wanted Lincoln to represent him in the litigation. One of Matson's adversaries, Dr. Hiram Rutherford, had known Lincoln since 1841, when he had met him on the judicial circuit in Taylorville, southwest of Springfield.[106] Years later, Rutherford recalled that because he believed that his views and Lincoln's "on the wrong of slavery being in perfect accord," he "determined to employ [Lincoln]; besides everyone I consulted advised me to do so."[107]

This advice may have confirmed what Rutherford had learned about Lincoln's ability from firsthand experience. In May 1843, the administrator of the estate of a deceased man named John H. McClelland brought suit in the Circuit Court of Coles County against Thomas Affleck and Dr. Rutherford. The administrator sought a court order preventing Affleck, who was the deceased's father-in-law, from collecting on notes and accounts in his possession which allegedly belonged to McClelland's estate.[108] Affleck hired Lincoln to represent him, and the matter eventually was settled by agreement in October 1846.[109]

It is not clear why Rutherford was joined as a defendant and, according to court records, he played no significant role in the case.[110] Apparently, Lincoln's representation was limited to Affleck. Nevertheless, it seems likely that, given his status as a party, Rutherford closely followed the case and observed Lincoln's performance in it.

Be that as it may, Rutherford decided to retain Lincoln and, upon hearing of his arrival, rode south from Independence to Charleston. There, he found Lincoln on the verandah of the Union Hotel, leaning his chair against a wooden pillar and regaling "bystanders and loungers . . . with one of his irresistible and highly flavored stories."[111] Rutherford waited for an opening. When Lincoln paused between anecdotes, Rutherford jumped in and pulled him aside. He told Lincoln what had been going on, "reminded him that we had always agreed on the questions of the day," and requested that Lincoln represent him.[112] Lincoln reacted in a totally unexpected manner.

According to Rutherford:

> *He listened attentively as I recited the facts leading up to the controversy with Matson, but I noticed a peculiarly troubled look come over his face now and then, his eyes appeared to be fixed in the distance beyond me, and he shook his head several times as if debating with himself some question of grave import. At length, and with apparent reluctance, he answered that he could not defend me because he had already been counseled with in Matson's interest, and therefore under professional obligations to represent the latter unless released.[113]*

Disappointed and angry, Rutherford would have none of Lincoln's attempts, "in his plausible way" to make Rutherford understand "that, as a lawyer, he must represent and be faithful to those who counsel with and employ him."[114] Rutherford bitterly answered that "my money was as good as any one's else," and left in a huff.[115] A few hours later, according to Rutherford, he received a message from Lincoln that he, Lincoln, had sent for whomever it was who had approached him on Matson's behalf earlier, and "if they came to no more decisive terms than at first he would probably be able to represent me."[116] Shortly after this, again according to Rutherford, there was another message that Lincoln "could now easily and consistently free himself from Matson, and was, therefore in a position, if I employed him, to conduct my defense [*sic*]."[117] Too late. Rutherford was a proud man. He "plainly indicated a disinclination to avail myself of [Lincoln's] offer." Rebuffed, Lincoln chose to return to Matson's service.[118]

CHAPTER 3

THE LAWYERS—LINCOLN

In October of 1847, Abraham Lincoln was thirty-eight years old. He stooped a bit, but when he stood tall, he was six feet four, his height accentuated by the fact that he was very thin.[1] At most, he weighed about 180 pounds.[2] Lincoln was a homely man who did little to enhance his appearance.[3] In 1847, he had yet to grow the beard that some thought would improve "his long sallow face" and, as his law partner put it, he "was not fastidious as to . . . dress."[4] Several months before the Matson trial, Lincoln spoke at the River and Harbor Convention in Chicago, which was attended by thousands of people from many different states.[5] Lincoln was well received despite the fact that "[n]o one who saw him [could] forget his personal appearance at that time. Tall, angular and awkward, he had on a short-waisted, thin swallow-tail coat, a short vest of the same material, thin pantaloons, scarcely coming down to his ankles, a straw hat and a pair of brogans with woolen socks."[6]

Lincoln's appearance often was the butt of his humor, a humor that made him popular with his colleagues, judges, juries, voters, and much of the general public.[7] His ability to tell a good story was legendary. "He was wise . . . , but O Lord wasn't he was funny," recalled Usher Linder, who also had a reputation as a raconteur.[8] Many of Lincoln's stories were not fit for mixed company, but, generally, he seemed able to gear his humor to his audience.[9] Moreover, even in the 1840s, it was not just country bumpkins who appreciated Lincoln's humor. In 1847, J. H. Buckingham, the erudite son of a Boston newspaper publisher, found himself with Lincoln and four other passengers in an overcrowded stagecoach on the Illinois prairie somewhere south of Chicago: "We started in a grumbling humor, but our Whig congressman [Lincoln] was determined to be good natured, and to keep all the rest so if he could; he told stories, and badgered his [Democratic] opponent, who it appeared was an old personal friend, until we all laughed, in spite of the dismal circumstances in which we were placed."[10]

In retrospect, Lincoln's humor and storytelling, at times, seem almost compulsive. He had a tendency to repeat the same stories again and again. "I have heard him," one of his law clerks recalled, "relate the same story three times within as many hours to persons who came in at different periods, and every time he laughed as heartily and enjoyed it as if it were a new story."[11] It may have been a defense mechanism. Anthony Thornton, an attorney who had offices in Shelbyville and rode the circuit with Lincoln for ten years, probably was on target in his conclusion that Lincoln told stories "to whistle off the meloncholy [*sic*]."[12]

The "meloncholy" was very real and "ineradicable."[13] Lincoln was subject to bouts of severe depression as well as brief violent fits of anger and moments of almost manic exuberance.[14] One of his legal colleagues recalled that when Lincoln was "thoroughly aroused & provoked[,] he was capable of terrible passion & invective."[15] His second law partner, Stephen T. Logan, agreed. Referring to the Lincoln that he knew in the late 1830's, Logan described a man who could lose it on occasion: "He was always very independent and had generally a very good nature. Though he had at times, when he was roused, a very high temper. He controlled it then in a general way, though it would break out sometimes— and at those times it didn't take much to make him whip a man."[16]

Numerous theories have been advanced to explain Lincoln's pattern of behavior. His first law partner, John T. Stuart, claimed that "it was due to his abnormal digestion. His liver failed to work properly—and his bowels were equally as inactive."[17] Other diagnoses range from "ante natal" trauma to a neurotic need to be loved to severe eye strain to mercury poisoning resulting from doses of what Herndon described as "blue mass," pills loaded with mercury that Lincoln took to combat his depression.[18]

Whatever the cause, Lincoln's condition could not have been helped by the fact that he was a very private, introspective man. His "nature," William H. Herndon tells us, "was secretive, it was reticent, it was 'hush.'"[19] Although he liked most people and was well-liked by most, Lincoln had few intimates.[20] Even Herndon, who often spent day after day with Lincoln, always addressed his partner as "Mr. Lincoln."[21] He also was "Mr. Lincoln" to his wife.[22] Lincoln, as his wife later said of her husband, "was not a demonstrative man, when he felt most deeply, he expressed the least."[23]

Lincoln may have come closest to showing his feelings through his choice of poetry. He was especially taken with sentimental poems, his favorite being a depressingly maudlin thing by the Scottish poet William Knox entitled "Morality," which mourns the futility of life. The first passage is representative of the poet's cheerless view:

Oh! why should the spirit of mortal be proud?
Like a swift-fleeting meteor, a fast-flying cloud.
A flash of lightning, a breath of the wave,
He passeth from life to his rest in the grave.[24]

While the sadness always lay beneath the surface, in the late 1840s Lincoln's mood swings were less frequent and less pronounced.[25] This may have been due to his having achieved a certain degree of respectability and order in his life.[26] Behind him, although still part of him, was the uncomfortable youth whose father was an uneducated, hardscrabble farmer, whose mother had died when he was nine, who had only about a year of formal education, who had bumped from one dead-end job to another, and who had failed as a storekeeper in a backwater crossroads hamlet. Behind him, too, were his insecurities about romantic commitment that had led him to call off engagements to two different women.[27]

In 1847, Lincoln was an established, married man, and he had married into what passed for high society in Springfield. His wife, Mary Todd, was a daughter of Robert S. Todd, a wealthy slaveholding merchant, banker, and Whig politician of Lexington, Kentucky. Mary Todd grew up in comfort with Henry Clay as a neighbor and family friend. Her older sister, Elizabeth, had married Ninian Edwards, Jr., whose father had been a governor of Illinois. The Edwardses were the arbitrators of Springfield society. Lincoln met Mary Todd at one of their Sunday soirees. Visiting her sister, Mary was a popular addition to the small town's social set.[28] She was, in the words of one contemporary, a "bright, witty and accomplished young woman, naturally fond of fun and frolic, but very staid and proper when it was in order to be."[29]

After one broken engagement, Lincoln and Mary Todd had married in 1843. By 1847, they had two sons, Robert Todd and Edward, ages four and one, respectively. The Lincolns lived in a modest, five-room house at Eighth and Jackson streets in Springfield that Lincoln had purchased three years earlier.[30] The house was small, but the Lincolns' prospects of moving up were good.[31] Those prospects were based on Lincoln's symbiotic careers as politician and lawyer.

Lincoln's political career had begun in 1832 with an unsuccessful run for one of his Sangamon County district's four seats in the Illinois House of Representatives. He finished eighth in a field of thirteen.[32] Two years later, he won a seat with 1,376 votes and a second-place finish. At twenty-five, he was the second-youngest member of the state legislature. His primary concerns were ensuring the move of the state capital from Vandalia to Springfield, promoting roads, canals, and railroads, and defending the Illinois State Bank, especially its central branch in Springfield.[33]

Lincoln had been in the legislature two years when, in 1836, he clashed with Usher Linder, then a freshman representative from Coles County. The two had first met a year earlier when Lincoln was in the county visiting family. Linder had known some of Lincoln's relatives in Kentucky, and the two fell into conversation. Linder was not impressed with Lincoln: "[H]ere I first met Abraham Lincoln, of Springfield, at that time a very modest and retiring man, dressed in a plain suit of mixed jeans. He did not make any marked impression upon me, or any other member of the bar. . . . The impression that Mr. Lincoln made upon me when I first saw him . . . was very slight. He had the appearance of a good-natured man, of plain good sense, and unobtrusive in his manners."[34]

Linder's lack of interest in his new acquaintance turned to respect when the two squared off in the Illinois House of Representatives. Linder led the Democrats in an assault on the Illinois State Bank. Lincoln, a Whig, was one of its chief defenders.[35] The two clashed again over a proposal to partition Sangamon County and over Lincoln's efforts to remove the state capital to Springfield in that county. Both showed themselves masters of legislative debate, especially "the power to hurt"—the hard personal shot directed at an adversary.[36] For example, when Linder opposed Lincoln's motion that the legislature's journal include his minority report against partitioning Sangamon County, his argument dripped with sarcasm: "Mr. Speaker, I would advise the Gentleman [Lincoln] to move for the printing of 3,000 copies of this report for the especial benefit of his constituents! Will not you gentlemen of the House, go to the expense of printing 3,000 copies for the benefit of Sangamo [sic]? But before you do, consider whether your constituents may not teach you another sort of courtesy."[37]

Similarly, Lincoln took off after Linder in the debate over the Illinois State Bank. Linder had offered a resolution to appoint a committee to investigate the bank's practices. Lincoln unleashed a stinging assault on the resolution and its author. In arguing that existing usury laws negated any need for a committee inquiry, Lincoln pointedly questioned both Linder's legal acumen and his ethical standards: "Does the gentleman from Coles know, that there is a statute standing in full force, making it highly penal, for an individual to loan money at a higher rate of interest than twelve per cent? If he does not he is too ignorant to be placed at the head of the committee which his resolution proposes; and if he does, his neglect to mention it, shows him to be too uncandid to merit the respect or confidence of any one."[38]

Linder left the legislature in February 1837 to serve as attorney general and soon moved to Alton.[39] In July, however, he briefly returned to the legislative halls as a spectator, where he witnessed William Lee Davidson Ewing, the representative from Fayette County, launch a "cutting and sarcastic" attack on the Sangamon County delegation.[40] Ewing accused Lincoln and his colleagues of "chicanery and trickery" in their campaign to move the state capital from Vandalia (in Fayette County) to Springfield (in Sangamon County).[41]

A man of "elegant manners" and "considerable notoriety, popularity and talents," Ewing was a formidable adversary.[42] He had been a colonel in the Black Hawk War, governor of Illinois, and a United States senator. Yet, Lincoln did not hold back. On behalf of the Sangamon County legislative contingent, he "retorted upon Ewing with great severity; denouncing his insinuations imputing corruption . . . , and paying back with usury all that Ewing had said."[43] It was that speech, "when everyone thought that [Lincoln] was digging his own grave," that Linder, "for the first time, . . . began to conceive a very high opinion of the talents and personal courage of Abraham Lincoln."[44]

Lincoln won the fight over the capital's move to Springfield. He served two more terms in the legislature where he became a leader of the Whigs in the house. Twice, his party nominated him for speaker and twice he was defeated by the Democratic majority.[45]

He also saw two of his favorite causes defeated—the Illinois State Bank and a comprehensive internal improvements program. The economic panic of 1837 and the economic malaise that followed bankrupted the state, killed off the internal improvements program, and doomed the Illinois State Bank. Lincoln fought to the last ditch to save the bank, which cost him support among his constituency and led him to decide against seeking another term in the state legislature.[46]

Lincoln's stint in the Illinois legislature saw him confronted with significant issues relating to slavery on two occasions. The first was during his first term in the house of representatives. In January 1837, having received memorials from sister legislatures in Virginia, Alabama, Mississippi, Connecticut, and New York requesting comment on the subject of abolitionism, the Democratic-controlled legislature took action.[47]

Led by Usher Linder, it passed a number of resolutions praising the allegedly beneficial effects of white civilization upon African natives, citing the poor condition of emancipated slaves as evidence of the foolishness of freeing them, and denouncing abolitionists.[48] One resolution, in particular, declared that the legislators "highly disapprove of the formation of abolition societies; . . . the right of property in slaves is sacred to the slave-holding States by the Federal Constitution, and they cannot be deprived of that right without their consent. . . ."[49]

The resolutions garnered unanimous support in the Illinois Senate. In the lower house, Usher Linder was instrumental in persuading all but six to cast their votes in support.[50] Six weeks later, two of that small minority, Lincoln and Dan Stone, a recently arrived graduate of Vermont's Middlebury College, recorded their "Protest" against the resolutions.[51] Dated March 3, 1837, the document is a curious one. In it, the two young Whig representatives from Sangamon County declared their belief "that the institution of slavery is founded on both injustice and bad policy," but agreed with the majority that "the Congress of the United States has no power under the constitution, to interfere with the institution of Slavery in the different States."[52] They also contended that "the promulgation of abolition doctrines tends rather to increase than to abate [slavery's] evils."[53]

Two years later, when the legislature considered two resolutions dealing with law and slavery, Lincoln wavered. The first resolution condemned the governor of Maine for refusing to surrender two men who had helped a slave escape and were charged in Georgia with stealing the slave. The second declared that citizens of free states should not interfere with the domestic relations of slave states. According to published reports, Representative Lincoln was anything but definite on how to vote on these measures:

January 5, 1839

Mr. Lincoln, on the first reading of the resolutions, had inclined to vote in favor concurring; but upon the second, he felt he wanted more time for deliberation. He now thought it would be better to postpone the subject indefinitely; and accordingly made a motion to this effect.[54]

After his decision against another run for the state legislature, Lincoln's respite from politics was brief. He had his eyes on the seat for the Seventh Congressional District. Anchored in Sangamon County, the district was safely Whig, but there was a problem or, to be more precise, there were two problems. John J. Hardin, the college-educated son of a United States senator from Kentucky, and Edward D. Baker, a friend so close that Lincoln had named his second son after him, also sought the Whig nomination. Both were popular candidates. Hardin won the nomination in 1843, but Lincoln persuaded the Whig district convention to rotate the nomination among the three contenders. This plan, the so-called "Pekin Agreement," resulted in Baker's nomination and election to Congress in 1844, and Lincoln's nomination and election on August 3, 1846. He won by the largest plurality in the history of the district, but was the only Whig among the seven representatives elected from Illinois.[55]

This is probably as good a place as any to point out, if it is not already apparent, that Lincoln's homeliness, ready humor, and bouts of depression should not obscure the fact that this was one highly intelligent, shrewd, and savvy man. "He was always calculating, and always planning ahead," recalled Herndon.[56] "Lincoln's perceptions were slow, cold, precise, and exact . . . he possessed originality and power of thought in an eminent degree."[57]

Moreover, despite his very real humility and his self-deprecating humor, Lincoln was a man on the make. As David Donald cogently explains in his classic biography:

> Membership in the Whig party meant something more than issues to Lincoln. He thought the party was grounded on principles in which he passionately believed. To him it embodied the promise of American life. Economically it stood for growth, for development, for progress. . . . This was a vision that attracted many of the wealthiest and best-educated members of society to the Whig party, but it was also one that appealed to young men who aspired to get ahead. Henry Clay, Lincoln's political idol, coined the term "self-made man" to describe Kentucky businessmen—but he might more accurately have applied it to Lincoln himself.[58]

Herndon put it quite simply. Lincoln's "ambition," he observed not unkindly, "was a little engine that knew no rest."[59]

Lincoln was elected to the House of Representatives on August 3, 1846, but was not scheduled to take his seat until December 1847, when the Thirtieth Congress convened for its initial session. This delay permitted him to devote fifteen months to his other vocation—the practice of law—and he did just that. The year 1847 was a busy one for Lincoln the lawyer. His fee book shows that he participated in more than a hundred cases that year.[60]

Lincoln's legal career had begun ten years earlier, when he was admitted to the Illinois bar.[61] He was fortunate that the standards for admission then were not very high. Unlike a few of his contemporaries who had gone to law school and many more who had "read law" as legal clerks in the offices of established practitioners, Lincoln had no formal training in law. His preparation consisted of his legislative experience in the Illinois house, observing some trials as a spectator, and reading Blackstone and a few other legal treatises.[62] Lincoln's real legal education began after he was admitted to the bar. He learned by doing, and he learned quickly and well. From the start, Lincoln demonstrated an aptitude for the courtroom.[63]

He also was lucky. Upon Lincoln's admission to the bar, John Todd Stuart, a Whig politician who had admired him as a legislator and had encouraged his legal studies, took Lincoln on as his law partner. Two years older than Lincoln, but with about ten years more legal experience, Stuart was a fellow Kentuckian who was related on his mother's side to Lincoln's wife. It was a good match. Stuart had a successful practice and, due to his political pursuits, little time for it. The day-to-day burden of the practice fell on Lincoln, who had no choice but to learn a good deal very quickly. In time, however, he grew weary of shouldering the load.[64]

In 1841, Stuart and Lincoln amicably went their separate ways, and Lincoln made another fortunate match. Stephen T. Logan, a former judge, may have been the most skilled attorney in Springfield. In April 1841, he took Lincoln on as a junior partner. While it is not clear how much Logan actually contributed to Lincoln's development as a lawyer, the junior partner could not have helped but learn from Logan's example. The partnership prospered and lasted until 1844 when Logan decided to take his son into the practice.[65]

By then Lincoln had established a reputation as one of the better lawyers in the area and could have linked up with one of his equals.[66] He did not do so. Instead, he chose to partner with William H. Herndon, who was only twenty-six years old, had just been admitted to the bar, had virtually no clients, and had a reputation as something of an unstable eccentric. Lincoln's choice has long baffled historians, who emphasize how very different the two men were.[67] In contrast to Lincoln, "Billy" Herndon, as Lincoln always called him, was "garrulous, windy, opinionated [and] prodigiously indiscreet."[68]

Historian David Donald, who wrote biographies of both men, acknowledges that Lincoln's choice of Herndon may have been an attempt to garner political support from younger "populist" Whigs of whom Herndon was a leader, but thinks it more likely that Lincoln was ready to be the boss and that he genuinely liked Herndon.[69] It would not have been the first time that an introspective personality found a vicarious outlet in a more expressive and exuberant one.

Soon after the partnership was formed, Lincoln and Herndon moved into an office on the top floor of the three-story Tinsley Building, which was across the street from the statehouse and housed the United States District Court. The single large room, in the historian John J. Duff's words, was an "incredibly dingy place even for a pioneer law office."[70] Gibson W. Harris, who clerked for Lincoln and Herndon from 1845 to 1847, has left us the following description of his place of employ:

The furniture, nearly all of it in a more or less dilapidated condition, comprised one small desk and a table, both of them quite plain, a sofa, or lounge, with raised head at one end, and half a dozen wooden chairs. Over the desk a few shelves had been enclosed; this was the office bookcase,

holding a set of Blackstone, Kents Commentaries, Chitty's Pleadings and a
very moderate number of other books. . . . The floor in our office was almost
never scrubbed, and the sweeping was done by the clerk."[71]

Obviously, Lincoln and Herndon did not spend much money on amenities. They probably did not have that much money to spend. In the 1840s, when he depended on his legal practice for most of his income, Lincoln probably made less than two thousand dollars (about forty thousand in 1999 dollars) a year.[72] The money came in small increments. Legal fees were remarkably low. Existing records show that Lincoln's fees typically averaged ten to twenty-five dollars a case. He handled a few cases for fifty dollars and, in 1845, received a biggie— one hundred dollars for an appeal to the Illinois Supreme Court.[73]

Although Lincoln was the dominant member of their two-man firm and its "rainmaker," he split receipts with Herndon on a fifty-fifty basis.[74] According to Herndon, the two maintained no records of their division of the firm's receipts. When a fee was received, it was divided immediately.[75]

They also divided the work. Herndon appeared in court on occasion, but concentrated his efforts on office work and attempting to keep the firm's records in order.[76] Lincoln's place was in the courtroom. Lincoln handled most of the firm's litigation and was well equipped to do so. His strength as a litigator was not based on a thorough grounding in legal theory. His former partner, Stephen Logan, did not believe that Lincoln "studied very much": "I think he learned his law more in the study of cases. He would work hard and learn all there was in a case he had in hand. He got to be a pretty good lawyer through his general knowledge of the law was never very formidable. But he would study out his case and make about as much of it as anybody."[77]

Herndon agreed. To him, Lincoln was "purely and entirely a case lawyer," that is, an attorney concerned less with legal theory and generalities than with what he needs to know to win a particular case.[78] When he had time, Lincoln hit the books to make the best case possible. "When I have a particular case in hand," Lincoln once stated, "I love to dig up the question by the roots and hold it up and dry it before the fires of the mind."[79]

Lincoln's real forte, however, and one that served him in good stead when, as often happened, there was neither time for research nor a place to do it, was his effectiveness at oral argument, especially when addressing juries.[80] Laurence Weldon, a lawyer who rode the circuit with Lincoln in the 1850s, echoed the sentiment of many of Lincoln's contemporaries who had witnessed Lincoln play a jury: "His speeches to the jury were very effective specimens of forensic oratory. He talked the vocabulary of the people, and the jury understood every thought he uttered. I never saw him when I thought he was trying to make a display for mere display; but his imagination was simple and pure in the richest gems of pure eloquence. He constructed short sentences of small words, and never wearied the mind of the jury by mazes of elaboration."[81]

Accolades such as this to the contrary, the consensus among recent students of Lincoln's legal career seems to be that, in fact, Lincoln was "a pretty ordinary lawyer" with "a relatively ordinary practice."[82] They correctly point out that the praise that Lincoln received came after his death when his status as a martyred president all but assured uncritical adulation and reflected the penchant of Victorian bar eulogies to laud even the most mediocre practitioner.[83]

Nevertheless, there are facts which call these conclusions into question. At the height of his career, Lincoln's prestige was such that East Coast attorneys and potential clients sought him out, requesting his assistance.[84] Others sought a more permanent professional relationship with Lincoln. In 1852, Grant Goodrich, a Chicago lawyer with an "extensive and paying practice . . . proposed to take Lincoln into partnership with him."[85] Eight years later, Erastus Corning, the president of the New York Central Railroad, offered Lincoln the position as the railroad's general counsel at a salary of ten thousand dollars per year.[86]

Corning's offer probably resulted, at least in part, from Lincoln's growing stature as a politician, but it also reflected the growing sophistication of Lincoln's legal practice, especially in the area of railroad litigation. By 1860, railroad law was the place to be and Lincoln's biggest and most frequent client was the Illinois Central Railroad. The company had him on retainer. In about eight years, he handled over fifty cases for it.[87]

None of this was true in 1847. In 1847, Lincoln did not handle any railroad cases.[88] In fact, in 1847, there were less than one hundred miles of railroad track in Illinois.[89] Lincoln's legal business in 1847 far more closely resembled the "ordinary" practice described by recent works. Lincoln had far fewer out-of-state clients in the 1840s and his practice was different from what it became in the subsequent decade. It was largely a difference in degree rather a difference in content.

Debt cases, which accounted for about 50 percent of Lincoln's docket even in the 1850s, amounted to up to 70 percent of his practice in the 1840s.[90] During that period, Lincoln also handled a wide variety of civil disputes, including actions relating to land, defamation, assault and battery, inheritance, and divorce, as well as a sprinkling of criminal cases.[91]

As best as can be determined, prior to the Matson case, Lincoln probably was involved in four cases involving slaves. Of the four, *Bailey v. Cromwell* (1841) is by far the best known.[92] Unfortunately, much of its notoriety has little to do with reality other than the fact that Lincoln was involved in it. Contrary to what has been written about it, *Bailey v. Cromwell* did not make new law. It turned on established precedent. It was not a suit for freedom. It was a commercial case. Lincoln did not represent Nance, the woman alleged to be a slave.[93] He represented a white man named David Bailey who agreed to purchase Nance as a slave from William Cromwell and then, apparently, sought to renege on the deal.

Cromwell had sued Bailey on his note, his written promise to pay. Bailey had given the note in lieu of cash for the purchase of Nance, who Cromwell claimed was his slave. Lincoln argued that his client owed Cromwell nothing because Nance, who had been represented to be a slave was, in fact, free and, therefore, not Cromwell's property to sell.[94]

Lincoln lost in the lower court, but prevailed on appeal. Citing the earlier case of *Kinney v. Cook* for the proposition "that the presumption of law was, in this State, that any person was free, without regard to color," the Supreme Court held that Cromwell's failure to prove that Nance was a slave doomed his case.[95] With somewhat felicitous language, Judge Breese put it this way:

> *The girl being free, and asserting her freedom in the only modes she could, by doing as she pleased, making purchases, contracting debts and controlling her own motions, could not be the subject of a sale, and no right to her services would pass by such sale.*
>
> *The sale of a free person is illegal, and that being the consideration of the note, that is illegal also and consequently no recovery can be had upon the note.*[96]

In June of 1845, in the Menard County Circuit Court, Lincoln litigated a case which, in fact, was more consistent with the mythology associated with *Bailey v. Cromwell*. He defended Marvin B. Pond, who had been indicted for harboring John Hawley, a black man whom William Hawley claimed to be a slave.[97] Lincoln did a first-rate job. The court quashed the first count of the indictment and the jury acquitted Pond on the other one.[98] As for John Hawley, the alleged runaway slave, the court ordered him "discharged, and that he go hence without day."[99]

About the same time, Lincoln represented J. Randolph Scott and George Kern, who were active in the Underground Railroad.[100] In September 1845, the state of Illinois brought indictments against them in Woodford, Illinois.[101] Both men were dedicated abolitionists. Once described as "a small man, but full of punch and pluck as an egg is of meat," Scott had emigrated to Woodford

County from Pennsylvania in 1836 and soon became a conductor on the Underground Railroad.[102] George Kern's involvement was a family affair. He and his three sons all were active in moving slaves north to freedom.[103]

The indictments against Scott and Kern charged that each "did harbor a certain negro . . . said negro then and there being a slave and thus owing service to a person . . . in the State of Missouri. . . ."[104] It is not clear what role Lincoln played in defending Scott and Kern. They had other counsel. Onslow Peters, a well-known Peoria attorney who later became a judge, argued on their behalf, as did William D. Briggs, one of Scott's "staunchest friends in the Anti-Slavery cause."[105] Whatever Lincoln's contribution, the defense succeeded. The case was transferred from Woodford County (which, apparently, had its share of pro-slavery "mobocrats") to the Tazewell County Circuit Court where, on April 8, 1847, the prosecutor withdrew the state's case against Scott and a jury found Kern not guilty.[106]

Judging from court records, Lincoln's appearance before the Illinois Supreme Court in *Bailey v. Cromwell* was the only time that he argued a slave case before that tribunal. But his appearance before the state's highest court was not extraordinary. He may have appeared before the Illinois Supreme Court more than any other attorney of his time.[107] Between 1837 and 1847, he handled at least eighty-three appeals.[108] In 1845 alone, Lincoln and Herndon had thirty-nine cases before the supreme court.[109] He also appeared before the federal courts, but his most common venues were the county trial courts that made up the Illinois Eighth Judicial Circuit, which included his home base of Sangamon County.[110]

Charleston, where the Matson case was tried, was in Coles County, which was not part of the Illinois Eighth Judicial Circuit. Nevertheless, in the years 1841 to 1847, Lincoln often attended court there. It was natural for him to do so because Coles County was flanked on three sides by counties that were in the Eighth Circuit, and the road connecting those counties ran through Charleston, the county seat of Coles County.[111]

In the Coles County Circuit Court, as in the courts of other counties, Lincoln ran into the same attorneys again and again, sometimes as allies, sometimes as adversaries. Two lawyers whose names repeatedly appear in the court records as Lincoln's cocounsel or opposing counsel in Coles County were Orlando B. Ficklin and Lincoln's old legislative adversary, Usher F. Linder.[112]

CHAPTER 4

THE LAWYERS—
FICKLIN, CONSTABLE, AND LINDER

Orlando B. Ficklin

ALL OF THE ATTORNEYS INVOLVED IN THE MATSON TRIAL WERE politicians with aspirations for higher office. At the time of the trial, the most successful in this respect was Orlando B. Ficklin, the lawyer who represented Jane and her children before the three justices of the peace. As noted earlier, in October 1847, Ficklin was a Democrat who represented Coles County and the rest of the Illinois Third Congressional District in the United States House of Representatives.[1] He had done so since 1843.[2] Prior to this, he had served three terms in the Illinois house.[3]

Ashmore's and Rutherford's choice of Ficklin was not based on his politics. He was not an abolitionist. In fact, his sentiments lay in the other direction. Initially a Whig and elected to state office as a Whig, Ficklin had become a Democrat in 1842 just prior to his first run for Congress.[4] Apparently, he found that party's southern sympathies and stance on slavery more in keeping with his own beliefs. These sympathies were reinforced in 1845 when Ficklin married Elizabeth, the daughter of Walter T. Colquitt, Democratic senator from Georgia and President Polk's floor leader in the Senate.[5]

In 1847, Ficklin was thirty-eight years old, just a few months older than Lincoln. Like Lincoln, he had been born in Kentucky and eventually had emigrated to Illinois.[6] Also like Lincoln, Ficklin was something of a mimic, a wit, and a storyteller. Thirty years later, caught up in the sentimental haze of memory, Linder recalled that Ficklin "could sing as good a song as any man I ever knew, and tell as good a story."[7] Ficklin "had a considerable vein of dry drollery about him, accompanied by a look and a comical lifting up of his eyebrows that would provoke a laugh from an anchorite."[8]

Ficklin had attended Transylvania University in Lexington, Kentucky, where he had studied law. After graduation, Ficklin was admitted to the Illinois bar in 1830.[9] While Rutherford described him as "a lawyer of recognized ability," not all of Ficklin's contemporaries agreed with this assessment.[10] Justice Gustave Koerner dismissed Ficklin's "legal knowledge" as "not extraordinary."[11] Usher Linder, his adversary in the Matson case as well as in several political campaigns, went much further, castigating Ficklin as, among other things, an "ignoramus and pettifogger."[12]

Linder's penchant for hyperbole notwithstanding, in the courtroom, Ficklin probably was not in the same class as Lincoln or Linder (at least when Linder was fairly sober). Still, after Linder, Ficklin probably was the best local lawyer available in Charleston, and he brought needed respectability to the abolitionists' side of the case. Moreover, as we have seen from his adroit maneuvering to add two justices of the peace so as to prevent antiabolitionist Judge Gilmer from being the sole arbitrator of the Bryants' fate at the initial hearing, Ficklin was able to put aside whatever personal beliefs he may have had and to approach the task of representing Jane and her children with a high degree of professional dedication and skill.[13]

Charles H. Constable

After his experience with Lincoln, Hiram Rutherford had retained Charles H. Constable to assist Ficklin in representing the Bryants. Charles H. Constable was eight years younger than the other three lawyers in the case. Unlike them, he was not a child of the Kentucky frontier nor was he a humorous storyteller with a gift of gab. Constable was born in Chestertown, Maryland, and, in the opinion of his client, Dr. Rutherford, he "was the best educated lawyer at the bar."[14] Rutherford may have been right. Constable had graduated from the University of Virginia, had studied law in Virginia, and had been admitted to the bar there. In 1840, Constable had migrated to Illinois, locating in Mt. Carmel on the Wabash River in Wabash County, about fifty miles south of Charleston. Four years later, he was elected as a Whig to the Illinois Senate. He had been a delegate for Wabash County to the Illinois constitutional convention in the summer of 1847, where, according to some reports, he "was one of the ablest . . . men in that body."[15] Like Ficklin, Constable was no friend of abolition.[16]

Constable was a solid advocate, but he lacked the flair of the other lawyers involved in the Matson case. Rutherford praised him as "a classical scholar, fluent and ready in debate, and of commanding physical presence."[17] Usher

Linder agreed that Constable was good looking, describing him as "one of the handsomest men I ever saw," and "a man of fine culture and elegant manners."[18] Linder also conceded that Constable was "really a good lawyer" who "prepared his cases with great care and accuracy," but did "not think he was a man of the most preeminent abilities, as very handsome or pretty men hardly ever are."[19]

Usher F. Linder

Lincoln's cocounsel in the Matson case, Usher F. Linder, requires far more copy than Ficklin or Constable if for no other reason than that he was Lincoln's co-counsel. But there is more. Linder was a friend of Lincoln's and a man who could influence him. An intriguing, if troubling, character, Linder has been virtually forgotten, or perhaps ignored, by most of those seeking to chronicle and to understand Lincoln's life.

Usher B. Linder was born in Hardin County, Kentucky, in 1809, the son of a hard-luck farmer who was trying to eke a living out of the unforgiving land-scape that made up an area appropriately known as the "Barrens."[20] In about 1822, the Linders moved to Indiana, but within five years, young Usher was back in Kentucky, studying law with his brother-in-law, Iredel Hart, a local prosecutor. Linder was admitted to the bar at eighteen and began practicing law.[21] By the summer of 1835, he had a wife and two children and, apparently, had had enough of Kentucky. In July, he moved to the little town of Greenup in Coles County, Illinois. There, his future began to brighten. After a short respite, Linder took up the law again and quickly made such a name for himself that, in 1836, Coles County sent him to the state house of representatives.[22]

In 1836, the capital of the state of Illinois was located in Vandalia in the south-central portion of the state. It was here that Linder met Theophilus W. Smith, a man whom Linder later maintained was "a most invaluable friend."[23] Linder's life may have taken a better tack had their paths never crossed. The fifty-two-year-old judge was a somewhat dubious role model for the young, ambitious lawyer-politician.

When he first met Linder at the private home in Vandalia in which they both rented rooms, Smith was an associate justice of the Illinois Supreme Court. He had been born in New York City and had been admitted to the bar there after studying law in the office of Aaron Burr. In 1816, Smith had moved to Edwardsville in southern Illinois. Elected as a Democrat to the state senate in 1822, he soon became one of the leaders of the movement to amend the Illinois constitution to legalize slavery in the state. That effort failed, but, in 1825, the

Democrat-controlled legislature elected Smith to a seat on the state's highest court.[24]

He was an unlikely jurist. Neither his temperament nor his inclinations suited him well for judicial office. Smith was a big "hulking" man with what Linder generously called an "ardent temperament."[25] During the campaign for a proslavery constitution in the 1820s, Smith attempted to horsewhip Hooper Warren, the editor of an opposition newspaper.[26] Another time, in a fit of anger, Smith had leveled a pistol at Governor Ninian Edwards. He had threatened the wrong man. Edwards grabbed the gun "and struck Judge Smith a blow which broke his jaw, and left upon his face a very ugly scar."[27]

But there was an even more disturbing side of Theophilus Smith. He exhibited an almost incessant lust for personal advantage which often expressed itself in convoluted schemes reminiscent of his old law teacher, Aaron Burr. When he was a state senator in the early 1820s, it quickly earned him the sobriquet "Tammany Smith" after the New York political machine.[28]

Smith's proclivity in this regard was so apparent that it was difficult to say a kind word about him without bringing it up. Thus, Gustave Koerner, who sat on the Illinois Supreme Court a few years after Smith left the bench, described the former justice as "an excellent lawyer, a man of fine talents and appearance, but of rather ambitious and intriguing character."[29] A judicial colleague and later governor, Thomas Ford, went further. After acknowledging that "Tammany" had a "tolerable share of tact and good sense," Ford left no doubt as to how he really felt about Smith: "He never lacked a plot to advance himself or blow up some other person. He was a laborious and ingenious schemer in politics; but his plans were always too complex and ramified for his power to execute them. Being unsuccessful himself, he was delighted alike with the mishaps of friends and enemies; and was ever chuckling over the defeat or blasted hopes of some one."[30]

Smith's behavior almost caught up with him in 1832 when, based upon "[n]umerously signed petitions from the people," the Illinois House of Representatives voted to impeach him.[31] The articles of impeachment charged the judge with selling a court clerk's office, swearing out vexatious writs returnable to himself, imprisoning a Quaker for not removing his hat in court, and suspending a lawyer for advising his client to apply for a change of venue from Smith's court.[32]

During his month-long trial before the state senate, Smith reportedly sent someone into the senate chamber after each adjournment to collect any notes of the trial which the senators may have left on their desks. Supposedly this tactic enabled him and his counsel to better direct their evidence and arguments.

Apparently, it worked. Fifteen of the twenty-two senators who voted found Smith guilty of at least one of the charges against him, but only twelve could agree on any one specification. A two-thirds vote being necessary for conviction, Smith secured an acquittal and continued to serve on the court.[33]

His impeachment years behind him, Smith was unchastened and running true to form when he approached Linder one night and, as Linder recalled years later, "asked me if I would not like to be a great man." When the freshman representative expressed an interest, Smith promised to "put you on the high road to become such, if you will follow my advice and instructions."[34]

Smith's immediate target was the Illinois State Bank at Springfield. The judge bore a personal grudge against what he described to Linder as "a most rascally institution."[35] A few years earlier, Smith had drafted the bill establishing the bank and had expected a sizable piece of its action. When none was forthcoming, he retaliated.[36] Smith drew up a string of resolutions for Linder to introduce into the legislature, "which resolutions," according to Linder, required the directors of the bank "to show how they distributed their stock, and poking great many uncomfortable questions at them."[37]

Now a Democrat, Linder introduced the resolutions which, in his words, "fell like a bombshell in the house," producing "a most excited debate, which lasted for some two or three weeks."[38] His primary opponent was Abraham Lincoln. During the debate, Smith furnished Linder "with facts and arguments," but Linder did the talking and he did it well.[39] Although the resolutions were adopted in only a watered-down version, Linder's drive and eloquence in support of them made him something of a celebrity.[40] According to his memoirs, "[i]t was in that debate that I won most of my laurels in the House of Representatives at that session, and the popularity which made me the Attorney General of the State."[41]

There is no doubt that Linder was, in the words of one contemporary, "a brilliant orator" with a genuine ability to relate not only to his fellow legislators, but also to jurors and constituents.[42] Despite his readiness to quote the classics and his somewhat dandified dress, Linder was anything but a fop. His ready, sometimes crude, sense of humor and storytelling ability made him a popular stump speaker.[43] Moreover, at a time when only men could vote and many of those men had a rough-hewn edge, Linder's reputation as a hard drinker with a penchant for violence only served to enhance his appeal to many.[44]

Of course, to some, these traits were a cause for concern. Soon after Linder was elected attorney general, the *Missouri Republican* characterized him as a "noisy . . . member of the [Illinois] House" who was not as "regular in his habits as an Attorney General is expected to be."[45] The incident that prompted this observation is a revealing one.

Apparently, when the Illinois legislature elected Linder attorney general, "some of the more decent members of his party," including state senator J. C. Reiley, refused to vote for him.[46] Incensed, Linder reportedly confronted Reiley in a barbershop "and drawing a pistol larger than the common pocket pistol, . . . fired at Mr. Reiley and wounded him in four places."[47] Reiley's wounds were not serious and, after Linder apologized, the matter was smoothed over, but the clouds over Linder's career as attorney general continued to gather.[48]

Although the law required him to live in Vandalia, Linder moved to Alton.[49] There, rumors of his failings in office became grist for the press. In the spring of 1837, the *Missouri Republican* reported that he was "connected in a most disreputable manner" to the escape of some prisoners from the Alton state penitentiary and that he was under investigation by the Madison County grand jury.[50] Other newspapers carried stories that Linder had been less than energetic in carrying out the duties of his office.[51] Linder fought back. On May 10, 1837, he wrote a letter to the Madison County grand jury requesting that it state "whether or not the evidence before you connected my name with [the prison warden's] conduct, or misconduct with the escape of the prisoners or reflected upon my integrity in the slightest. . . ."[52]

The foreman of the grand jury wrote back that Linder's name "was not called in question in the slightest manner by the witnesses who testified" before the grand jury.[53] Linder had the correspondence published in the *Illinois State Register and People's Advocate*, which took his part, editorializing that "the Attorney General has been faithfully attending to his duties on the circuit, except during some short time when he was confined by severe indisposition.—The assiduity with which Mr. LINDER has attended to his duties may be estimated by the fact which we learnt, is, that he has already convicted more criminals than were before confined."[54]

The warden was indicted, but subsequently acquitted.[55] Linder did not act as prosecutor, but was permitted by the court to make a statement. Linder took the opportunity to make, in the *Republican's* view, "a vulgar and abusive speech against the late editors of this paper and those connected with them in politics."[56]

Not surprisingly, the attacks on Linder continued. On September 2, 1837, the *Sangamo Journal* noted that the *St. Louis Republican* had reported that "the grand jury of Madison county, at the late term of court, presented U. F. Linder, attorney general of this State, for palpable omission of duty. A bill of indictment was found, and . . . he was removed from office."[57]

The story turned out to be wishful thinking on the *Republican's* part. For better or worse, Usher Linder was still the attorney general of Illinois and was still a resident in Alton when, in November 1837, he became a prime mover in

the events that culminated in the murder of the abolitionist editor Elijah Lovejoy as he attempted to prevent an armed mob from attacking a warehouse and
destroying his printing press.

It is not entirely clear what motivated Linder's actions in the tragedy that
ensued. He was no friend of blacks—slave or free. Linder considered the United
States to be "a white man's government made by white men and for the benefit of the white race."[58] He had no use for abolition or abolitionists.[59] Yet what
Linder did in Alton in 1837 probably was prompted as much by political expedi-
ency as by anything else. For the past several months, Linder had been taking a
beating in the press. He needed an issue, a distraction. In Lovejoy, Linder saw
the perfect foil—an outspoken abolitionist, a man disliked by most and hated
by many—a voiceless majority. If Linder could provide that voice, there was
political capital to be gained on a statewide basis.[60]

Linder began to dog Lovejoy's steps. When the abolitionist convened an
antislavery convention, Linder and his friends gained access to the meeting.[61]
With an advantage in numbers, they voted down an antislavery report and adopted resolutions proposed by Linder which, among other things, declared that
free blacks should not have the same rights as other free men, that because
the Constitution protects property rights, even the slaveholding states have no
right to abolish slavery, and that antislavery activities "ought to be discountenanced by an intelligent community."[62]

About a week later, after Lovejoy almost convinced a skeptical meeting of
Alton's "leading individuals" of his right to publish what he believed, Linder
followed with a speech described by one Lovejoy sympathizer as "unequaled
by anything I ever heard for an excited, bitter, vindictive spirit."[63] In it, Linder
blasted Lovejoy "as a fanatic, as a dangerous man in the community."[64] To another observer, Linder's words were "[a]ll aimed to stir up the mob spirit and
intimidate and drive Lovejoy from the city."[65] Linder knew what he was doing.
After the meeting, he reportedly told another participant that Elijah Lovejoy
would be "killed within two weeks."[66] He was off by about a week.[67]

Usher Linder, who had been conspicuously absent on the night of the riot
which led to Lovejoy's murder, played a very active role in the trials of the warehouse's defenders and its attackers.[68] As attorney general, he had no duty or
absolute right to take part in the prosecution of the warehouse defenders. However, after both sides consented, the judge granted a petition by "[a]bout sixty
of those in sympathy with the mob" to permit Linder to assist the city attorney
in prosecuting William Gilman, the first of Lovejoy's cohorts to be tried for
breach of the peace.[69] As a private attorney, he acted as cocounsel in the defense
of the accused rioters.[70]

While all of the other lawyers in the two cases confined themselves to the questions at issue, Linder insisted on injecting the issues of abolitionism and race into the proceedings. His closing argument is a study in racist demagogy: "[Lovejoy's press was] brought here to teach rebellion and insurrection to the slave; to excite servile war; to preach murder in the name of religion; to strike dismay to the hearts of the people, and spread desolation over the face of this land. . . . I might depict to you the African, his passions excited by the doctrines intended to be propagated by that press. As well you might find yourself in the fangs of a wild beast."[71]

Linder was quite proud of his involvement in the Alton trials. At a hearing the next year, he "boasted in open court, in tones of triumph, that he had cleared all the men recently indicted for riots in Alton except one, who he said was fined for ringing a bell."[72] His elation was short-lived. It all backfired. Usher Linder returned to Coles County in 1838, his political career in tatters. To many, Alton had a "widespread reputation" as "the city of blood."[73] Linder found himself, in his words, "severely assailed and maligned" for his role in the events leading up to Lovejoy's murder.[74] He was condemned as the "man who had made himself conspicuous in exciting and sustaining the Alton riots," and, although he was not present in the city on the night Lovejoy died, he was tagged as "the ringleader of the mob."[75]

In June 1838, Linder resigned his office as Illinois attorney general.[76] It is not clear why he did so. Linder gives no explanation in his memoirs. It may have been the criticism of his performance in office that led to his decision. In a letter written in 1895, his son, Daniel W. Linder, who had been born the year that his father left office, gave an alternative explanation. He maintained that his father had resigned after learning that "he had by his eloquence and power as a lawyer sent an innocent man to the penitentiary."[77] Linder obtained a pardon for the prisoner, but the incident left him shaken. According to his son, Linder often told him "that he never felt worse in his life as at that moment[,] he immediately resigned his office, and swore he never would prosecute another man until he was thoroughly convinced before hand of his guilt."[78]

A third possibility is that Linder simply wanted to get back to the legislature. After his resignation, Linder did not leave Alton. Earlier he had announced his candidacy for a seat from Madison County in the Illinois House of Representatives.[79] His campaign went nowhere and things began to unravel. Not surprisingly, alcohol was involved.

Apparently, in early 1838, before he had resigned as attorney general, perhaps in contemplation of his run for the state assembly, Linder had publicly gone on the wagon. He had become "the high minded and eloquent advocate" of a move to suppress saloons in Alton.[80] Given the number of taverns in Alton and Linder's fondness for the bottle, this could not last long and it did not last long. As was his wont, Linder switched sides. After what one newspaper condemned as "a mock show of reformation," Linder "appeared in the police court as an advocate of those who met the city temperance ordinance with defiance repudiating the very sentiments and arguments he had a few weeks before urged in favor of its adoption."[81]

Linder started drinking and pulling guns on people again. In July 1838, he was arraigned "on a charge of attempting to shoot Mr. Wm. Hartnet, a respectable citizen of this place, and with whom Mr. Linder and family boarded."[82] Linder had difficulty coming up with the five hundred dollars needed for bail. Alton was not working out. It was time to go home—back to Coles County.

Apparently, when Linder returned to Coles County, it did not take long before his legal practice was up and thriving; at least that is the impression that he gives in his (not always reliable) memoirs.[83] Just how long it took and how successful he was are open questions, but it was not until March 1842 that Linder expanded his practice to include all the other counties which shared the Fourth Circuit with Coles County. As might be expected, Linder announced this move with no phony display of modesty:

U. F. LINDER

Attorney and Counselor at Law WILL hereinafter practice in all the counties of Judge Wilson's Circuit; also in the Federal and Supreme Courts of Illinois. References are deemed unnecessary, inasmuch as he flatters himself that he is pretty generally known professionally; having practiced assiduously eight years in Kentucky and seven in Illinois.—He is determined to lend his whole energies to his profession, to make up for lost time, and hard times, his punctual attention will be given to all cases instructed to him either in law or in equity.[84]

It probably was no oversight that Linder did not include among his credentials his tempestuous tenure as attorney general. Be that as it may, the move home worked. It seems clear that at least by the mid-1840s, Linder was a prominent and respected member of the circuit-riding fraternity of attorneys which included the Circuit Court of Coles County among its regular stops.

Linder's path to political recovery was a bit more problematical. In his 1842 announcement of his expanded legal practice, Linder referenced *"lost time"* and *"hard times"* and promised to "lend his whole energies to his profession." The "hard times" and the time "lost" probably were due to Linder's attempted involvement in Coles County politics.

Linder now was a Whig—a timely conversion, made perhaps because Coles County now tilted Whig.[85] Unfortunately for the prodigal son, Coles County was home to numerous Whig incumbents and aspiring Whig politicians, all with party credentials better than Linder's. In 1838, Cole County's seat in the state senate was held by a Whig, and both of its state representatives were Whigs—James T. Cunningham and Orlando B. Ficklin. Cunningham had been elected in 1837 to fill Linder's seat in the legislature when Linder had resigned to become Illinois attorney general and he was easily reelected in 1838.[86] Ficklin was to become the bane of Linder's attempt at a political comeback.

In 1838, Ficklin had been elected to the Illinois house as a Whig.[87] In 1842, when he became a Democrat, his conversion provided an opening on the Whig ticket in Coles County. Ignoring his pledge to "lend his whole energies to his profession," Linder pounced. He ran, he lost, and he lost badly. There were too many Whig candidates for the three Coles County seats in the legislature. The Whig vote was split too many ways, enabling Ficklin and a Democratic colleague to take two of the three seats. One of the founders of Coles County, George M. Hanson, a Whig, won the other seat. Linder placed fifth with about 11 per cent of the vote.[88]

It was around this time, perhaps in an effort to raise his political profile, that Linder became a coeditor of the *Charleston Courier*, a local newspaper that had been founded by his coeditor, W. W. Bishop, a fellow Whig.[89] Linder's foray into journalism ended in 1844, the year that he again faced off against Orlando Ficklin, this time for the right to represent Coles County and the rest of the Illinois Third District in Congress.

Ficklin had been elected to the seat in 1843, an election that had been delayed about a year due to problems in redistricting after the 1840 census.[90] Before Linder was nominated by the Whig convention in Vandalia, he, perhaps disingenuously, had denied any appetite for office. In a letter to his friend and political ally Congressman John J. Hardin, Linder claimed that his only goal was to help Henry Clay be elected president, to "ask him for nothing," to "fall back upon my own humble resources, . . . and live like a gentleman." I "have held office," he wrote Hardin, "but never expect or desire it again[.] [I]t is my desire to live and die a 'big private.'"[91]

Linder's avowed reluctance to run may have been prompted by the challenge he would have to face in Ficklin. The Democrat had won rather handily the year before against Justin Harlin, a man for whom Linder had "the most profound respect."[92] Moreover, in Ficklin, Linder believed that he would have "a wiley [sic] opponent . . . to contend with."[93] His appreciation of Ficklin's abilities did not mean that Linder admired the man. To the contrary. In another letter to Harlin in early 1844, Linder referred to Ficklin as the "most contemptible" man in Congress and, with classic Linder venom, condemned his future opponent as a "political Harlot."[94]

Perhaps it was this very venom that drove Linder to run against Ficklin in 1844. Or maybe it was because he believed that the Democrats were "more divided and dispirited in this state, than ever I have known them; and the opinion is beginning to prevail in both parties that the state will go for Clay," the Whig candidate for president and a man that Linder idolized.[95] Of course, Linder's decision to run may also have just been the result of what he called "the political itch."[96] He had been out of the political spotlight since Alton and his ill-fated days as attorney general, and as he himself admitted, "It must be flattering to a man's vanity to reach so honorable an elevation" as a seat in Congress.[97]

Linder promised that his campaign would be "no boys-play" and that he would give Ficklin "the hottest canvass he has ever had."[98] Linder did his best to live up to his boast. Loading his family into a two-horse, four-seated buggy, he "visited every place of importance and some places of hardly any importance or note in the congressional district."[99] His son recalled that it was "one of the most exciting campaigns" that the Third District had ever seen.[100] His father lost.

When the final vote was tallied, Ficklin had won big—by a larger margin than that by which he had won in 1843.[101] Still, Linder's defeat had a silver lining. Although he had been fairly well trounced in the rest of the district, Linder had won a majority in Coles County.[102] Building on this local success, Linder ran for a Coles County seat in the assembly in 1846 and won easily.[103] It was the first time that he had won an election in a decade.

So what was Usher F. Linder like in 1847, at the time of the Matson trial? We can say what he did not look like. Linder probably did not look like the "tall and gangling" individual described by some of Lincoln's biographers.[104] According to a description in the *Peoria Democratic Press* for February 10, 1847, Linder was a man "about five feet eight inches in height, rather robust, short neck, impudent face, prominent eye, brown hair and fresh complexion and a devil may care carriage and sanguine temperament."[105]

The article also points out that Linder "is a very popular speaker and one of the best in the [assembly], but . . . speaks too often, with too much levity, and some times uses language not the most choice."[106] In sum, he had not changed much in ten years. He still was a masterful orator. For example, his friend Bishop found it "idle to attempt to describe" Linder's speech in June 1846 to the initial muster of Coles County volunteers for the Mexican War. "We would just as soon," Bishop wrote in the *Charleston Republican*, "attempt to transfer to paper the dash of lightning, or the roar of artillery—he spoke for some two hours, being frequently interrupted by enthusiastic bursts of applause."[107]

Despite his travails, Linder had not lost his sense of humor, which, by 1847, was becoming legendary among his legal colleagues.[108] His oratory also retained its sting, its "power to hurt," which had manifested itself when he first battled Lincoln in the state legislature ten years earlier.[109] Linder's verbal onslaughts enraged his political opponents and caused his friends to fear for his physical safety. During the 1844 presidential campaign, for instance, Linder made a pro-Clay speech at the Illinois Statehouse. The speech, which Linder characterized as "the very best I ever made in my life," provoked "gross personal" insults and threats from some of those in the audience and an escort to his hotel by friends who feared that he would be attacked "by some of those ruffians who insulted [him] from the galleries."[110]

Usually, Linder did not need much help in defending himself. Never one to shrink from a violent confrontation, he always was ready to strike a blow or fire a few shots in his own behalf. The Democratic mayor of Quincy learned this the hard way. According to Linder, the mayor "had been going around the country attacking my personal character."[111] In a speech at a Whig convention in Quincy, Linder "opened upon him . . . and held him to the scorn and indignation of my auditors."[112] Then the mayor made a near fatal mistake. He escalated the level of the dispute and physically attacked Linder with "a large hickory cane."[113] After fighting the man off, a battered and bloody Linder went to a friend's house, "got my head dressed . . . armed myself with a good revolver," and went to the mayor's house "determined if I met him in his own parlor to Plaster its walls with his brains."[114] Fortunately for all concerned, the mayor was nowhere to be found.

Linder's fiery temper was merely the most extreme manifestation of a fundamental instability that plagued him throughout his life and was blatantly obvious to contemporaries. The 1847 article in the *Peoria Democratic Press*, referred to earlier, noted that Linder's "political opinions and course and life have been some what unstable."[115] John M. Palmer, who called Linder "the most remarkable man I have ever met," noted that Linder "combined all the qualities of a great man and a great lawyer, except plain, common 'horse sense.'"[116]

Linder's boozing did not help matters. He tried to deal with the problem. In 1846, the year that Coles County sent him back to the state legislature, Linder was persuaded by a legislative colleague to again take up "the temperance cause."[117] In retrospect, Linder regretted that he "had not stood by it," but he did not, and like his oratory, his humor, and his temper, Linder's drinking became the stuff of legend.[118]

In letters to his wife while riding the circuit, David Davis, then a state judge whom Lincoln later appointed to the United States Supreme Court, regularly informed her of whether Linder was drunk or sober.[119] Sometimes, Linder's cases had to be postponed because he was too intoxicated to proceed.[120] But this was a few years in the future. In 1847, the bottle had yet to get the better of him and Usher Linder still was a force in the courtroom. In 1847, he was still, in his own words, "in the hey-day of life, being in the very prime of my youthful manhood."[121] In 1847, in the words of Hiram Rutherford, Linder still was "an orator certainly remarkable."[122]

On a more somber note, in 1847, Linder still was a racist. He still was the same man who, ten years earlier, at the Alton trial, had compared "the African" to "a wild beast."[123] And in the Matson case, he was Lincoln's cocounsel.

CHAPTER 5

THE LAW

JANE AND HER FOUR CHILDREN WERE RUNAWAY SLAVES. IN 1847, WHEN it came to runaway slaves, the federal Fugitive Slave Act of 1793 and the United States Supreme Court's decision in *Prigg v. Pennsylvania* (1842) dominated the legal landscape.[1] Congress had promulgated the Fugitive Slave Act of 1793 to implement Section 2(3) of Article IV of the United States Constitution, which read as follows:

> *No person held to service or labor in one State ["slaves"], under the laws thereof, escaping into another, shall, in consequence of any law or regulation therein, be discharged from such service or labor, but shall be delivered up on claim of the party to whom such service or labor may be due.*

The act of 1793 implemented Section 2(3) by establishing a somewhat summary procedure for recovering runaways. The statute authorized a slave owner or owner's agent to seize a purported fugitive, take him or her before a federal or state judicial officer, and offer written or oral sworn testimony that the accused was the claimant's slave "under the laws of the State or Territory from which he or she fled."[2] If the judge agreed, he had no choice but to provide the claimant with a certificate of ownership of the individual in question.[3] The statute gave the accused fugitive no right to habeas corpus, no right to produce evidence, no right to cross-examine witnesses, and no right to a jury trial.

At this juncture, it is critical to understand that Section 2(3) and the Fugitive Slave Act cut against what was generally considered "the determinative English precedent."[4] This is no small point. In the first half-century of the republic, despite nationalistic diatribes against reliance on "foreign" law, American legal argument and judicial decisions often cited and quoted English decisions and

English treatises as authoritative precedent. This was especially true of English cases decided prior to July 4, 1776, because these cases arguably were part of the laws of the colonies which they had brought with them into the new nation.[5]

The English case of *Somerset v. Stewart* was one such decision.[6] Decided in 1772, *Somerset* involved the legal status of a slave who had been brought from Virginia to England where he then had escaped. Recaptured, he was about to be shipped to Jamaica for sale when he was brought before the Court of King's Bench on a writ of habeas corpus secured through the efforts of Granville Sharp, an English opponent of the slave trade. William Murray, Lord Mansfield, was called upon to decide whether England, where there were thousands of slaves but no laws permitting slavery, would give effect, on English soil, to the laws of Virginia which protected a master's right "to detain, imprison, and transport his slave."[7]

Because there is no verbatim transcript of the hearing, it is not altogether clear what Chief Justice Mansfield's opinion actually said.[8] Later, Mansfield maintained that all he had held was that "the master cannot by force compel [Somerset] to go out of the kingdom."[9] No matter. The version that reached America included the following:

> [T]he state of slavery is of such a nature, that it is incapable of being introduced on any reasons . . . but only [by] positive law which preserves its force long after the reasons, occasion, and time itself from whence it was created, is eased from memory: It is so odious, that nothing can be suffered to support it, but positive law.[10]

What this meant was that slavery was contrary to natural law (i.e., was an unnatural condition) and could only be recognized if established by "positive law" (i.e., law enacted or adopted by government). Where there was no such "positive law" recognizing slavery, there could be no slaves.[11] Thus, "[t]he language that reached America as the text of Lord Mansfield supported the conclusion that a slave became free upon setting foot in a free jurisdiction."[12]

Northern judges were not immune to the contradiction between natural and federal law.[13] In *State v. Hoppess* (1845), an Ohio judge voiced the dilemma facing many northern jurists and articulated the distinction most believed that they had to draw between morality and the law:

> True, the great principles of natural right asserted in the Declaration of Independence, and lying at the foundation of our institutions, if permitted to operate, would liberate all. . . . Nor is it necessary to refer to charts,

*ordinances, and the written declarations of men, as the foundation and
recognition of those natural rights of freedom, inherent in man as the gift of
God, and impresses upon our nature by the hand of omnipotence himself.
. . . Slavery is wrong inflicted by force, and supported alone by the mu-
nicipal power of the state or territory wherein it exists. It is opposed to the
principles of natural justice and right, and is the mere creature of positive
law. Hence, it being my duty to declare the law, not to make it, the question
is not, what conforms to the great principles of natural right and univer-
sal freedom—but what do the positive laws and institutions which we, as
members of the government under which we live, are bound to recognize
and obey, command and direct.*[14]

What the "positive laws and institutions" (the United States Constitution
and the Fugitive Slave Act) did "command and direct" was that escaped slaves
"be delivered up on claim" of their masters.[15] The courts found their hands tied.
Some northern legislatures attempted to fill the void and protect fugitive slaves.
By the early 1830s some of the free states, including Ohio (1804), Pennsylvania
(1820, 1826), and Illinois (1833), had addressed the problem of overeager slave
catchers with statutes that made it illegal to kidnap free blacks for the purpose
of enslavement.[16] The Pennsylvania statute of 1826 went further, establishing
what amounted to a mandatory procedure that had to be followed before an
alleged runaway could be seized.[17]

Beginning in the mid-1830s, as their movement grew stronger in the North,
antislavery forces there sought to take advantage of the vagueness of the Fugitive Slave Act of 1793 by attempting, through personal liberty laws, to graft on
to it rights that were not provided for in the act, or, for that matter, contem-
plated by the Congress that had passed it.[18] Massachusetts (1837), Connecticut
(1838), New York (1840), and Vermont (1840) required a jury trial in fugitive
slave cases.[19] The act's opponents also favored giving alleged fugitives the right
to confront their accusers and present evidence in their defense.[20]

While there were some skirmishes in lower courts concerning state efforts to
temper the Fugitive Slave Act, the major battle was fought in the United States
Supreme Court. *Prigg v. Pennsylvania* (1842) involved a slave catcher who failed
to follow Pennsylvania's 1826 personal liberty law and was prosecuted, bringing
the constitutionality of that law into question.[21]

In his "lead opinion," which was the official opinion in *Prigg,* Justice Joseph
Story began by emphasizing the importance of the Constitution's fugitive slave
provision, which, in his words, was "a fundamental article without which the
Union could not have been formed."[22] He then addressed the English decision

in *Somerset's Case*, stressing the limits that the Constitution put on natural law and the rights of the free states to determine the status of fugitive slaves on their soil.[23]

Story went on to hold that the Fugitive Slave Act of 1793 was a constitutional exercise of congressional power "necessary and proper" to implement the fugitive slave provision of the Constitution, and that the Pennsylvania statute was unconstitutional because "it purports to punish as a public offense against that State the very act of seizing and removing a slave by his master which the Constitution of the United States was designed to justify and uphold."[24]

Story could have stopped there. He chose not to do so. His sights were on the entire antislavery arsenal of statutes, decisions, and arguments that were aimed at denying the Fugitive Slave Act its efficacy and, in Story's view, threatened the very foundation of the union.[25] Story maintained that the power to legislate on the subject of fugitive slaves was "exclusive in the National Government."[26] While states had "police power" to "arrest and restrain runaway slaves, and remove them from their borders, and otherwise secure themselves against their depredations and evil example, . . . such regulations can never be permitted to interfere with or to obstruct the just rights of the owner to reclaim his slave, derived from the Constitution of the United States, or with the remedies prescribed by Congress to aid and enforce the same."[27]

With regard to the language in the 1793 statute permitting a master to prove his case before a state magistrate, Story said the following:

> As to the authority conferred upon state magistrates, while a difference of opinion has existed, and may exist still, on the point in different States, whether state magistrates are bound to act under it, none is entertained by this Court that state magistrates may, if they choose, exercise that authority unless prohibited by state legislation.[28]

Prigg proved to be a two-edged sword. In declaring the Fugitive Slave Act an exclusively federal concern and denying the rights of states to legislate in this area, the Supreme Court shot down northern efforts to give civil rights to accused fugitives, but, in recognizing that the states had discretion as to whether their officials need assist in the enforcement of the Fugitive Slave Act, it also provided the antislavery forces with a new weapon. Between 1842 and 1847, Massachusetts (1843), Vermont (1843), Ohio (1843), Connecticut (1844), New Hampshire (1846), and Pennsylvania (1847) passed laws that essentially prohibited state assistance in capturing and jailing fugitive slaves.[29]

The Massachusetts statute was the prototype.[30] Providing fines and jail time for noncompliance, the 1843 Act further to Protect Personal Liberty declared:

Sect. 1. No judge of any court of record of this Commonwealth, and no justice of the peace, shall hereafter take cognizance or grant a certificate, in cases that may arise under the third section of the [Fugitive Slave Act of 1793], to any person who claims any other person as a fugitive slave within the jurisdiction of this Commonwealth.

Sect. 2. No sheriff, deputy-sheriff, coroner, constable, jailor, or other officer of this Commonwealth, shall hereafter arrest or detain, or aid in the arrest or detention or imprisonment, in any jail or other building belonging to this Commonwealth . . . , of any person, for the reason that he is claimed as a fugitive slave.[31]

That is how the law under the Fugitive Slave Act stood in 1847 when Jane Bryant and her children found themselves in the Coles County jail. That probably is why Robert Matson's first move in the case was to make a sworn statement before Judge Gilman that the Bryants "were his slaves in the state of Kentucky," that they were now in Illinois, and that they "refuse to return" to his service in Kentucky.[32] He was attempting compliance with Section 3 of the act which required judicial officers to issue a certificate of removal to any claimant who could by "oral testimony or affidavit" prove that an individual owed "service or labor to the person claiming him or her."[33] The problem was that the Fugitive Slave Act did not apply to the situation. It applied to slaves who had escaped from one jurisdiction to another.

Jane and her children did not enter Illinois as fugitives. Matson had brought them there voluntarily. This was not a singular occurrence. Masters often brought or sent their slaves into free states. When slave owners took up residence in a free state, they often brought their slaves with them. It was not unusual for slaves to accompany masters as their personal servants when the master visited the North on business or for pleasure. Some slaves merely passed through free states with their owners on the way from one slave state to another. The status of slaves who were voluntarily brought to free soil raised questions which, as emotions over slavery heated up, became increasingly more difficult to answer in a consistent manner.[34]

The Supreme Court of the United States had not attempted to do so in *Prigg*. In that case, Chief Justice Taney voiced the view of the entire Court when he made it clear that the case before the Court involved slaves who had fled to another jurisdiction and not those "whom their masters voluntarily take into a non-slaveholding state."[35] Taney made this point because *Prigg*, the Constitution, and the Fugitive Slave Act of 1793 dealt only with slaves who fled their masters—i.e., *fugitive* slaves. The problem of what to do about "slaves whom their masters voluntarily take into non-slaveholding states" was largely left up to the states, who looked to each other for precedents on how to decide the issue.

There were different responses, but on some issues there was general agreement. Virtually all of the courts that confronted the question concurred with the 1806 decision of Justice Bushrod Washington (George's nephew) in *Butler v. Hopper* that the Fugitive Slave Act did not apply to a slave voluntarily "carried" by a master into a free state.[36]

The "Butler" in *Butler v. Hopper* was Pierce Butler, a senator for South Carolina. For years, Butler had kept a Negro servant in Philadelphia. When the slave sued for his freedom, Justice Washington declared him free on the ground that if a master took up residence in a free state or territory, his or her slaves in the state or territory became free as a result of that residence.[37] Most courts agreed with this premise, but often this road to freedom was a long and winding one.

In *Vaughn v. Williams*, a case decided in 1845, a slave owner named Tipton had moved with three slaves from Kentucky to Illinois in 1835 and had declared his intention to become a citizen of that state.[38] In 1836, Mr. Tipton took the slaves across the border to Missouri, a slave state, where he sold them to a Mr. Vaughn. A year later, the slaves escaped to Indiana. Eight years passed. In 1844, Vaughn learned where the slaves were living, crossed into Indiana, obtained a warrant under the Fugitive Slave Act, and apprehended the slaves. Then things began to get uncomfortable.[39] Mr. Vaughn soon found himself confronted by an ever-increasing crowd of angry Hoosiers who, in the judge's words, "expressed a strong interest on behalf of the Slaves."[40] A compromise was reached, and the slaves were placed in a wagon purportedly to be transported to court for a judicial resolution of the matter. The crowd became larger and more vocal. Suddenly, a "shout was raised, and the wagon was driven rapidly. The fugitives escaped, and have not since been seen by the plaintiff."[41]

Apparently, Owen Williams, the defendant in the case, had played a leading role in the rescue, or, again to use the judge's words, "took active agency in the proceedings on behalf of the slaves."[42] Vaughn sued Williams under the provision of the Fugitive Slave Act that allowed a master to recover five hundred dollars from any person who aided a fugitive slave to escape. In instructing the jury, Justice McLean made it clear that under the law and the facts, the plaintiff had no chance to recover:

Having been brought to the State of Illinois, which prohibits slavery, by their master from the State of Kentucky, and kept at labor six months, under the declaration of the master that he intended to become a citizen of that State; and [the master] having actually exercised the rights of a citizen by voting, there can no doubt that the slaves were thereby entitled to their freedom. This conforms to decisions repeatedly made by the Supreme Court of the State of Missouri.[43]

McLean's reference to Missouri law is significant because slave states, such as Missouri, also usually recognized that a master who took slaves into a free state and "by the length of his residence there indicates an intention of making that place his residence & that of his slave . . . does by such residence declare his slave to become a free man."[44]

One of the leading southern authorities on this point was *Rankin v. Lydia*, decided by the Kentucky Court of Appeals in 1820. That case involved the fate of Lydia, a fifteen-year-old black girl who had been born a slave in Kentucky in 1805.[45] Two years later, her master, John Warrick, moved to the Indiana Territory, taking Lydia and her mother with him. In 1814, Warrick sold his rights in Lydia, now age nine, and after a series of transactions, she ended up back in Kentucky with John Rankin, "who still holds and claims her as a slave for life, she being a person of color."[46]

Lydia sued for her freedom in the circuit court of Shelby County, Kentucky, and won. The court of appeals affirmed. It based its decision on the language in Article VI of the Northwest Ordinance, which declared that "there shall be neither slavery nor involuntary servitude" in Indiana or the other territories northwest of the Ohio River.[47] In the court's view, when John Warrick, Lydia's original master, opted to live in Indiana, his claim to "every atom of property he there possessed had its right of possession and enjoyment based upon that ordinance."[48] It governed his rights to whatever he claimed to own and "[a]s between him and Lydia [Article VI] then spoke equally loud—that she was not his slave—that his right to her was extinct; or in other words, that she was on her own."[49]

Moreover, the fact that Lydia had been returned to Kentucky, a slave state, the state, in fact, where she had been born a slave, was of no effect. Warrick's right to Lydia's service *during the seven years' residence of Lydia, in Indiana, was not only suspended but ceased to exist; and we are not aware of any law of this state which can or does bring into operation the right of slavery once destroyed. . . . The purchaser from Warrick could not receive from him the right of slavery in Lydia, for he had none to convey. She was not the slave of the purchaser while he remained in Indiana after his purchase; and is it to be seriously contended that so soon as he transplanted her to the Kentucky shore, the noxious atmosphere of this state, without any express law for the purpose, clamped upon her newly forged chains of slavery, after the old ones were destroyed. For the honor of our country. we cannot for a moment admit, that the bare treading of its soil is thus dangerous, even to the degraded African.[50]*

The rule applied even in the Deep South. In *Lunsford v. Coquillon* (1824), a Louisiana court freed a slave then in Louisiana who earlier had been taken by her prior master to live in Ohio:

We conclude that the constitution of the state [of] Ohio emancipates, <u>ipso facto</u>, such slaves whose owners remove them into that state, with the intention of residing there . . . and the plaintiff was accordingly as effectively emancipated, by the operation of the constitution, as by the act and deed of her former owner—that she could not be free in one state, and a slave in another. . . .[51]

Rankin and other southern decisions were careful to distinguish between situations in which it was established that the master and his or her slaves had taken up *residence* in a free state and those in which master and slave were *temporarily* in a free state. In the latter situation, when the master was merely visiting or passing through, the predominant southern judicial view was that the slave remained a slave and gained no rights by virtue of his or her time on free soil.[52] In the words of the court in *Rankin*:

Different then is the case of the sojourner from that of him who moves with the intention of residing. The former is subject only to particular laws, <u>and has the title of his property secure</u>, while he who enters and actually resides is subject to every law.[53]

In *Strader v. Graham* (1844), the Kentucky Court of Appeals went so far as to hold that the right of a master to retain ownership of his or her slaves remained inviolate even if the slaves performed services in a free state so long as their purpose in being there was transient.[54] The case involved two slaves whom their master had taken from Kentucky to Ohio and Indiana where they performed as musicians. When this point was raised in support of proving them free men, the court would have none of it. In the court's words, the fact that the slaves had performed services in free states was "immaterial . . . they were still sojourners for a transient purpose, not inhabitants or residents, and voluntarily returned with [their master]."[55]

In a subsequent decision in the case, the court of appeals went out of its way to hammer home the point that the slaves in question could never have become free "by being temporarily in a free State with their master . . . having control over them."[56] The court refused to accept the premise

[t]hat in consequence of such a fact, and by force of the mere general prohibition of slavery in the fundamental or declaratory law of the [free] State, which might be thus visited, the relation of master and slave, as existing under the laws of their own State, would be affected.[57]

There were, of course, cases which involved factual situations which did not fit neatly into the master in residence/master in transit dichotomy. The Missouri Supreme Court wrestled with a number of these in the early 1830s, leading it to modify its approach to the problem.

As noted earlier, in the case of *Winney v. Whitesides* (1824), the Missouri Supreme Court had held that a master's residence in a free state liberated those slaves that he or she had brought into the state to be residents there.[58] In *Winney,* the court had implied that the key to determining whether or not the master (and his slaves) were, in fact, in residence was the master's intention to do so, and that such intention could be determined by the "length of his residence" there. In brief, the longer a master stayed in a free state, the more likely that he or she intended to become a resident.[59]

Six years later, in *Vincent v. Duncan* (1830), the Missouri Supreme Court was confronted with a case in which the master had spent virtually no time in Illinois, but had hired out his slave to labor in the saltworks in the Salines near Shawneetown a year prior to the adoption of the Illinois Constitution of 1818, which specifically permitted slaves to be used there.[60]

The court held that because the constitution had not been in effect for at least a year during which time the slave had worked in the Salines, the question was governed by the Northwest Ordinance, which, in the court's view, "was made to prevent the introduction of slaves into the Territory of which Illinois was then a part."[61] The court then referenced, without naming, *Winney v. Whitesides* and other decisions in which it had decided "that if the owner of slaves took them with him into Illinois, with intent to reside there, and did reside there, keeping his slaves, it was a fraud on the [Northwest] Ordinance, and the slaves became free."[62]

But here, Vincent's master had not resided in Illinois and had demonstrated no intention to do so. He had remained in Kentucky. Proof of his owner's intent would not have freed Vincent even though he had been sent to a place where the Northwest Ordinance forbade the introduction of slavery and had worked there as a slave. Fully realizing this, the court held that if a master "stay in Kentucky, and send a slave over to reside [in Illinois], it is equally a violation of the provisions of the ordinance" and the slave was free.[63]

This decision, as Paul Finkelman astutely points out in his *An Imperfect Union*, represented a significant shift in Missouri law.[64] Without articulating it as such, the Missouri Supreme Court had rejected the abstract "'intention to reside with a slave' test in favor of a factual determination: 'Did the master actually introduce slavery into a free state?'"[65]

The Missouri Supreme Court made this change explicit in *Julia v. McKinney*.[66] In this 1833 case, the plaintiff sued for her freedom on the ground that her former master had moved to Illinois from Kentucky and, before sending her to be sold in St. Louis, kept her as a slave and hired her out for two days in Illinois.

The defendant argued that Julia's master had not intended to make Illinois Julia's residence, had declared this intention, and that, under *Winney v. Whiteside*, "what the owner intended, is to be the criterion to govern the question of freedom or slavery."[67] The court disagreed. It maintained that in *Winney*, it was the fact of the slave's residence in Illinois which had freed her, not the owner's declared intent to take up residence there.[68] Similarly, in Julia's case, the facts counted more than intent:

> Is it true that if a person says he does not intend to do an act and yet does it, that act is not done? The Constitution of Illinois does not regard the intention to introduce or not to introduce slavery but prohibits the act. If a person says he does not intend to introduce slavery, yet he does introduce it de facto, can the innocent intent save him from forfeiture? We think it cannot unless he can also show that his case raises a reasonable and necessary exception. But in this case the evidence is, that the owner did intend and did in fact introduce slavery into Illinois, but declared that she did not intend to continue it for any length of time; but that she would take the

slave to Missouri and hire her out. But suppose the owner did not intend to make Illinois the place of the slave's residence permanently, but only for one month; yet slavery is introduced and continued for the mere convenience of the owner without any circumstances which raise a just or even a reasonable exception in her favor.[69]

Initially, northern states also generally adhered to the "in residence" v. "in transient" approach.[70] The 1780 Pennsylvania statute that mandated the gradual abolition of slavery in the state also provided that slaves that were brought into the state were not entitled to their freedom unless their master's "sojourn" exceeded six months.[71] New York gave masters similar rights for nine months.[72] Judge Duncan of the Pennsylvania Supreme Court explained the rationale of the Pennsylvania statute in the case of *Butler v. Dalaplaine* (1821):

It was well known to the framers of our Acts for the Abolition of slavery, that southern gentlemen, with their families, were in the habit of visiting this State, attended with their domestic slaves, either for pleasure, health, or business; year after year passing the summer months with us, their continuance scarcely amounting to six months. If these successive sojournings were to be summed up, it would amount to a prohibition—a denial of the rights of hospitality.[73]

In time, however, as a result of growing antislavery sentiment, many northern judges rejected not only the "sojourner" exception, but any exception at all. Chief Justice Lemuel Shaw of the Massachusetts Supreme Judicial Court led the way in the 1836 case of *Commonwealth v. Aves.*[74] The subject of the lawsuit, Med, was an eight-year-old slave girl who had accompanied her mistress, Mary Slater, as a personal attendant on a trip from New Orleans to Boston. Mrs. Slater had placed Med in the temporary care of her father, Thomas Aves, when the Boston abolitionist Levin H. Harris filed a petition for a writ of habeas corpus to secure Med's release.[75]

Chief Justice Shaw ruled in the little girl's favor. After noting that slavery had been abolished in Massachusetts in 1789, that federal law applied only to fugitive slaves, and that slavery was "contrary to natural right," Shaw concluded "that an owner of a slave in another State where slavery is warranted by law, voluntarily bringing such slave into this State, has no authority to detain him against his will, or to carry him out of the State against his consent, for the purpose of being held in slavery."[76] The chief justice did not base this conclusion on Massachusetts precedent—there was none—but rather on his assumption that the law was "established . . . that the moment the master carries his slave into a country where domestic slavery is not permitted, he becomes free."[77]

In freeing Med, Shaw had subscribed to the most liberal interpretation of *Somerset* and, in so doing, had obliterated the distinction, so important in southern decisions, between slaves whose masters had taken up residence in a free state and those whose masters merely were there temporarily.[78] And Massachusetts was not alone. A year later, in *Jackson v. Bulloch*, the Supreme Court of Connecticut held that the state's 1774 statute forbidding slaves from being brought into Connecticut "to be disposed of, left or sold" within the state meant that "no slave shall be brought from any place and suffered to remain in the state."[79] From this premise, the court concluded that, despite her master's claim that his stay in Connecticut was only temporary and that he intended to return to Georgia, his slave Nancy had been "brought and left in this state contrary to the act of 1774; and, therefore, that she cannot be claimed or treated as a slave, under our laws."[80]

Other northern decisions were decided to the same effect, and, in the 1840s, both Pennsylvania and New York repealed their statutes permitting sojourning masters to retain ownership of their slaves.[81]

In general then, by 1847, the law with regard to slaves voluntarily in free states came down to this: an increasing number of northern states agreed with Shaw's decision in *Aves* that a slave became free the moment he or she was voluntarily brought into a free state no matter how long he or she stayed there. The remaining northern states and all of those in the South held that slaves remained bound if their presence in a free state was of a transitory nature. For these states, slaves who had spent time in free states were emancipated only if they or they and their master took up permanent residence there, or, at least according to the Missouri line of cases, the master's actions with regard to a slave amounted to the introduction of slavery into a free state. This position was far more complicated than the "free soil, free man" equation. It required evidence of the permanency of the master's and/or the slave's residence which could involve objective factors such as the duration of the stay and subjective ones such as intent.[82]

While all of this had been going on, the Illinois legislature and the Illinois courts had remained relatively inactive with regard to slaves who had escaped or been brought into the state. Although Illinois's statutes prohibited the kidnapping of free blacks, unlike many of its northern neighbors, the state did not promulgate personal liberty laws aimed at providing civil rights to alleged fugitive slaves.[83] To the contrary, in the words of Senator Stephen Douglas, Illinois legislation "had been friendly to every constitutional obligation."[84] Section 149 of the Illinois criminal code made it a misdemeanor to "harbor or secrete any negro, mulatto, or person of color" who was "a slave or servant" of anyone residing "within the limits and under the jurisdiction of the United States" or to "in any wise hinder or prevent the owner or owners of such slaves or servants from retaking them in a lawful manner."[85]

Things began to heat up in the early 1840s. In October 1843, in what was probably the most famous fugitive slave trial of the period, Elijah Lovejoy's younger brother, Owen, was tried before Justice John Dean Caton in the Bureau County Circuit Court. The indictment against him charged Lovejoy with "keeping . . . In his dwelling house, conveying . . . from place to place, feeding, clothing, and . . . comforting" a runaway slave named Nancy in violation of Section 149 of the Illinois criminal code.[86]

The lead prosecutor in the case was Norman H. Purple, a strong opponent of abolitionism.[87] He was assisted by B. F. Findley, the local state's attorney. Lovejoy's supporters had raised money to retain Alvin Stewart, a prominent abolitionist lawyer from Utica, New York, to lead Lovejoy's defense, but Stewart was not available. Lovejoy was represented by Chicago antislavery lawyer James H. Collins, but played an active role in his own defense.[88]

Because of the defendant's celebrity, the case received statewide attention. Emotions ran high on both sides. Part of the lore of the case is a story that on the day that it was called for trial, an ardent proslavery sympathizer, who was behind Lovejoy's indictment, approached Findley, offered him money, and urged him "to be sure and convict this preacher and send him to prison."[89] Findley reportedly refused the cash and replied: "Prison! Lovejoy to prison! Your prosecution will be damned sight more likely to send him to Congress."[90]

The trial lasted for almost a week. The courtroom was packed.[91] According to Justice Caton, who was presiding, the prosecution established the fact that "a large fat negro woman was domiciled in Mr. Lovejoy's house for several days."[92] There also was evidence that Lovejoy knew that she was a slave and that he knew that she had escaped from her master while they were passing through Illinois on their way from Kentucky to Missouri.[93]

The closing arguments took several days. Apparently, Collins alone spoke for seven hours in defense of Lovejoy, drawing heavily on Lord Mansfield's opinion in the *Somerset* case.[94] Lovejoy assisted in his defense and, by all accounts, he was eloquent. According to one observer, Lovejoy "quoted with effect" lines from the English lawyer-poet William Cowper's "The Task," which celebrated the decision in *Somerset*:

> *"'Slaves cannot breathe in England, if their lungs*
> *Receive our air, that moment they are free—*
> *They touch our country and their shackles fall.'*

'And,' said [Lovejoy] 'if this is the glory of England, is it not equally true of Illinois, her soil consecrated to freedom by the ordinance of 1787, and her constitution.'"[95]

Apparently, Justice Caton bought this argument. Instructing the jury that Nancy remained a slave and was subject to recapture if she "came within this state without the consent of the master," Caton told the jurors that it was not so if her master had brought her into Illinois:

> *By the Constitution of this State, slavery cannot exist here. If therefore, a master voluntarily brings his slave within this State, he becomes from that moment free, and if he escape from his master while in this State, it is not an escape from slavery, but is going where a free man has a right to go; and the harboring of such a person is no offense against the law; but the tie between the slave and the master can only be severed by the voluntary act the latter.*[96]

Lovejoy was acquitted.[97]

For all of its notoriety, Lovejoy's case had little value as precedent because it merely was a circuit court decision. Illinois Supreme Court rulings were what really mattered and, prior to the Matson case, that court had rendered two decisions which touched on issues in that case. In 1843, the same year that Lovejoy was acquitted in Bureau County, the supreme court decided *Eells v. People.*[98] The case involved a *fugitive* slave, that is, a slave who had fled into Illinois rather than one who, like Nancy in the Lovejoy case or the Bryants, had been voluntarily brought into the state. Six of the nine justices affirmed the lower court finding that Dr. Richard Eells, a noted abolitionist, was guilty of violating Section 149 of the Illinois criminal code by "harboring and secreting" a fugitive slave belonging to one Chauncey Durkee of Missouri.[99]

Chief Justice William Wilson and Justices Samuel Drake Lockwood and Thomas C. Browne dissented in words of import to the Matson case. Writing for the three, Lockwood argued, among other things, that Eells's indictment was defective because it did not allege how the escaped slave had entered Illinois. To the dissenters, the omission was critical:

The person being in this State, and by our laws presumed to be free, the question arises, what takes him out of the operation of this rule? Did he escape from Missouri? Then he is a fugitive from labor, and the secreting him is an offense against the act of Congress. Did his master bring him here, and hire him out? Then he becomes free.[100]

There was no Illinois precedent for the dissenters' assertion that a slave brought into the state and hired out "becomes free." Lockwood cited no authority from other jurisdictions in support of this position, but he may have been relying on the Missouri Supreme Court's decision in *Julia v. McKinney* (1830).[101] It will be recalled that in that case, the court held that bringing a slave into Illinois for a month, treating "the slave in all respects as slaves are treated in states where slavery is allowed," and, in particular, hiring her out to another, amounted to a de facto introduction of slavery into the state and, therefore, operated to free the slave.[102]

Again, Lockwood's position was expressed in dissent and the majority decided *Eells* as a fugitive slave case and not one of a slave voluntarily brought into Illinois. However, during the same December 1843 judicial term, the Illinois Supreme Court decided *Willard v. People,* a case that did involve a slave who had been brought into the state by her master.[103] In some respects, this case foreshadowed the Matson case four years later, but some of its similarities were obscured by the manner in which it reached the supreme court.

It all began when Sarah W. Lisle decided to return to her home in Louisiana after an extended visit with two of her sisters in Jacksonville, Illinois.[104] Lisle's planned departure did not sit well with Julia Green, who had made the trip north with Lisle. Green, a teenage "mulatto girl, and a person of color, and . . . a slave owing service, as such to Sarah W. [Lisle]," took off.[105] Her freedom was short-lived. She soon was recaptured, and two local men, Julius A. Willard and his son, Samuel, were arrested and charged under Section 149 with "secreting" Julia Green, a fugitive slave.[106]

From then on, many of the actual facts of the matter became irrelevant. It was only the facts as averred in the indictment that were important and many of these "facts" were pure fiction. As the indictment had it, Julia Green had "escaped from the possession and custody of [Lisle] while in the State of Illinois and passing from the State of Kentucky to the State of Louisiana, through the State of Illinois."[107] Gone from the record were the nearly four months that Lisle and Green had spent in Illinois. Gone too, at least for the time being, was any possible argument that Green had been "resident" in Illinois or that her master had done anything that could be construed as introducing slavery into the state. According to the indictment, the two were just passing through.

Samuel Willard's case was heard in the March 1843 term of the Circuit Court of Morgan County before Justice Lockwood sitting as circuit judge.[108] Willard's lawyers filed a demurrer to the indictment which argued, in effect, that even if the facts as alleged in the indictment were true, it did not state a violation of law because Green had been emancipated the moment that she had entered Illinois.[109] Lockwood disagreed. He maintained that "by comity . . . a person passing through a state with what was property in his own state retained the right thereto during transit."[110]

Having lost on their demurrer, Willard's lawyers could have withdrawn it and proceeded to trial. For reasons which are not completely clear, they chose not to do so.[111] They stood by their demurrer. Justice Lockwood fined Willard thirty dollars and costs and the case went up to the Illinois Supreme Court on the facts as (incorrectly) stated in the indictment.[112]

For his appeal, Willard's defense team had added a new member, the formidable James H. Collins, "as combative as an English bull-dog."[113] Willard's counsel repeated the argument that had been rejected below. Relying on *Somerset*, *Commonwealth v. Aves*, and their progeny, they argued that "if the master bring his slave into a state where slavery does not exist, such slave becomes free."[114] They also contended that Section 149 was unconstitutional and conflicted with the Fugitive Slave Act of 1793.[115] Neither argument prevailed. They lost a unanimous decision.

Justice Scates wrote the majority opinion. After determining that Section 149 was a valid "police regulation" that did not conflict with the Fugitive Slave Act of 1793, Scates turned to the defendant's claim that Julia had been emancipated the moment that she had entered Illinois.[116] Scates held that although not required to recognize a master's "right of transit with a slave," Illinois had "expressly done so" in promulgating Section 149.[117] Scates saw this as a good thing. To do otherwise—to deny comity—would be to deny slave owners in transit "their constitutional right, as citizens of one of the states, to all the rights, immunities, and privileges of the citizens of the several states."[118]

Moreover, the results would be disastrous. To hold that slaves voluntarily brought into Illinois were freed upon entering the state

> . . . *would be productive of great and irremediable evils, of discord, of heart burnings, and alienation of kind and fraternal feeling, which should characterize the American brotherhood, and tend greatly to weaken, if not to destroy the common bond of union amongst us, and our character, interest,*

and feeling. Thousands from Kentucky, Virginia, Maryland, Tennessee and the Carolinas, and other southern states have found free and safe passage with their slaves across our territory to and from Missouri. It would be startling, indeed, if we should deny our neighbors and kindred free and safe passage, which foreign nations would hardly dare deny.[119]

Willard earned a somewhat dubious distinction in upholding the right of slave transit. It was the last major northern state court decision to do so.[120] While some in Illinois condemned it, others applauded the decision. The *Chicago Express*, a Democratic newspaper which stood against both slavery and abolitionism, commented that *Willard* (and *Eells*) issued "a solemn warning to abolitionists to mind their own business."[121]

This then is where the law of Illinois stood in October 1847 when the issue of runaway slaves was raised in the Circuit Court of Coles County, and Abraham Lincoln stood at the bar of that court advocating the interests of Robert Matson.

CHAPTER 6

THE TRIAL

In early October 1847, as the days grew shorter and the wind carried a chill, the upcoming Matson trial monopolized conversation in the taverns and livery stables and by firesides in Coles County. The case was the biggest thing to happen there since, perhaps, the "winter of the deep snow" in 1830–31 or, maybe, "the night of the falling stars" on November 12, 1833, or the "sudden freeze" of December 20, 1836. It seemed that everyone was talking about the case.[1] Then, for a day or two, it looked as though the trial might not take place.

Lewis Hutchason, the sheriff of Coles County, had been something of a bit player in the unfolding drama. He had carried out Judge Gilman's order to arrest and jail the Bryants.[2] On Friday, October 8, with less than perfect spelling, the sheriff opted for a larger role. He gave notice that on Thursday, October 14, he would "proceed to higher out to the highest Bidder for one Month the following Nigrows[:] one Nigro Woman[,] Three Nigro girls and one Nigro Boy."[3] Matson saw the proposed auction as an opportunity to shortcut the judicial process by leasing the Bryants and taking them back to Kentucky. Orlando Ficklin, Ashmore's attorney, saw what Matson saw. Prior to the opening session of the Circuit Court of Coles County, Ficklin went before the court and obtained an order enjoining the auction until after a ruling on his petitions for habeas corpus.[4]

That proceeding was held in the late afternoon of Saturday, October 16, 1847, in the Coles County courthouse in Charleston. Built in 1835, the courthouse was the first brick structure in Charleston, replacing a log building in the southern part of town. It dominated the village square. It had cost five thousand dollars. It was ugly. Constructed in the then prevailing architectural style of an old Kentucky tobacco barn, the courthouse was perfectly square with a four-sided "hip roof," each side of the roof a triangle running up to a steeple in the center.[5] According to the original specifications, the steeple was "'to extend 5 feet, with a ball about 10 inches in diameter, to be covered with gold leaf, and a spear to extend six feet above the ball with a fish or chicken on the top.'"[6] Apparently, neither the gold ball, nor the fish, nor the chicken was included in the final design. As constructed, the top of the courthouse roof was surmounted by a wooden cupola that housed a bell.[7]

The Coles County courthouse's sole courtroom was on the first floor and, on the afternoon of October 16, 1847, that courtroom was crowded, in Ficklin's opinion, "with sympathizers for Matson."[8] For or against Matson, the spectators anticipated a high-stakes trial involving an explosive issue with a palpable potential for violence. In the days that had preceded it, Ashmore and Rutherford had found themselves reviled and "denounced as harborers of runaway negroes."[9]

The parties' counsel were an impressive foursome who promised an entertaining show. Ficklin was a sitting congressman, Lincoln would take his seat in Congress in two months, Linder was a state representative and a former Illinois attorney general, and Constable was a state senator. The first three—Lincoln and Linder for Matson, and Ficklin for the Bryants—were well-known performers on the judicial circuit. Constable may not have been as entertaining as the other three, but he could hold his own and was, by far, the best looking of the quartet.

These four would argue the Bryants' right to freedom before Chief Justice William Wilson and Associate Justice Samuel Hubbell Treat of the Illinois Supreme Court who were sitting as circuit court trial judges. Two judges on the bench was quite unusual. Chief Justice Wilson was there by assignment—Coles County was part of the Fourth Judicial Circuit, which he traversed twice a year. The fact that Wilson had brought along Justice Treat from the neighboring Eighth Circuit to hear the case with him is testament to the importance that Wilson attached to the matter.

The two judges represented a total of thirty-four years of supreme court experience, most of it Wilson's. At fifty-three, the chief justice was seventeen years older than Treat. Wilson had studied law in his native Virginia and then moved to Kentucky and, later, to Illinois. He had been in Illinois only a few years when, in 1819, at the age of twenty-five, he had been appointed an associate justice of the state's highest court.[10] He quickly became known as a painstaking, conscientious judge who was credited by his contemporaries with bringing a heretofore unknown dignity to the supreme court.[11] Six years later, he was elected chief justice, a position to which he was reelected for four consecutive terms.[12]

Everyone seemed to like and respect the chief justice. William Caton, who served on the supreme court during part of Wilson's tenure, hailed him as a man "of good parts . . . a thorough gentlemen, courteous and affable, pleasant, and of a very cheerful disposition."[13] Caton recalled that "often when tired of hard thinking and of listening to dry discussions in the conference room [Wilson] would break in and tell a good story, which would be relief and rest to all."[14]

Some of Wilson's affability may have been the product of more than "a very cheerful disposition." In 1835, Gustave Koerner, then a young applicant for the bar, made an interesting discovery when he visited Justices Wilson and Theophilus Smith in their hotel room to be examined for admission as an attorney: "The room was whitewashed, perfectly bare with the exceptions of the two bedsteads, a deal table and a couple of chairs. Wilson, complaining of being sick, was stretched out on one of the beds, held a small phial of medicine in his hand and swallowed once or twice in the course of the conversation a few drops. It was opium, which he was in the habit of taking for a chronic disease of the stomach."[15]

Opium was a common (and sometimes abused) palliative at the time. Whatever the extent of Wilson's "habit," it apparently had no adverse impact on his professional competence. Koerner, for example, considered Wilson "a good lawyer, and a fine writer."[16] This seemed to be the general consensus. In his *Reminiscences*, published in 1879, Usher Linder remembered Wilson as "an able judge, both of the Supreme Court and the courts *nisi prius*."[17] Caton's judicious evaluation of Wilson probably expressed the majority view: "He did not know all the law there is, nor does any man, but . . . he had the capacity to understand the law when it was read to him, or was stated to him in argument, with the reasons in support of it, and this is a capacity of the greatest value in a judge."[18]

Samuel Hubbell Treat, who shared the bench with Wilson at the Matson trial, had a similar reputation as a judge. Born on a farm near Cooperstown in central New York, Treat had studied law and then moved to Springfield, Illinois, in 1834 at age twenty-three to practice law. Seven years later he was appointed to the supreme court.[19]

Neither Treat nor Wilson was an especially "political" judge. According to Linder, Treat "was a sterling Democrat, and as true as steel to that great and noble old party, but he never suffered his politics to mingle in the slightest degree with his judicial opinions or deliberations."[20] Wilson came from the other side of the political aisle. He was a Whig; yet, as one contemporary recalled, Wilson was "a judge, and nothing else: in no sense was he a politician."[21]

The justices' judicial resumes offered some strong hints as to how they might rule in the Matson case. In the indentured servant cases of the 1820s and 1830s, while Wilson consistently voted to uphold the indenture system, he insisted that the law be precisely applied.[22] Moreover, he was part of unanimous courts in *Kinney v. Cook* and *Bailey v. Cromwell* in 1841 which held that Illinois law presumed that all men and women were free. Treat, who had just joined the court in time for the *Bailey* case, was part of the unanimous court in that case.[23] The two justices had disagreed in *Jarrot v. Jarrot*, in which the Illinois Supreme Court held that French slavery was prohibited in Illinois. Wilson voted with the majority, filing a concurring opinion. Treat dissented without opinion.[24]

In the two 1843 Illinois Supreme Court decisions dealing with runaway slaves, Justices Wilson and Treat had not seen eye to eye. In *Willard v. People*, the case closest to the Matson case, Wilson and Treat joined with the rest of their supreme court brethren in affirming the conviction of the Jacksonville abolitionist Julius A. Willard for assisting an escaped slave in violation of the Illinois criminal code.[25] Justice Breese wrote the majority opinion, a majority that included Justice Treat. Wilson disagreed with the majority. He joined in a concurring opinion by Justice Lockwood. However, both opinions, majority and concurring, clearly held that "the slave does not become free by the Constitution of Illinois by coming into the State for the mere purpose of passing through it."[26]

In *Eells v. People*, Wilson and Treat split over the sufficiency of an indictment for assisting a fugitive slave in violation of the Illinois criminal code.[27] Treat voted with the majority, which held that the indictment was sufficient and that state law was not preempted by the Fugitive Slave Act. Chief Justice Wilson joined Justice Lockwood's dissent. He agreed with his old friend that the state law was preempted and that the indictment was insufficient because it did not specify the manner in which the alleged fugitive had entered Illinois. In his (and Wilson's) dissent, Lockwood was unequivocal: "Did the master bring him here, and then hire him out? Then he becomes free."[28]

Justice Treat's sympathy for slaves and those accused of being slaves may have been stronger than reflected by his supreme court votes. As discussed earlier, in 1845, while presiding as a trial judge, Treat had ordered the discharge of Joseph Warman, a free black who had been arrested and jailed as a fugitive slave.[29]

In 1842, while holding court in Springfield, Treat twice made rulings which favored accused runaways. In the case of Daniel, an African American who was arrested because he did not have a "certificate of freedom" as required by state statute, Treat reportedly declared the law unconstitutional and Daniel went free.[30] That same year, Treat was confronted with a claim under the Fugitive Slave Act that one James Foster, a black who had resided in Springfield for two or three years, was a slave who had escaped from Arkansas. Although the federal statute required only the master's affidavit to establish an alleged runaway's identity, Treat insisted that the claimant prove that Foster was his slave by the testimony of "disinterested witnesses."[31]

Because there is no written transcript of the proceedings, is not clear how the Matson trial unfolded. It is not even clear if there was live testimony or if the court relied solely on affidavits and/or the record from the prior hearing. In his opinion, Chief Justice Wilson refers to "depositions read in evidence" and "oral testimony adduced," but it is unclear whether he is referring to "oral testimony" presented to him and Justice Treat by live witnesses or to "oral testimony" that was given before the justices of the peace and included in the record of that hearing.[32]

Apparently, it was the general practice in Illinois habeas corpus proceedings for the applicant to submit his or her petition supported by affidavits and for the respondent to reply by affidavit.[33] While that may have been done in this case, no affidavits were found in the court file.[34] The file also does not include a record of the initial hearing, but there is some indication that the evidence presented in that hearing "was written down with a view to submitting it to the . . . circuit court."[35]

If the court did receive live testimony, neither Matson nor the Bryants probably testified. The same rules that barred them from doing so at the prior hearing would have operated to keep them off of the witness stand in the habeas corpus proceeding.[36]

There is no question that there was oral argument in the case, but it is not altogether certain who said what or when it was said. The general consensus is that, in advocating Matson's cause, Usher Linder argued that because slavery was recognized by the United States Constitution, all of the states had an obligation to protect an owner's interest in his or her slaves just as the states had the duty to protect an owner's rights in any other species of property.[37] According to Ficklin, Linder demonstrated a "bitter and malignant prejudice" toward abolitionists in general, and bitterly denounced Rutherford and Ashmore for harboring runaway slaves.[38] Ficklin also maintained, albeit thirty-eight years later, that Linder's bold and eloquent speech "would have been vociferously cheered in the hall of the legislature in the 'Palmetto' state [South Carolina]."[39]

As for the other side, according to Ficklin, Constable "stoutly maintained that the negroes who had been manumitted by the voluntary act of their master, should not be again remitted to slavery and be revived to go forth to unrequited toil, at their master's will, and be subjected to his lash at the will and discretion of that master."[40]

Ficklin and Constable apparently relied upon the Ordinance of 1787, the Illinois Constitution, and "upon the English and American decisions, (which were abundantly furnished to the court)."[41] In referring to "English . . . decisions," Ficklin may have been alluding to Lord Mansfield's 1772 decision in *Somerset*, a staple of abolitionist lawyers.[42] They also may have quoted from another abolitionist favorite, the famous speech made in 1794 by the Irish lawyer John Philpot Curran in defense of Hamilton Rowan, who had been charged with sedition:

> *I speak in the spirit of British law, which makes liberty commensurate with and inseparable from British soil; which proclaims even to the stranger and sojourner the moment he sets foot upon British earth, that the ground on which he treads is holy and consecrated by the genius of universal emancipation, no matter in what language his doom may have been pronounced, no matter what complexion incompatible with freedom or Indian or African sun may have [burnt] upon him, no matter in what disastrous battle his liberty may have been cloven down; no matter what solemnities he may have been devoted upon the altar of slavery; the first moment he touches the sacred soil of Britain the altar and the God sink together in the dust; his soul walks abroad in her own majesty; his body swells beyond the measure of his chains that burst from around him and he stands regenerated and disenthralled by the irresistible genius of universal emancipation.*[43]

Reportedly, Ficklin later said that he would "never forget how Lincoln winced when Constable quoted from Curran's defense of Rowan."[44]

Constable's purported speech and Lincoln's purported reaction to it are part of the lore of the Matson case. It makes for good theater. In fact, it is a showstopper. Some historians love it.[45] Most likely it never happened. The source of the story seems to be a 1907 magazine article about the trial that was written by early Lincoln biographer Jesse W. Weik. In that article, Weik purportedly quotes Ficklin's comments on Lincoln's reaction to the use of Constable's speech.[46] Ficklin may have said the words Weik attributes to him, but in his own 1885 newspaper article about the case, an article from which Weik appears to have drawn most of his "quotes," Ficklin mentions neither Lincoln's winces nor Constable's supposed use of Curran's speech.[47]

In that 1885 article, Ficklin quotes Curran's speech for illustrative purposes as part of his explanation of why he and Constable cited English legal precedents in arguing the Bryants' case. The reason that they relied on English decisions, according to Ficklin's article, was because in 1847, "[t]he English people were unquestionably more inveterately hostile to African slavery than the American and the rule deduced from the decisions of their courts is broader and more far-reaching than ours."[48]

Then to illustrate this inveterate hostility, Ficklin's article quotes from Curran's defense of Rowan. In fact, Ficklin acknowledges that, in contrast to Curran's "British soil," crossing onto Illinois soil did *not* automatically free a slave. Rather, a master "possessed in this country the right of passage in transit for his slaves over the soil of free states and the right to visit watering places with body servants and nurses, and that he was protected in his property while so doing, but that the moment he located even for a brief period of time, the slave became free, for slavery could not have a 'local habitation' on Illinois soil under the constitution and laws of the state."[49]

Lincoln was on the same page. According to Ficklin's recollection of the trial, Lincoln based his argument on Matson's *intent* in bringing Jane and her children into Illinois:

> "This then," [Lincoln] explained, "is the point on which the whole case turns: were these negroes passing over and crossing the State, and thus, as the law contemplates, in transitu, or were they actually located by consent of their master? If only crossing the State that act did not free them, but if located, even indefinitely, by consent of their owner and master, their emancipation logically followed. It is, therefore, of the highest importance," he continued, "to ascertain the true purpose and intent of Matson in placing these negroes on the Black Grove farm."[50]

Ficklin recalled that the "fact that General Matson had at such a time when he placed a slave on his Illinois farm, publicly declared that he was not placed there for permanent settlement, and that no counter statement had ever been made publicity [sic] or privately by him, constituted the web and woof of the argument of Mr. Lincoln."[51]

In sum, Lincoln's position was that Jane and her four children were part of a group of seasonal workers who came to Illinois in the spring and returned to Kentucky in the autumn, that it was their master's publicly declared intention that they not become permanent residents of Illinois and, therefore, that they were *in transitu* and remained slaves.[52]

Ficklin described what happened "[a]fter the argument was concluded and the court took time to consult and advise with respect to their decision"[53:]

> *It was a time of agonizing suspense with the attorneys on either side, neither one had the least intimation from the judges what their decision would be, nor could any token be discerned from their manner on the bench or expression of countenance during the argument. . . . [E]ach side was hopeful, but without any confidence of success. Linder was never known to be more in earnest or more sensitively alive to the interest and success of his client. Lincoln was calm, thoughtful and considerate; Constable was all anxiety and profoundly excited, but not without hope of success.[54]*

The court's decision was not long in coming. In an order entered the same day as the hearing, Justices Wilson and Treat "considered and adjudged" that Jane Bryant and her four children "be discharged from the custody . . . of . . . David R. Hutchason or of Robert Matson and all persons claiming them by[,] through or under him as slaves, and they be and remain free and discharged from all servitude whatsoever to any person or persons from hence forward and forever."[55] The Bryants were free. Moreover, the court went out of its way to ensure that the Bryants remained free. The justices "further adjudged that this proceeding be certified to said negroes as evidence of their freedom."[56]

Jane and her children had won. Matson had lost, and lost not just five of his slaves. In the same order that freed the Bryants, the court ruled that "Robert Matson pay all costs due and owing by reason of the arrest of said negroes including the costs of this application [for *habeas corpus*], and that executions issue from this court therefore . . . ."[57] The adverse decision also doomed Matson's suits against Rutherford and Ashmore.

Postmortems of the lawyers' performances in the case probably began before the ink was dry on the court order, and the game still goes on today. Of course, Lincoln's approach and presentation have received the most scrutiny, but the actions of all of the lawyers have been analyzed.

Years later, Orlando Ficklin characterized Usher Linder's efforts as "eloquent and bold" and praised his "trenchant wit and fervid eloquence."[58] However, most of those who have commented upon it have not been impressed with Linder's argument that slave ownership was entitled to the same protection as the ownership of any other type of property. The historian John J. Duff, whose analysis is perhaps the most insightful, finds Linder's argument a "pedestrian"

one "which did not particularly illuminate the issue."[59] Duff's point is well tak-
en. If the previous decade of runaway slave litigation established nothing else,
it demonstrated that the contention that free states must protect a slave owner's
property rights had only marginal relevance to situations such as Matson's,
where the slaves had not escaped into Illinois but were voluntarily brought into
the state by their master.

In contrast, Lincoln's argument shows that he completely understood what
the case was all about. Nevertheless, contemporaries and historians alike have
condemned Lincoln's arguments as "feeble," "pitiably weak," "spiritless, half-
hearted, and devoid of his usual wit, logic, and invective."[60] The criticism cen-
ters on Lincoln's presentation to the court in which, laying the groundwork for
his case, he stressed that if Jane and her children were merely *in transitu*, i.e.,
just passing through the state or, at least, not intended by Matson to be permanent residents, then Matson's claim to their continued servitude was a good
one. On the other hand, he acknowledged that if Matson intended otherwise,
they were free.[61]

Lincoln's critics maintain that in making this concession, "Mr. Lincoln *gave
his case away!*"[62] They contend that to prove his case that the slaves were *in
transitu*, Lincoln needed strong evidence that he did not have. They argue that
Lincoln had only the word of Joe Dean, "an ignorant, worthless fellow, who was
easily and ruthlessly impeached."[63] They blast Lincoln for not realizing that the
evidence did not support his case. One commentator goes so far as to speculate
that Lincoln may not even have studied all of the evidence.[64]

Lincoln's performance does not deserve this criticism. A lawyer can only
play the cards as dealt. The facts and law being what they were, Lincoln used
"the only sensible argument which he could have advanced."[65] As noted earlier,
there had been only one Illinois Supreme Court decision on point, and Lincoln
must have had that case in mind in putting together his argument. *Willard v.
People* stood for the proposition that a slave did not become free merely by
passing through Illinois (*in transitu*).[66] This holding put Illinois at odds with
many northern courts which, by the mid-1840s, had come in line with the Massachusetts Supreme Court's decision in *Commonwealth v. Aves* that even a brief
sojourn in a free state liberated a slave brought there.[67]

The Illinois Supreme Court's decision in *Willard* was consistent with most
southern court decisions that held that slaves brought into free states on a transitory basis remained slaves and only those who took up permanent residence
were freed.[68] However, the Illinois Supreme Court had not spoken with regard
to the second half of this equation, i.e., what happened if the slave was *not* just
passing through. Moreover, the decisions from other jurisdictions, North and

South, were all over the map as to what constituted "permanent" residence and what factors should be considered in making that determination.[69]

That was where Lincoln saw his opening. He had to convince the court that the operative factor in determining permanency was the master's (Matson's) intent. If there was no intent to establish permanent residency, there was no permanent residency.[70] Therefore, Lincoln laid the groundwork for his argument and what he hoped to prove. Contrary to what his critics said, this approach was not "pitiably weak" and did not "[give] his case away." It was a painful necessity.

No less an observer than Lincoln's adversary, Orlando Ficklin, maintained that, far from admitting away his case, Lincoln presented

his opponents [sic] points and arguments with such amplitude and seeming fairness and such liberality of concessions of their force and strength that it increased in his adversaries their confidence of success. . . . [B]ut his trenchant blows and cold logic and subtle knitting together and presentation of facts favorable to his side of the case, soon dissipated all hope that any advantage was likely to be gained by Lincoln's liberal concession, but rather that he had gained from the court a more patient and favorable hearing and consideration of the facts on which he relied for success.[71]

Lincoln apparently had a bad witness in Joe Dean, but he made the best of it. According to Ficklin, the facts relating to Matson's intentions "were plausibly, ingeniously and forcibly presented [by Lincoln] to the court, so as to give them all the effect and significance to which they were entitled and more."[72]

The real problem for Lincoln was the reality of the situation. That reality was that his client had brought Jane and her children to Illinois as slaves, they had remained in Illinois for two years as slaves, and they had worked for Matson in Illinois for two years as slaves. Matson's declarations aside, Jane and her children simply were not "in transit."

Given this situation, Lincoln's case was doomed from the start. Given this situation, it is difficult to determine how much credit Ficklin and Constable deserve. Some historians have been hard on them. They have attacked the Bryants' lawyers for, in Duff's words, "having missed the boat" by not utilizing *Bailey v. Cromwell*, the 1841 case in which the Illinois Supreme Court held "that the presumption of law was, in this State, that every person was free, without regard to color."[73] One noted legal historian goes so far as to brand their failure to reference *Bailey* as "ineptitude bordering on professional incompetence."[74]

This is an unfair overstatement. First, there can be no doubt that both Chief Justice Wilson and Justice Treat were very familiar with the holding in *Bailey*.[75] Both of them had voted with the unanimous court that had handed down the ruling in that case. More important, while citing *Bailey* certainly would have helped the Bryants' case, it was not dispositive. *Bailey* created a presumption of freedom, but it was not an irrebuttable presumption. The presumption could be overcome "by showing some legal claim to [the alleged slave's] services."[76] The claimants in *Bailey* had lost because "[t]his presumption [they] did not attempt to rebut, by any proof whatever."[77]

Lincoln did not make this mistake. He knew *Bailey*. His was the winning argument before the Supreme Court in that case. Lincoln's argument in the Matson case was aimed at rebutting the *Bailey* presumption by showing that the Bryants had been slaves in Kentucky and still were slaves because Matson was a citizen of Kentucky and had no intent to establish his slaves permanently in Illinois.

Regarding Ficklin and Constable, it seems likely that to the extent that they referenced English and American decisions which attacked slavery and relied upon *Somerset* and *Aves*, they did so to give their argument a legal and emotional context. Like Lincoln, they seem to have understood the real issues in the case.

Confronted with the Illinois Supreme Court decision in *Willard*, Ficklin and Constable had no choice but to admit, as they apparently did, "that the master possessed . . . the right of passage in transit for his slaves over the soil of free states" and that when he did so, he "was protected in his property," but they also knew where the line was drawn.[78] Such protection ceased, they argued, the "moment [a master] located [in Illinois] even for a brief period of time."[79]Then, "[t]he slave becomes free, for slavery could not have a 'local habitation' on Illinois soil under the constitution and laws of the state."[80]

The Bryants' attorneys rightfully attacked Matson's primary evidence. They maintained that his yearly declarations that his slaves merely were temporarily visiting in Illinois were self-serving statements made "with a design to be used in future for his own benefit . . . and therefore of no more significance as evidence in the case than any other declarations or verbal statements made in his own interest."[81]

As Ficklin told it years later, the court did not initially seem inclined to buy into his and Constable's argument. However, as they went on, the two judges, in Ficklin's words, began "drifting around to the position Constable and I had taken. Our triumph was complete."[82] Ficklin was right.

In his written opinion, Chief Justice Wilson made clear his personal feelings about slavery and the dilemma that it represented:

> *Slavery is unquestionably to be deplored as a great evil in any form, and by none more than those who find it so interwoven with their political institutions, that any rash and injudicious attempt to remove it might endanger the whole structure. The removal of this deforming feature from our fair and happy form of government, would leave it almost without blemish; but until means can be devised by which that can be done with safety and justice to all parties, it is the duty of every good citizen to conform to the Constitution and the laws of the United States, as they exist; and the Courts, by carrying them into effect, in the spirit in which they were adopted, will show a due respect to the institutions of our sister States, and at the same time vindicate those of our own.*[83]

Wilson spent several paragraphs discussing Article IV of the Constitution and the Fugitive Slave Act of 1793, correctly concluding that neither applied to the facts before him because "[t]here can be no pretense that [Jane Bryant] is a fugitive from [Matson's] service in Kentucky. Indeed, it is not controverted that it was by his direct and voluntary act that she was brought here in 1845, and kept within his employ up to within the last few days."[84]

The chief justice gave due consideration to Lincoln's arguments, especially the contention that Matson had "retained his citizenship in Kentucky, and professed the intention of leaving his servants in Illinois but temporarily."[85] In fact, despite Joe Dean and despite Lincoln's alleged lack of preparation, Wilson acknowledged, at least for the sake of argument, that "Mateson [*sic*] consistently expressed the intention of keeping his negroes here but a short time—said that he only stopped them here until he could get ready to remove them to a farm in the western part of Kentucky."[86] But he and Treat rejected Lincoln's conclusion. At first, it sounded as though the court merely had decided that Lincoln's proffered criteria for establishing domicile were irrelevant, that time of residence was critical and, that given the Bryants' two years in Illinois, they were not *in transitu*:

> *[W]e cannot perceive that these circumstances are entitled to the consideration in this case claimed for them. Neither the place of residence, nor the declared intentions of [Matson], countervail the fact that he voluntarily domiciled his servants here for two years or upwards.*

*In connection with the Constitution of Illinois, we are clearly of opinion
that [Matson], by bringing Jane into the State of Illinois, and domiciling
them here, has forfeited all claim to their services, and entitled them to be
discharged therefrom.*[87]

Then the justices went farther, but not all the way. While it later was claimed
by Illinois abolitionists and others that the decision in *Jane* put Illinois courts
"in step with the rest of the North on the adoption of the *Somerset* principle,"
that conclusion simply is not correct.[88] Although the Bryants' lawyers may have
pushed hard in that direction and although Wilson and Treat leaned closer to
that position, the justices were not prepared to hold that Illinois soil freed any
slave the moment he or she set foot on it. They were uncomfortable with the
concept and with its English source.

In his opinion, Wilson went to some pains to point out "that the loudest cries
for emancipation, and the fiercest denunciations against the slaveholder" were
heard from England, "whose cupidity first planted slavery upon our shores, in
defiance of the prayers and protest of the colonies, and who now hold a tenth of
the human race in a state of bondage as onerous as that of the African."[89]

Wilson and Treat were not ready to reject the unanimous holding of the
Illinois Supreme Court in *Willard* that gave masters a right of transit through
Illinois with their slaves, but they made it clear that slaves in transit had to be,
in fact, in transit. While they freed Jane Bryant, who had lived in Illinois for
two years, the duration of her stay had nothing to do with her right to freedom. In the judges' view, the only question was whether the slaves had become
domiciled in Illinois.[90] "Even if," wrote Wilson, "from some contingency, they
had remained *but a day*, the circumstance of [Matson] having transferred their
domicile from Kentucky, and fixed it in Illinois" would have resulted in their
freedom.[91]

Lincoln lost the Matson case and, as described earlier, Hiram Rutherford
never forgave Lincoln for his role in representing a slaveholder. Why did Lincoln do it?

CHAPTER 7

THE COILS OF FRIENDSHIP

A FEW WEEKS AFTER THE MATSON TRIAL, LINCOLN LEFT FOR WASHINGTON to begin his term in Congress. Orlando Ficklin also was a member of the seven-man Illinois delegation. Soon after their arrival, the two men ran into each other on Pennsylvania Avenue, not far from Ford's Theater. Their conversation turned to the Matson trial and, as Ficklin recalled years later, "Lincoln, with earnest tones remarked, 'Ficklin, do you know that I think the latter part of your speech was as eloquent as I ever listened to?'"[1]

That's it. His compliment to Ficklin is the only comment that we have from Lincoln pertaining to the Matson case. He left nothing in writing on the subject and Herndon never mentioned the matter.[2] Lincoln's silence as to his motivation and the importance of the answer to that question have led to a mythology that attempts to square Lincoln's representation of a slaveholder with his status as the "Great Emancipator."

The myth is simple. Because of his hatred of slavery, Lincoln held back at the Matson trial, giving it less than his best effort. Once again, Jesse W. Weik probably started it all. In his 1897 magazine article about the trial, he claimed that Lincoln *"gave his case away."*[3] Albert Beveridge, the first great Lincoln biographer, maintains that observers at the trial noted that Lincoln "was pitiably weak and halfhearted in making his argument."[4] According to Beveridge, "[a]ll thought that Lincoln's speech was fatal to his client."[5]

Beveridge's somewhat restrained account was eagerly adopted and magnified by later biographers. To one, "Lincoln's heart was not in the case."[6] To another, "he showed no zeal in such a cause."[7] Then the myth, full blown—"Lincoln's arguments in behalf of a cause his conscience detested were spiritless, half-hearted, and devoid of his usual wit logic and invective."[8]

There is anecdotal evidence to support the view that Lincoln was "[g]reat in court anywhere he thought he was right,"[9] but when he believed that he was wrong, in the words of one contemporary, attorney Samuel C. Parks, Lincoln "was the weakest lawyer I ever saw."[10] In describing a murder case in which he, Leonard Swett, and Lincoln defended Thomas Patterson, Henry C. Whitney attributed Lincoln's poor showing to the fact that he believed his client guilty, saying that "Swett was a most effective advocate, and when he closed in the afternoon I was full of faith that our client would be acquitted. Lincoln followed the next morning, and while he made some good points[,] the honesty of his mental processes forced him into a line of argument and admissions that were very damaging. We all felt that he had hurt our case. In point of fact our client was convicted and sent to the penitentiary for three years."[11]

With this background in mind, those who contend that, in the Matson case, Lincoln was advocating a cause that he hated, ground their position, at least in part, on the substance of the argument that he made to the court. They contend that in focusing on whether the Bryants were permanently domiciled in Illinois or merely passing through (*in transitu*), Lincoln gave away his case.[12] Nonsense. As pointed out earlier, given what he had to work with, Lincoln made the strongest argument possible.[13]

The issue of whether or not Lincoln was as effective as he could have been in presenting Matson's case is something of a distraction. The real question is not how Lincoln handled the case, but why he represented Matson in the case.

One theory, which has gained some recent currency, links Lincoln's representation of Matson to his identification with certain core Whig values and principles which found expression in Lincoln's self-image and in his approach to society, politics, and the practice of law.[14] This school of thought posits that a predominant element of Whig thought was a concern with self-control, both individually and collectively.[15] Whigs, it is argued, viewed the "passions" as "dangerous and strong," and saw it as the task of responsible citizens, allied with political institutions, to keep them under control.[16] To do otherwise was to invite social disintegration and mob rule.[17] Obviously, law and the judicial system played a critical role in maintaining order.[18]

With regard to slavery, Whigs accepted the fact that, like it or not, slavery was protected by the Constitution and that there was nothing, short of destroying the union, that could be done about it in those states where it was extant.[19] Two corollaries to this proposition were that strident abolitionism threatened to ignite passions that could burn out of control and destroy the union and that enforcement of the Fugitive Slave Act was essential to preserving the union.[20] As a result, while there were Whig abolitionist lawyers who represented fugitive

slaves and their abettors, other Whig lawyers, who strongly believed that national unity depended upon effective enforcement of the Fugitive Slave Act,
appeared on behalf of slave owners.[21]

In many respects, Lincoln's attitudes and beliefs appear to fit rather neatly
into this paradigm. Lincoln was a man who abhorred disorder and lawlessness and feared their consequences. He had good reason to do so. It may be,
as David Donald has maintained, that "Lincoln's efforts to impose rationality
on public life reflected his internal struggle to bring coherence to his own, still
unshaped personality," but Lincoln also had practical observation to go by.[22] He
lived in an Illinois where mob violence and civil disorder on a grand scale were
everyday facts of life. In the decade preceding the Matson trial, Illinois had
endured the Alton riot in 1837, Ogle County vigilantism in 1841, the five-year
Regulator-Flathead conflict in Massac County, and the "Mormon War" in 1846.
During each of these disruptions, the civil authorities had proven to be power-
less, and the rule of law had disappeared. Each had resulted in wanton loss of
life and destruction of property.[23]

From the very beginning of his political career, Lincoln inveighed against
mob rule. In an early speech in the Illinois legislature in support of the state
bank against attacks by Jacksonian Democrats. Lincoln drummed on a theme
he was to repeat again and again, saying, "I am opposed to encouraging that
lawless and mobocratic spirit, whether in relation to the bank or any thing else,
which is already abroad in the land; and is spreading with rapid and fearful
impetuosity, to the ultimate overthrow of every institution, or even moral principle, in which persons and property have hitherto found security."[24]

A year later, on January 27, 1838, in the wake of the fiery death of a mulatto at
the hands of a mob in St. Louis and Lovejoy's death in Alton, Lincoln addressed
the Young Men's Lyceum of Springfield on the dangers of "the increasing disregard for the law which pervades the country."[25] To Lincoln, that disregard
threatened the very existence of the United States: "[W]henever the vicious
portion of the population shall be permitted to gather in bands of hundreds
and thousands, and burn churches, ravage and rob provision stores, throw
printing presses into rivers, shoot editors, and hang and burn obnoxious persons at pleasure, and with impunity; depend upon it, this Government cannot
last."[26]

Lincoln did not limit his criticism to those who ran amuck in support of
slavery. He was equally hard on those of its opponents who took to the streets,
those who, in Lincoln's words, "would shiver into fragments the Union of these
States; tear to tatters its now venerated constitution; and even burn the last copy
of the Bible, rather than slavery should continue a single hour."[27]

For Lincoln, the paramount danger was a loss of collective self-control, "the growing disposition to substitute the wild and furious passions, in lieu of sober judgments of Courts."[28] It was not only the heated debate over slavery that troubled him. He was wary of enthusiasm in general and was concerned about where it could take people even in the best of causes. For example, although he did not drink and advocated temperance, Lincoln had no use for prohibitionists who "addressed drunkards and dramshop-keepers 'in the thundering tones of anathema and denunciation,' blaming them for 'all the vice and misery and crime in the land' and condemning them as persons to be 'shunned by all the good and virtuous as moral pestilences.'"[29]

If unbridled emotion was the poison, the law was the antidote. He was unequivocal in his belief that the nation's laws had to be obeyed: "Let every American, every lover of liberty, every well wisher to his posterity, swear by the blood of the Revolution, never to violate in the least particular, the laws of the country; and never to tolerate their violation by others."[30]

He did not limit his admonishment to "good" or just laws: "When I so pressingly urge a strict observance of all the laws, let me not be understood as saying there are no bad laws, . . . I mean to say no such thing. But I do mean to say, that, although bad laws, if they exist, should be repealed as soon as possible, still while they continue in force, for the sake of example, they should be religiously observed."[31]

Lincoln's resolute belief that even bad laws "should be religiously observed" extended to laws which protected slavery and slave owners. Although he strongly believed that slavery should not be permitted "to find new places to live in," was to support the Wilmot Proviso during his one term in Congress, and would make opposition to slavery in the territories the cornerstone of his first presidential campaign, Lincoln, in 1847, did not believe that anything could be done about the peculiar institution where it already existed.[32]

In his 1837 protest to the Illinois legislature's proslavery resolutions, Lincoln described slavery as "founded on . . . injustice," but he also declared his belief "that the Congress of the United States has no power under the constitution to interfere with the institution of slavery in the different states."[33] Writing to Whig abolitionist William Durley in October 1845, Lincoln proclaimed it "a paramount duty of us in the free states, due to the Union of the states, and perhaps to liberty itself (paradox though it may seem) to let slavery in the other states alone."[34]

So far Lincoln fits the Whig mold, but when it came to putting his beliefs into practice, especially with regard to the enforcement of laws dealing with runaway slaves, the concordance begins to break down a bit. According to one of his contemporaries, Lincoln would not represent runaway slaves "because he did not want to be a party to a violation of the Fugitive Slave Law," but this recollection is not entirely accurate.[35] While Lincoln did not join the coterie of lawyers who regularly represented fugitives and those who assisted them, on several occasions, as discussed earlier, he successfully defended men accused of harboring runaway slaves.[36] In the state legislature, when given the opportunity to censure the governor of Maine for protecting two men who had violated Georgia law by assisting a slave to escape, Lincoln had waffled inconclusively.[37]

This deviance from the Whig norm is significant when analyzing Lincoln's behavior in the Matson case. There was no threat to the Constitution at issue. The case did not involve the Fugitive Slave Act but rather slaves who had been voluntarily brought into Illinois. Lincoln's willingness to represent those slaves appears to demonstrate that he did not believe that doing so threatened the union's existence. Why then, did this good Whig, who supposedly believed slavery immoral, represent Matson?

The exponents of the Lincoln as a Whig school maintain that his representation of Matson, while it was not done to uphold a particularly important law, was consistent with "a Whiggish attitude toward the law and the rule of law in American society."[38] According to this interpretation, Whig lawyers such as Lincoln were more concerned with utilizing the legal system to promote order than they were in promoting an ideology through the system: "[They] believed that the court system provided a neutral means to resolve disputes and maintain order. A lawyer's role in this system was to represent either side in a dispute—it didn't matter which side the lawyer took."[39]

Lincoln, so the argument goes, did not choose his clients to fit within some political agenda. He believed that his professional obligation was to represent a client's interest in the most effective manner possible and not to make moral judgments or to use the law as an instrumentality. Following "a model of professional responsibility that refused to hold a lawyer morally accountable for his choice of clients," Lincoln "was able to represent [Matson] because he was able to suspend his moral judgment."[40]

This theory may explain why Lincoln was "able" to represent Matson, but it fails to explain why he *chose* to represent the slaveholder. After all, he did not have to take the case. There was no professional imperative that required him to do so, and Matson already had very competent counsel in Usher Linder.

One explanation offered for Lincoln's willingness to be Matson's lawyer is that the fact that his client was seeking to drag Jane and her children back into slavery simply was not that important to Lincoln. According to Lincoln biographer Benjamin Thomas, Lincoln represented Matson because "the slavery issue had not yet seared into his conscience to the point of inducing him to place the plight of a few hapless blacks above the abstract legal aspects of the question."[41] To Allen C. Guelzo, Lincoln's representation of Matson merely underscored his "indifference to slavery as injustice to blacks."[42] Lincoln, it is argued, failed to grasp "the fundamental horror and sin of slavery . . . that it profoundly damaged black people day by day, for too many score years. . . ."[43] Phillip Shaw Paludin, for one, maintains that although Lincoln was a compassionate man in many respects, "[t]here is very little evidence of Lincoln's sensitivity to the suffering of slaves in bondage."[44] Proponents of this interpretation reject as suspect the recollections of those who would attest to such empathy and deem Lincoln's own comments on slave suffering "ambiguous" and devoid of righteous "fury and outrage."[45] They dismiss Lincoln's 1837 protest in the Illinois legislature as a politically timed and motivated device which demonstrated little more than his "vague understanding that slaves might suffer" because although he asserted that slavery was founded on injustice, he said nothing about the day-to-day tortures that slaves endured, and attacked abolitionists, the very people who sought to end those tortures.[46]

This argument, that Lincoln represented Matson because he was indifferent to the plight of slaves, fails to sufficiently credit the insights of a very insightful man.

In the spring of 1864, Lincoln wrote, "I am naturally anti-slavery. If slavery is not wrong, nothing is wrong. I can not remember when I did not so think, and feel."[47] While Lincoln's antislavery feelings took time to mature, his public statements prior to the Matson trial demonstrate that for at least ten years before that episode he had thought and felt that slavery was "wrong." Lincoln's earliest recorded statement on slavery is that 1837 protest in the Illinois legislature. Not content with simply joining the tiny minority that voted against the proslavery resolutions, he went on record with a protest which unequivocally declared "that the institution of slavery is founded on both injustice and bad policy. . . ."[48]

Contrary to the arguments of those who would diminish the significance of Lincoln's declaration by arguing that he also attacked abolitionism in his protest, that he waited too long before making it, and that he failed to acknowledge the horrors of slavery, Lincoln's declaration that slavery was "founded on . . . injustice" was a big deal. Even Guelzo, who plays down its significance, acknowledges that in going public in this way, Lincoln took a "risk."[49] The statement demonstrated courage born of strong belief. This fact can be better understood when Lincoln's declaration is painted on the dark canvas that was Illinois in 1837.

In March 1837, Lincoln's position on slavery was a highly unpopular one. Only six state legislators voted against the proslavery resolutions and only one joined Lincoln in his protest.[50] In March 1837, state law still sanctioned slavery in Illinois.[51] In fact, there were slaves held in Springfield, at least one of them the property of his own brother-in-law.[52] In March 1837, a statement against slavery could have adverse political consequences for the speaker or even worse.[53] In March 1837, Elijah Lovejoy had only a few more months to live before he was shot dead for saying much the same thing as Lincoln had said.[54]

To be sure, Lincoln did take a swipe at abolitionists in his protest, but not at their fundamental hatred of slavery. He discouraged the "promulgation" of abolitionist doctrines as counterproductive. This, of course, was consistent with his belief that the Constitution protected slavery in the South and that active abolitionism would lead only to violence and disorder which could destroy the union itself.[55]

It also is true that Lincoln's protest did not dwell on the evils of slavery. That was not his purpose. He wanted to go on record that he did not agree with the legislature's resolutions and that he did not agree because slavery was unjust.[56] He did wait several weeks to file his protest, and this delay, as some have suggested, may have been because he did not want to risk the success of his campaign to move the state's capital to Springfield. Be that as it may, the fact that remains is that he did file the protest "in his own well considered language which [stood] of record for the inspection of all who [chose]."[57]

Lincoln remained true to the sentiments of his 1837 protest. In an address before Springfield's Washington Temperance Society in 1842, Lincoln equated drunkenness with slavery and looked forward to the ultimate triumph over both:

> And when the victory shall be complete—when there shall be neither a slave nor a drunkard on the earth—how proud the title of that Land, which may truly claim to be the birth-place and the cradle of both those revolutions, that shall have ended in that victory. How nobly distinguished that People, who shall have planted, and nurtured to maturity, both the political and moral freedom of their species.[58]

In his letter to William Durley in 1845, Lincoln emphasized "that we should never knowingly lend ourselves directly or indirectly, to prevent slavery from dying a natural death—to find new places for it to live in, when it can no longer exist in the old."[59]

Moreover, Lincoln was fully cognizant of, and painfully troubled by, the re-
alities of slavery and the egregious human toll that it exacted. Some attribute
this awareness to two trips that he made down the Mississippi River to New Orleans, one in 1828 and another in 1832. According to the purported recollections
of his companion on the first trip, Lincoln was so disturbed by a slave auction
that he clenched his fists and muttered, "[T]hat's a disgrace! If I ever get a lick
at that thing I'll hit it hard."[60] John Hanks, who claimed to have traveled to New
Orleans on the second trip, told Herndon over thirty years later that after wit-
nessing "Negroes chained—maltreated—whipt & scourged" in New Orleans,
"Lincoln's heart bled" and he "was sad—looked bad—felt bad—was thoughtful
and abstracted. . . ."[61]

The authenticity and reliability of these reminiscences are dubious and many
historians, especially those who maintain that Lincoln had little or no empathy
for slave suffering, have rejected them.[62] However, there remain other sources
that are far more difficult to ignore.

In a letter to his friend Joshua Speed's sister in 1841, Lincoln recounted his
experiences on another river trip during which he encountered a dozen slaves,
chained together, on their way further south. There can be no doubt that Lincoln grasped the pathos of their situation: "In this condition they were being
separated forever from their childhood, their friends, their fathers and moth-
ers, and brothers and sisters, and many of them, from their wives and children,
and going into perpetual slavery where the lash of the master is proverbially
more ruthless and unrelenting than any other where."[63]

It has been argued that, far from demonstrating Lincoln's compassion for
slaves, his letter to Mary Speed shows his insensitivity to their plight because,
in the letter, he also comments on their apparent cheerfulness and fails to take
the opportunity to condemn slavery.[64] Regarding the first point, it should be
noted that Lincoln was reporting what he observed—that the slaves appeared
to be "the most cheerful and happy creatures on board," but in no way did this
observation diminish his dismay for their situation.[65] Speaking of their gaiety,
he mused, "How true it is that 'God tempers the wind to the shorn lamb,' or
in other words that He renders the worst of human conditions bearable. . . ."[66]
Lincoln's failure to explode against the evils of slavery was not surprising. As
noted earlier, he "was not a demonstrative man, what he felt most deeply, he
expressed the least."[67]

The impact of this experience on Lincoln's sensitivity to the evils of slavery
is clearly demonstrated in a letter he wrote to Mary Speed's brother, Joshua,
in 1855. "I confess," he wrote with regard to fugitive slaves, "I hate to see the
poor creatures hunted down, and caught, and carried back to their stripes and

unrewarded toils."[68] Then his letter revisits the trip about which he had written to Mary Speed in 1841. After fourteen years, Lincoln still could not get over the slaves he had seen, shackled together with irons: "That sight was a continual torment to me; and I see something like it every time I touch the Ohio, or any other slave border. It is hardly fair for you to assume that I have no interest in a thing which has, and continually exercises, the power of making me miserable."[69]

In view of Lincoln's hatred of slavery and the "continual torment" of which he writes to Speed, it seems unlikely that he took the Matson case because he was indifferent to the plight of slaves. His purported conference with Rutherford before the trial supports this conclusion. Rutherford maintained that he purposely sought out Lincoln to represent the Bryants. At the time, Lincoln apparently had a reputation among Illinois abolitionists as an attorney who "was not afraid of a negro case," and his name had been recommended to Rutherford by "everyone whom [he] consulted."[70] Moreover, it seems that during some previous conversation or conversations that the two had had, Lincoln may have said something that led Rutherford, an abolitionist, to believe that their views "on the wrong of slavery [were] in perfect accord."[71]

When Rutherford asked Lincoln to represent him, he did not give Lincoln much wiggle room. He "reminded [Lincoln] that we always agreed on the questions of the day"—in effect, saying to Lincoln, "[A]re you against slavery or not?"[72] Confronted so starkly with the question, a visibly nonplussed Lincoln reluctantly answered that he already had talked to someone who was acting "in Matson's interest" and was under a professional obligation to represent Matson "unless released."[73] A few hours later, he offered his services to Rutherford, who turned him down.[74]

At that point, after the hypocrisy of representing a slave owner has been brought home to him, Lincoln simply could have stayed out of the case. He did not do so and it seems unlikely that some abstract Whig faith in the necessity for orderly dispute resolution accounts for his actions. Something else must have been at work, something that compelled Lincoln to remain in the case as Matson's counsel, and, in fact, led him to take on Matson's case in the first place.

Ego, money, and loyalty each may have played a role in Lincoln's decision. Of the three, money seems the least likely to have led Lincoln to represent Matson. Not that money was not an important consideration. Even those historians who argue that the willingness of Whig lawyers to represent just about anyone stemmed from their faith in the need for the neutral judicial resolution of dispute acknowledge that money also played a role in dictating their moral neutrality.[75] Legal fees were low, competition fierce, and, economically speaking, a morally repugnant client often was better than none at all.[76] Lincoln was not averse to making a fee, but selling out for a few dollars appears unlikely. Lincoln was not a greedy man. In Joseph Gillespie's words, "[h]is love of wealth was very weak" or as Herndon would have it, Lincoln had "no avarice of the get."[77]

Ego is a more likely motivation. Lincoln was not above promoting himself and the Matson case was a high-profile case. It had everything. The consequences were profound—slavery or freedom. The legal questions were complicated and controversial—the effect of free soil on the status of those slaves who reached it. The cast of characters was dramatic: a mother protecting her children, an "aristocratic" master, two supreme court justices, and two of the most prominent attorneys in the state as adversaries—one a sitting congressman, the other a former Illinois attorney general.

Considering that he was toiling in a legal practice which, at that time, usually involved small claims, petty crimes, and disputes over pigs, horses, and other barnyard animals, it would not be surprising that Lincoln might have wanted to be a part of a bigger show on one side or the other.[78] Still, to choose Matson's side—slavery's side—probably required more than a mere desire for the spotlight. Some person or persons must have convinced Lincoln to put aside his strong personal feelings about slavery and to take Matson's cause.

Rutherford's recollection of his attempt to retain Lincoln as counsel indicates that a third party had enlisted Lincoln to Matson's cause. Rutherford states that in responding to his request, Lincoln said that "he had already been counseled with in Matson's interest."[79] A few hours later, Lincoln sent a message to Rutherford concerning the possibility that he might be able to represent the abolitionist. In that message, Lincoln referred to "the man who had approached him in Matson's behalf."[80]

Orlando Ficklin thought that he knew who that man was and the critical role that he had played in persuading Lincoln to represent Matson. Speaking years after the fact, Ficklin maintained that it was at Thomas A. Marshall's "earnest solicitation . . . that Lincoln took a hand in the case."[81] This may have been what happened, but Ficklin's recollection may have been colored by subsequent events. There is no question that Marshall was involved in the Matson controversy. Although apparently he played no role in the habeas corpus proceeding, Marshall was Linder's cocounsel in Matson's damage suits against Rutherford and Ashmore.[82]

There also can be no dispute that, at some point, Marshall and Lincoln became close friends and political allies. Together, they helped establish the

Republican Party in eastern Illinois in the mid-1850s.[83] When he was in Charleston to debate Douglas in their 1858 race for the United States Senate, Lincoln stayed overnight at Marshall's house. He stayed there again in January 1861, when he stopped in Coles County on his way to Washington to be inaugurated.[84] While Lincoln was president, the two communicated regularly on politics, military topics, and other issues of the day with Lincoln always ready to listen to Marshall's opinions.[85]

Yet, all of that was years later. It is difficult to assess how close their relationship was in 1847, or whether Marshall had enough influence with Lincoln at that time to persuade him to take Matson's side. In 1847, Marshall had been in Illinois about eight years. Born in Frankfort, Kentucky, in 1817, Marshall was the scion of a family famous in that state. His father served two decades on the Kentucky Court of Appeals, and his uncle was Henry Clay. After attending Kenyon College and lectures in law at Transylvania University in Lexington, Marshall practiced law in Vicksburg, Mississippi. In 1839, he moved to Coles County, where he had purchased a large tract of land known as Dead Man's Grove. Two years later, he relocated to Charleston and resumed the practice of law. In 1847, prior to the Matson case, Marshall had been a delegate to the Illinois constitutional convention.[86]

There is no mention of Marshall in Lincoln's papers prior to 1847, but, apparently, they did know one another at that time. According to court records, Lincoln and Marshall appeared as cocounsel in at least two cases in the Circuit Court of Coles County prior to 1847.[87]

If Marshall was close enough to Lincoln to influence him in favor of Matson, he may have done so. Although he was born in Lexington, Marshall grew up in Paris, Kentucky, in Bourbon County. His father represented that county in 1827 and 1828, just a few years before Robert Matson did so. Both were Whigs and supporters of Henry Clay.[88] No doubt the Marshalls knew Matson and, given Ficklin's assertion that Thomas Marshall was the responsible party, it is definitely possible that his influence was at least a factor in Lincoln's decision to represent Matson. In this respect, the Clay connection may have played an important role. At this stage in his career, Lincoln idolized Henry Clay.[89] Not only was Marshall Clay's nephew; he had been married in Clay's home.[90]

Marshall may have persuaded Lincoln to represent Matson but it seems more likely that Usher Linder was "the man who had approached [Lincoln] in Matson's behalf." He had some influence over Lincoln. The two had a somewhat unusual relationship. Clearly, there was some kind of friendship there, but how close and how constant is difficult to say. Lack of documentary sources is only part of the problem. The situation is further complicated by Lincoln's somewhat ambivalent view of friendship and Linder's inability to stay on any one course for very long.

As David Donald has pointed out in his *We Are Lincoln Men*, Lincoln was a man with many friends, but few intimates.[91] To political ally Richard Oglesby, Lincoln "was not a man of strong attachments . . . the warm friend of few men. . . ."[92] Joseph Gillespie, who had known Lincoln since the late 1830s and believed him "tender hearted," "extremely just and fair minded," acknowledged that Lincoln "was by some considered cold hearted or at least indifferent toward his friends."[93]

Some of Lincoln's friends did, in fact, see him this way. Ninian W. Edwards, at whose home a young Lincoln had spent many a social evening, concluded that his brother-in-law was "not a warm hearted man" when, during Edwards's visit to the White House, Lincoln "asked no questions about old friends."[94] Edwards thought that Lincoln "[s]eemed to be ungrateful" to those who had helped him along the way.[95] Lincoln's first law partner agreed. In an interview with Herndon in June 1865, John T. Stuart told him that Lincoln "did forget his friends . . . There was no part of his nature which drew him to do acts of gratitude to his friends."[96]

"Acts of gratitude" could be expanded to include words of praise. Lincoln was not one to laud the achievements of others. When Lincoln praised Ficklin for his argument in the Matson case, Ficklin "doubly prized" the compliment because, in Ficklin's experience, "Lincoln seldom paid compliments in the presence of the person complimented."[97] Apparently, Lincoln's reticence in this respect ran even deeper than that. He seldom praised anyone, present or not, living or dead. "[D]o you remember," Oglesby wrote Herndon in 1866, "that Mr. Lincoln was never given to praise much—of any living man, and was not good at Eulogy upon the dead."[98]

These proclivities do not appear to have applied to the relationship that Lincoln shared with Linder. It appears to have been much closer to a true friendship, developing over time. It began in 1838 when the mutual respect that the two had developed as adversaries in the legislature turned to friendship when Linder became a Whig and the two began riding the judicial circuit together. Lincoln trusted Linder as a lawyer and shared confidences and clients with him. They appeared together as cocounsel in litigation, and, when Lincoln was unable to attend to a case, he sometimes referred it to Linder.[99]

Soon after the Matson case, during his sole term in Congress, Lincoln traded political insights with Linder. These were not just superficial observations, but rather the kind of confidential, practical, and candid counsel that one shares with a trusted ally. Thus, in February 1848, with regard to their candidate

Zachary Taylor's campaign for the presidency, Lincoln advised Linder, "in kindness," to "simply go for General Taylor" and avoid getting caught up in the merits of the origins and prosecution of the Mexican War.[100] A month later, he went to some lengths to explain to Linder in some detail why he and other Whigs had opposed the war and had sought an alliance with the abolitionists. Not only did Lincoln single out Linder to receive this information; he relied on Linder to pass the word along to other local Whig leaders.[101]

Having Linder as a political ally, not to mention as a friend, was not always easy. Linder's intemperate oratory, penchant for intrigue, and repeated shifts in political allegiance doubtless strained his relationship with Lincoln, but also demonstrated the strength of the bond between the two. The examples are many. In the incident in 1844, when enraged opponents threatened Linder with bodily injury for a fiery pro-Clay speech at the Illinois Statehouse, it was Lincoln who had to come to Linder's rescue. In words that Linder no doubt embellished in his memoirs, Linder claims that Lincoln told him:

> Linder, Baker and I are apprehensive that you may be attacked by some of those ruffians who insulted you from the galleries, and we have come to escort you to your hotel. We both think we can do a little fighting so we want you to walk between us until we get you to your hotel; your quarrel is our quarrel, and that of the great Whig party of this nation, and your speech upon this occasion is the greatest one that has been made by any of us, for which we wish to honor, love and defend you.[102]

Linder's political instability must have given Lincoln pause. Sometimes, it was difficult to tell which side Linder was on at any particular point in time. The summer of 1849 was one such point. In May and June of that year, Lincoln was attempting to line up support for his bid to be nominated for commissioner of the General Land Office over the front runner, Justin Butterfield. Apparently, Lincoln believed that he had Linder safely on his side. Then, in early June he received a letter from two of his allies in Coles County warning "against treachery in the camp . . . . We have this day heard [Linder] dealing out glowing eulogies upon your competator [sic] Butterfield."[103] They cautioned Lincoln that unless Linder had given him "a written line of confidence, be assured that it will be against you."[104]

It is not clear whether this intelligence was correct or what, if anything, Lincoln did about it.[105] What is clear is that Lincoln did not receive the appointment and that Linder was publicly outraged about the fact that Lincoln was denied the post. In the autumn of 1849, he made a speech in the Illinois legislature which ferociously attacked Thomas Ewing, his own party's secretary of the Department of the Interior, whom Linder blamed for Lincoln's rejection. It was classic Linder hyperbole: "Such a man as Ewing has no right to rule the cabinet of a republican president. He is universally odious, and stinks in the nostrils of the nation. He is a lump of ice, an unfeeling, unsympathizing aristocrat, a rough, imperious, uncouth, and unamiable man. Such a minister, in a four year's administration, would ruin the popularity of forty presidents and as many heroes."[106]

Whatever effect Linder's tirade may have had, when the smoke cleared, he and Lincoln were still friends. They remained friends after Linder, believing that "the Whigs were merged with the Abolitionists in the Republican Party," switched back to the Democratic Party.[107] In 1856, Linder's eighteen-year-old son, Daniel, shot a man and faced the death penalty if convicted. According to Linder, some Republicans "seemed to avail themselves to wreck vengeance upon me in the death of my son."[108] Lincoln was not one of them. He consoled Linder and his wife and offered to defend their son free of charge.[109]

Linder kept pushing the envelope. In the Illinois 1858 senatorial campaign between Lincoln and Stephen Douglas, Linder's active support for Douglas was critical to the Democrat's campaign. A Republican "truth squad" followed Douglas on his campaign swing through the state, rebutting his speeches after the Democratic candidate "would be in bed asleep, worn out by the fatigues of the day."[110] Douglas telegraphed Linder to join him and to accompany him on the stump "to help fight off the hell-hounds."[111] Douglas was emphatic—"For God's sake Linder, come."[112] The message was leaked to the Republican press, which had a field day, relentlessly referring to Linder as "For God's sake Linder." Of course, Linder being Linder, reveled in the nickname and did his best to defeat Lincoln.[113]

Linder was elected as a delegate to the 1860 Democratic national committee.[114] The friendship continued to survive. When the Lincolns were preparing to move to Washington, Mary Lincoln made a gift to the Linders of some dishes and silverware.[115] "Being a man of strong Southern proclivities," and believing that "the abolition of slavery would be everlastingly ruinous to the South," Linder "differed from . . . Lincoln on the question of emancipation."[116] Yet, Lincoln remained a friend, indeed, a friend in need.

To be sure, as president, Lincoln did not appoint Linder to the government job that Linder had requested, but this was not surprising.[117] Lincoln was besieged by office-seekers and Linder not only was a Democrat, but was a very partisan Democrat. What Lincoln did do for his friend was far more significant. Again, Linder's son Daniel was involved.

Prior to the war, Daniel had moved to the South. After Fort Sumter, he had enlisted in the Confederate army, was captured, and faced years in a military prison. Distraught, Linder wrote to the president seeking his assistance. Lincoln was neither "cold hearted" nor "indifferent" to this friend. He did not "forget" Usher Linder. Lincoln ordered Secretary of War Edwin M. Stanton to administer the Oath of Allegiance to "the son of my friend U. F. Linder, discharge him, and send him to his father."[118] Apparently, the matter was very important to Lincoln. He acted "without hesitation," but took the time to meet with Daniel before sending him to Illinois.[119] At the time, Attorney General Edward Bates recorded in his diary that "[t]he Prest: is anxious to gratify Linder the father who is his old friend."[120]

Indeed, it was a curious friendship. Superficially, the two men were eerily similar. They were born within a month of each other in 1809, in Kentucky, not ten miles apart. Both were largely self-educated. Both had outstanding oratorical abilities. Both admired Henry Clay. They rivaled one another as storytellers to the point where one who knew them both believed that Lincoln "was some like Linder."[121] Both were popular with their colleagues. Both were very good lawyers.[122] Yet, they were very different men. As Linder acknowledged, "I am one of those who stand a very great distance from the sublime character of Lincoln."[123]

Lincoln seldom, if ever, drank; Linder was a drunk.[124] Lincoln hated and feared violence; Linder once beat up another lawyer in open court, shot a member of his own party, and literally went gunning, revolver in hand, for a political opponent. Lincoln usually spoke with measured restraint; Linder was prone to careless inflammatory rhetoric. Lincoln was frugal and apparently uninterested in material appearances; Linder dressed like a dandy and once boasted to have "made hundreds and thousands of dollars on [the] circuit, and I spent it liberally."[125] Lincoln hated slavery and longed for its demise; Linder's deep-seated racism caused him to equate abolition with "the ruin of the white race."[126] At the time of the Matson trial, Lincoln's star was rising; Linder's was past its apogee.

Those who knew Linder probably would have agreed with one of his friends who concluded that he was "learned in everything but how to take care of himself."[127] One who knew him well, Joseph Gillespie, in his introduction to Linder's *Reminiscences,* wrote that when Linder's virtues were measured against his failings, one could only conclude that "he was the worst enemy to himself."[128] While there can be no doubt that Lincoln enjoyed Linder's unquestioned affability and, as Gillespie notes, "admired him greatly as a speaker," it may have been Linder's weaker side that most endeared him to Lincoln and cemented the friendship.[129] Lincoln and Linder shared the same "worst enemy."

It was as though Lincoln was attracted to Linder as some sort of reverse image—emotionally, an anti-Whig, that is, Linder was what Lincoln himself could have been (and still might become) but for self-control. In this respect, Lincoln's relationship with Linder was not unique. Lincoln "had a knack for forging relationships whose surface peculiarities raised eyebrows but that worked on some sort of subterranean level."[130] As noted earlier, Lincoln and his law partner, William Herndon, differed in many respects, not the least of which were Herndon's impetuosity and weakness for alcohol.[131] Herndon's conduct, as he acknowledged, "frequently was an embarrassment to Lincoln," yet Lincoln, in his treatment of Herndon, "was the most generous, forbearing, and charitable man I ever knew."[132]

An integral part of Lincoln's relationship with Herndon was Herndon's need to be bailed out of trouble and Lincoln's willingness to do so, sometimes literally, as when Herndon's public drunkenness landed him in jail.[133] So too with Linder. When he got drunk riding the circuit, Lincoln was there to pour him into the saddle and make sure that his inebriated friend made it to the next courthouse.[134] Lincoln protected Linder from the dangerous consequences of his colleague's often reckless oratory, as when he rescued Linder from the mob angered by a speech he had just delivered.[135] Then there were his efforts on behalf of Linder's somewhat wayward son.

Theirs was an unbalanced relationship. Linder was like the "swift-fleeting meteor" of Lincoln's favorite poem "Mortality," destined for self-destruction. In helping his friend, Lincoln reaffirmed his personal victory over emotion and his own self-doubts. But there was a quid pro quo. Dealing with Linder often required Lincoln to suspend his critical judgment and to put aside his personal values and standards. That is what he did with regard to the Matson case. Linder was confronted with a difficult situation, needed assistance, and asked his friend Lincoln for help.

It could not have been an easy decision for Lincoln, but he agreed to assist his friend. Then, when Rutherford's request brought home the hypocrisy of his position, it is likely that Lincoln, after telling Rutherford that the arrangement to represent Matson had yet to be finalized, went back to Linder and asked to be released from his commitment. His friend agreed to do so and Lincoln informed Rutherford that he was "free" to represent him, only to have his services rejected. No doubt chagrined, Lincoln felt that he owed it to Linder, who had been good enough to release him, to assist him in representing Matson.[136]

After Lincoln returned to Illinois from Washington in 1849, he reembarked on the practice of law with, in his words, "greater earnestness than ever before."[137]

In the next decade or so he handled thousands of cases, but not one of them involved a runaway slave or an abolitionist.[138]

Lincoln's return preceded by about a year the passage of the Fugitive Slave Act of 1850 which added teeth to the slave rendition process.[139] It may well be, as has been suggested, that Lincoln did not accept fugitive slave cases because he viewed the new law, "which had been championed by his political heroes, Daniel Webster and Henry Clay," as essential to the protection of slave owners' rights guaranteed by the Constitution and to the preservation of the union.[140] Still, there are factors which militate against this conclusion and lead in another direction.

After his stint in Congress, Lincoln not only did not take cases that fell within the reach of the fugitive slave law; he did not take any cases involving slaves or abolitionists. This, of course, is in marked contrast to the years before his departure when he was involved with various aspects of slavery in *Bailey v. Cromwell, People v. Pond*, the *Scott* and *Kern* cases, and, of course, the *Matson* case. Moreover, while Lincoln's representation of fugitive slaves and their abettors arguably could undermine the fugitive slave law, he could have represented slave owners in such cases which, if anything, would have aided its enforcement. Finally, although Lincoln had no personal involvement in slave cases, apparently he had no problem with his junior partner, William H. Herndon, representing fugitive slaves, which Herndon did at least once in 1857, and again in 1860.[141]

It seems quite plausible that Lincoln's avoidance of slave litigation after the Matson case can be attributed to his experience in that case. As others have pointed out, Lincoln's views about slavery and what could or should be done about it evolved over the years.[142] To some extent this evolution was a product of the times. In the 1830s and 1840s, Illinois politicians seldom had the need and almost never had the desire to address the issue. Lincoln was no exception. Prior to the 1850s, when the admission of new states made its expansion a pressing national issue, slavery was "on the periphery of Lincoln's field of vision."[143] He had the luxury of keeping his as yet unformed ideas about it to himself—saying little and doing less.

There were, however, a few occasions when the slavery issue forced itself into Lincoln's public life and he made very difficult choices. One was his politically dangerous vote in the Illinois legislature in 1837. Another was his decision to represent Matson. The moral dilemma that that case had presented, the conflicting loyalties that it had engendered, apparently troubled him to the point where he chose to avoid them in the future and the best way to do so was to steer clear of such cases. Lincoln's 1855 letter to Joshua Speed, which was referenced earlier, provides a glimpse of Lincoln's inner turmoil which the Matson case made manifest, and which he chose not to experience again, at least not at the bar:

> *You know I dislike slavery; and you fully admit the abstract wrong of it. So far there is no cause of difference. But you say that sooner than yield your legal right to a slave . . . , you would see the Union dissolved. . . . I . . . acknowledge your rights and my obligations, under the constitution, in regard to your slaves. I confess I hate to see the poor creatures hunted down, and caught, and carried back to their stripes, and unrewarded toils; but I bite my lip and keep quiet.*[144]

POST TRIAL BRIEFS

The Bryants

THE COURT'S DECISION IN THE MATSON CASE FREED JANE BRYANT AND her four children. No longer were they "the Matson slaves." How free they were to determine their own destinies is an open question. We can only speculate about what Jane and her husband, Anthony, actually wanted to do with the rest of their lives or with their children's futures. What we do know is that on October 17, 1847, as required by the Illinois Black Laws, Hiram Rutherford, Gideon Matthew Ashmore, and Samuel C. Ashmore posted a surety bond of "one Thousand dollars, current money of this United States" because the Bryants were African Americans "desirous of settling in this State and county."[1]

But the Bryants did not settle in Illinois. According to one story, fearing Matson's "vindictiveness" and concerned "lest her children should be kidnapped and carried back into slavery,"[2] Jane accepted an offer from the American Colonization Society to emigrate to Liberia. Abolitionists in Independence raised money to pay for the Bryants' passage to Africa. Gideon Ashmore accompanied them across the state to Quincy, Illinois, where they boarded a steamboat to travel down the Mississippi River to New Orleans and the voyage to Liberia. The trip across Illinois served as a fund raiser, with stops in Springfield and in Jacksonville to drum up money from local abolitionists. One of the contributors in Springfield was "Billy" Herndon, Lincoln's law partner.[3]

The Bryants made it to Liberia, but, apparently, did not prosper there. In an account of his seven-week trip to Liberia, Elder Samuel S. Ball reported to the August 1848 annual meeting of the Colored Baptist Association of Illinois that the Bryants were "truly in a deplorable situation."[4] The money that had been raised on their behalf proved only enough to get them across the ocean "and they arrived in Liberia without one dollar."[5] In Monrovia, the country's capital, their situation went from bad to worse. According to Elder Ball's report:

> *They were placed on the outskirts of the town, and were all going through the fever. They all shed tears on seeing me, and began to represent their distress. They informed me that they had on one occasion sent all around Monrovia to beg a chicken, and could not get one; but were told if they had the money they could get one. The old gentleman [Anthony Bryant] wanted the three Kentucky delegates and myself to try to raise as much money as would bring him and his family back to the U. States, but this we could not do: he then wished us bring him and his little boy back; but this was out of our power.[6]*

Robert Matson

The decision in *In the Matter of Jane* was not appealed. Apparently, before the ruling came down, Matson had decided to abide by the court's decision. This, at least, was Chief Justice Wilson's conclusion. In his opinion, Wilson observes that Matson "showed every disposition to submit to the result of an adjudication upon his claim."[7]

Tradition has it that after he lost at trial, an angry Robert Matson left Illinois for Kentucky and never paid Lincoln a dime. Matson may have been angry, but the evidence indicates that he may have paid Lincoln his fee, or at least some of it. On December 7, 1848, Thomas Lincoln wrote his son about selling a note from a "Robert Mattison" for "twenty dollars in goods . . . with out recourse on any body. . . ."[8]

There also is evidence that if Robert Matson left for Kentucky, he did not stay there for too long. On November 23, 1848, Matson was back in Illinois, this time in Gallatin County, south of Coles County, just across the Ohio River from Kentucky. There, on that date, Robert Matson married Mary Ann Corbin, his housekeeper, the woman whose reputed dispute with Jane Bryant had triggered the chain of events that culminated in the trial.[9]

Two years later, the national census of 1850 recorded Robert and Mary Matson as residing in Fulton County, Kentucky, in the southwestern tip of the state. The census records indicate that the couple had four children living with them at that time: two in their teens, little Mildred, who was born in Coles County, and Henrietta, three months, who was born after the couple had married.

Robert Matson's occupation is identified in the census report as "farmer," and the appraised value of his property is one of the higher of those listed.[10]

The Matsons had at least two more children, the second just four years before Robert's death.[11] In 1859, he died in Fulton County, near Matson's Switch.[12] Mary died there in 1874. They lie buried on the family farm, which is located on the highway that runs between Union City, Tennessee, and Hickman, Kentucky, and which, at last report, still was owned by Matson's descendants.[13] His epitaph reads as follows:

> *General Robert Matson born Bourbon Co., Ky January 1796, died January 26, 1859 aged about 64 years old as a soldier he was brave and as a legislator incorruptible. An affectionate husband, an indulgent parent, and a good citizen, he died contented and by all respected as an honest man.*[14]

Gideon M. Ashmore and Hiram Rutherford

The decision freeing the Bryants mooted Matson's suits against Gideon Ashmore and Hiram Rutherford. On May 9, 1848, appearing on Matson's behalf, Thomas Marshall moved to dismiss the actions. The court granted the motions, assessing costs against Matson in favor of the defendants.[15] In all likelihood, neither Ashmore nor Rutherford ever received a penny from Matson.[16] Their efforts were rewarded in years.

After escorting the Bryants across Illinois to the Mississippi on the first stage of their trip to Liberia, Gideon Ashmore disappears from the scene. Apparently, he eventually moved to Arena in Iowa County, Wisconsin. There, on January 25, 1892, Ashmore died at the age of eighty-two.[17]

Hiram Rutherford remained in Independence, Illinois, for the rest of his life, another fifty-three years.[18] Tradition has it that in addition to providing him the satisfaction of seeing the Bryants go free, the Matson trial also gave Rutherford, then a widower, the pleasure of meeting Harriet, the woman who would become his second wife. They married in 1848 and had eight children together. When the babies started coming, Rutherford moved his office out of the family's two-story frame house into a small structure across the street. The house and office are still standing as part of a historic compound in what is now Oakland, Illinois.[19]

Rutherford was a pillar of his community. For many years, he served on the county board and as school treasurer. He was a founder of the Oakland National Bank. Rutherford died in 1900 at age eighty-four.[20]

Charles H. Constable

If Charles H. Constable made an eloquent appeal for freedom on behalf of the Bryants at the Matson trial, it was an aberration in his career. Constable's support of slavery or, at least, his strong opposition to its abolition in the South, was a dominant element of his life, along with his thirst for office. Both affected his political loyalties and his relationship with Lincoln.

In 1848, when his party's candidate, Zachary Taylor, was elected president, Constable was a Whig. He sought a diplomatic appointment to one of the Latin American countries. He wrote to Lincoln and David Davis to aid his cause. His letters have an unbecoming pleading quality about them. In his May 5, 1849, letter to Lincoln, Constable said that he had a growing family, that his law practice was becoming less profitable and that, while he would prefer a diplomatic appointment, he would take almost any government job.[21] In his letter to Davis, Constable wrote, "This is very important to me, failure is defeat indeed."[22]

Davis and Lincoln dutifully wrote letters on Constable's behalf. In his letter to Secretary of State John M. Clayton, Lincoln described Constable as "a Marylander by birth, who came to our state ten years ago, who fought the Whig battles faithfully with us ever since, and is now a favorite with us all."[23] Constable did not receive an appointment.

His next goal was a place on the federal bench in the Washington or Oregon territories. Again, Lincoln and Davis went to bat for him with Whig congressmen and senators.[24] Again, Constable was not successful.

By 1851, Constable was thinking about changing parties. His increasing inclination toward the Democrats almost led to a fistfight with Lincoln. It happened on the judicial circuit. Constable was visiting Lincoln and Davis in the room that they were sharing in a tavern in Paris, Illinois. He began complaining about the "old fogyish" Whig party's treatment of bright young men as compared to the way that the Democrats did things. According to one of Lincoln's first biographers, Josiah Holland, Lincoln listened quietly until Constable accused the Whigs of ingratitude toward him.[25] Then, Lincoln "turned fiercely upon him, and said, 'Mr. Constable, I understand you perfectly, and have noticed for some time that you have been slowly and cautiously picking your way over to the democratic party.'"[26]

"[S]orry and nervous" about the quarrel, Davis was able to reconcile the two men, but by 1856, to use Lincoln's words, Constable had "gone over hook and line" to the Democrats.[27] That year, he was a Democrat presidential elector-at-large on the Buchanan ticket. In 1861, after moving to Clark County, Constable was elected as a Democrat to the bench and began his ill-fated career as judge of the Illinois Fourth Circuit.[28]

One contemporary described Constable as "the finest circuit judge I think I ever saw," but he was a vociferous opponent of Lincoln's war policies.[29] After rendering a couple of antiadministration decisions which earned him the deep antipathy of local Republicans, Constable touched off a powder keg.[30] In the spring of 1863, he released four suspected Union army deserters and ordered the two sergeants who had arrested them held for trial on charges of kidnapping.[31] Their hearing never was completed. About three hundred Union troops seized the Coles County courthouse, released the sergeants, and arrested Constable.[32]

In the hearing that followed, the court acquitted Constable of any wrongdoing, but he was a marked man.[33] Constable did not improve his standing when, on June 17, 1863, he was elected to a leadership position at a meeting of an estimated forty thousand opponents of the Lincoln administration convened at Springfield, Illinois. The convention passed several resolutions calling for the withdrawal of Lincoln's recent Emancipation Proclamation and the restoration of peace on the basis of the union as it was before the commencement of hostilities. It also condemned Constable's arrest.[34]

None of this went over well with Union soldiers stationed or on leave in the vicinity. On January 29, 1864, several of them confronted Constable and forced him to swear an oath to support "the Administration, Abraham Lincoln, all proclamations now issued and all that may hereafter be issued. . . ."[35]

The festering situation finally exploded on March 28, 1864. It was a Monday and the first day of the spring session of Judge Constable's court in Charleston. The town was crowded with furloughed soldiers seeking some liquid refreshment before rejoining their regiment and Democrats planning to attend a speech by a local Democratic congressman.[36] To this day, no one can say who fired the first shot, but the fusillade that followed left nine men dead.[37] The Coles County grand jury indicted only two of the accused rioters who, after a change of venue ordered by Judge Constable, were tried and acquitted.[38]

Despite these difficulties, Constable remained a judge until his death in 1865.[39]

Orlando B. Ficklin

Writing years after the Matson trial, Orlando Ficklin recalled that his "Democratic Friends . . . were greatly concerned, that being counsel for the Ashmores, who were pronounced abolitionists, might destroy all future prospects for political promotion."[40] Their concerns proved unjustified. In 1851, he was again elected to Congress as a Democrat.[41]

That same year, Coles County suffered through a deadly epidemic of Asiatic cholera and Ficklin had a scare. He went down while working in the fields of the family farm. Carried home and put to bed, Ficklin revived enough to summon his wife, children, and servants to his bedside. Then, according to the *History of Coles County*, Ficklin bid them good-bye and kissed each one, "concluding with his old colored cook, and prepared to die of cholera."[42] False alarm. After falling asleep for a few hours, Ficklin awoke—"himself again."[43]

In 1856, Ficklin was a district delegate to the Democratic National Convention in Cincinnati, which nominated James Buchanan for president.[44] Four years later, he was a delegate-at-large to the Democratic convention in Charleston, South Carolina, which ended in anarchy. About six weeks later, Ficklin attended the adjourned convention in Baltimore, which nominated his old colleague Stephen Douglas for the presidency and saw southern delegates walk out.[45]

Although he "valued him highly" as a friend, Lincoln's election to the presidency dismayed Ficklin.[46] He "believed [correctly] that the election of Lincoln and Hamlin by sectional votes, on sectional platforms would lead to disunion."[47] Ficklin disagreed with fighting a war to reunite the union. In his words, "[T]he sword would cut asunder but could never unite the states and the people, that our federal union of states could only be held together by the bonds of fraternity and brotherhood. . . ."[48]

He also deplored the social disruption wrought by the war and the government's crackdown on opposition. In December 1862, he wrote:

> *Freedom of speech of the press, and freedom from arrest, except for crime, are the birthright of every American freeman, these have been stricken down with ruthless hands by the party in power, and an attempt has been made to nullify the constitution and the laws of our state not only in respect to the liberty of her citizenry, but also by flooding the state with a class of miserable, imbecile and wholly worthless freed negroes, than which a greater scourge and heavens curse could not be inflicted on the people of a free state.*[49]

In June 1863, Ficklin attended the huge antiadministration convention in Springfield that attacked the Emancipation Proclamation. Like Constable, he was elected to its leadership.[50] After the Charleston riot in March 1864, friends and families of some of the accused rioters paid Ficklin one thousand dollars to travel to Washington to attempt to persuade President Lincoln to free the prisoners.[51] Ficklin made the trip that July and exchanged correspondence with the president in which he argued that the military should turn the prisoners over to the civil authorities.[52] There is no way of determining how much Ficklin's entreaties influenced Lincoln, but in early November 1864, over the objections of the army, Lincoln ordered the prisoners sent to Coles County for civil prosecution.[53]

After the war, Ficklin still had the respect and held the confidence of a majority of his Coles County neighbors. In 1870, they sent him to the Illinois constitutional convention and, eight years later, returned him to the Illinois House of Representatives at age seventy.[54] One of his neighbors never wavered in his gratitude for the role that Ficklin had played in representing Jane Bryant and her children. Hiram Rutherford attended Ficklin's funeral in 1886: "I sat by and heard with pleasure the many good and kind things said about him by his fellow members of the bar, but strange to say, the best and greatest event of his life was not mentioned. They did not know perhaps that in his last journey, he would reach St. Peter's gate, bearing as a ticket pass the shackles of five slaves, for the good apostle to look upon and honor."[55]

Usher F. Linder

For thirteen years after the Matson case, Usher Linder continued to practice law on the circuit from his office in Charleston. For a while, he retained his ability to mesmerize a jury. "Logical, concise, and clear in argument," Linder was still, in 1851, "eloquent as an advocate—the terror of his opponents before a jury."[56] Henry Clay Whitney, who, as a young lawyer, rode the circuit with Linder in the 1850s, remembered him as "the most brilliant orator that ever lived in Illinois."[57]

In those years, Linder also retained his famous sense of humor. Typical was an incident in 1856 when Linder was regaling a group with stories about Leonard Swett, "the sharpest lawyer in Illinois," who, according to Linder, always obtained acquittals for his clients in murder cases by proving them insane: "He carries around with him a little doctor, who knows all about insanity, and swears 'em all crazy as loons. The jury comes in with a verdict of insanity every time."[58]

Linder went on to describe several cases in which the acquitted accused were "just as sane as I am, sir."[59] A bemused listener politely introduced himself as Dr. Roe, a well-known physician and "the little doctor you are talking about."[60]

Embarrassed but unfazed, Linder apologized, explaining that "he did not know the man was Dr. Roe of Bloomington" and assuring his listeners that "if this man ever swears I am insane, I will believe him myself."[61]

However, as the decade played itself out, there was less and less laughter. Excessive drinking drove Linder's legal career on a downward spiral. He began to neglect his clients' needs. It got to the point that Judge David Davis felt the need to address the problem. "Mr. Linder," Davis said from the bench in open court, "I must give you some advice. You must drink less and work more or you will roll in the gutter."[62]

Linder ignored the advice and things got worse. In 1859, enraged, drunk, or both, Linder physically attacked another lawyer, Elisha Starkweather, in court. Citing the assault and alleging that Linder carried a pistol, Starkweather petitioned the court to require Linder to post a bond insuring that he keep the peace. The petition was granted and Linder posted a five-hundred-dollar bond.[63]

Politically too, Linder's life ran a ragged course downhill. Coles County elected him to the state legislature in 1848 and again in 1850. As we have seen, Linder switched from the Whigs to the Democrats, supported Douglas against Lincoln in 1858, and earned the sobriquet "For God's Sake, Linder."[64] His election as a delegate to the Democratic National Convention in 1860 was the last time that he was elected to any office and the last time that he served the people of Coles County.[65]

He remained a racist. To the extent that he supported the war against the South, Linder supported it as a war to save the union, not, as he made clear in his memoirs, as a war to "emancipate the negro, or to make him the equal of the white man."[66]

Linder moved to Chicago in 1860 and spent the last sixteen years of his life there, apparently living from hand to mouth. While his efforts to persuade Lincoln to intervene on behalf of his Confederate son were successful, Linder's attempts to touch his friend for a federal appointment were unavailing. In March 1864, he wrote Lincoln from Chicago on the state of his fortunes and his need for assistance. "I have been, now," he wrote, "four years at this place, and notwithstanding I have exerted a diligence and prudence, hardly common to me, no prosperous wind has yet filled my sail."[67] Linder modestly stated that if Lincoln "should think me loyal, competent and worthy—and upon these considerations offer me a place where I can be of service to the country, I will accept it however humble or insignificant it may be—and bring to the discharge of the duties thereof all the zeal and talents I have, be they great or small."[68]

No job was forthcoming. A year later, two days after Lincoln's assassination, Linder gave a moving eulogy at a meeting of the Chicago Bar Association which one observer called "a masterpiece of eloquence."[69] The *Chicago Times* found his remarks "affecting beyond account . . . more than one, as he listened to the tremulous tones of the speaker, was visibly moved to tears."[70]

It was Linder's last hurrah.

In the early 1870s, seeking "support in my old age," he submitted his name "for nomination to the humble office of Justice of the Peace, which they failed to give me, and for which I have no complaint to make against them."[71] In 1874, an old acquaintance, Orville H. Browning, ran into Linder on the streets of Chicago. "He looks old and broken," Browning recorded in his diary, "and was poorly and meagerly dressed, and I suspect is poor and needy."[72]

Hoping to leave some legacy to his children, Linder spent his last years writing his *Reminiscences*, which was published in 1879, three years after his death. While the bulk of this "charming" but "inconsequential" memoir is devoted to the old man's recollections of colleagues at the bar, the memoir does provide a glimpse of how the author viewed his own involvement in events long past.[73] He was not too hard on himself.

Linder acknowledged that he and John Hogan were "severely assailed and maligned for the part [they] took in attempting to settle and compromise matters between [Elijah] Lovejoy and his enemies," yet this man who used his formidable eloquence to stir up murderous feeling against the abolitionist refused to take any responsibility for Lovejoy's death.[74] Speaking specifically of Hogan but implying that it was about himself as well, Linder maintained that "he did all that mortal man could do to bring about peace between those hostile elements."[75] According to Linder, "[i]nstead of participating in the riot that resulted in [the] death of Lovejoy, I, for weeks before its occurrence, did all that I could to prevent such a catastrophe."[76]

Linder's *Reminiscences* says nothing about the Matson case, but his description of his legal practice in central Illinois would seem to indicate that he had no regrets about the role that he had played in the matter: "[U]p to 1860 I led a career of proud legal success on the Wabash circuit which makes my heart still swell with pride when I think of it. I made hundreds and thousands of dollars on that circuit, and I spent it liberally: was not mean or penurious in its distribution; and I can lay my hand upon my heart and say that I never prosecuted or oppressed an unfortunate man in my character as a lawyer."[77]

NOTES

Abbreviations

ALPL   Abraham Lincoln Presidential Library
BCCCR   Bourbon County Circuit Court Records, Public Records Division, Department for Libraries and Archives, Frankfort, Kentucky
CHS   Chicago Historical Society
LPAL   Martha L. Benner and Cullom Davis, et al., *The Law Practice of Abraham Lincoln: Complete Documentary Edition*, DVD–ROM (Urbana: University of Illinois Press, 2000)
LOC   Library of Congress
MHS   Missouri Historical Society
WHS   Washington (Illinois) Historical Society

Introduction

1. Willene Hendrick and George Hendrick, eds., *On the Illinois Frontier: Dr. Hiram Rutherford, 1840–1848* (Carbondale: Southern Illinois University Press, 1981), p. 139.

2. Quoted in D. T. McIntyre, "History of the Matson Slave Trial in 1847," typewritten manuscript, Albert J. Beveridge Papers, Container 404, LOC, Manuscript Division. See also Hendrick and Hendrik, *On the Illinois Frontier*, p. 142.

3. Henry Clay Whitney, *Life on the Circuit with Lincoln* (1892; Caldwell, Idaho: The Caxton Printers, Ltd., 1940), p. 315 n.4.

4. John J. Duff, *A. Lincoln: Prairie Lawyer* (New York: Rinehart & Company, Inc., 1960), p. 130.

5. Benjamin Quarles, *Lincoln and the Negro* (New York: Oxford University Press, 1962), p. 25; Peter Burchard, *Lincoln and Slavery* (New York: Atheneum Books for Young Readers, 1999), p. 30.

6. Benjamin P. Thomas, *Abraham Lincoln* (1952; New York: Book-of-the-Month Club, Inc., 1986), p. 118.

7. David Herbert Donald, *Lincoln* (New York: Simon & Schuster, 1995), pp. 103–4.

8. Brian Dirck, *Lincoln the Lawyer* (Urbana: University of Illinois Press, 2007), p. 149.

9. Mark E. Steiner, *An Honest Calling: The Law Practice of Abraham Lincoln* (DeKalb: Northern Illinois University Press, 2006), pp. 136, 177.

10. Albert C. Guelzo, *Abraham Lincoln: Redeemer President* (Grand Rapids: William B. Eerdmans Publishing Company, 1999), p. 126. See also Phillip Shaw Paludan, "Lincoln and Negro Slavery: I Haven't Got Time for the Pain," *Journal of the Abraham Lincoln Association* 27 (Summer 2006), found at www.historycooperative.com (December 12, 2006).

Chapter One

1. Northwest Ordinance (July 13, 1787).

2. John W. Allen, "Slavery and Negro Servitude in Pope County, Illinois," *Journal of the Illinois State Historical Society* 42 (1949), p. 11.

3. Paul Finkelman, "Slavery, the 'More Perfect Union,' and the Prairie State," *Illinois Historical Journal* 80 (1987), p. 249; Thomas Ford, *A History of Illinois from Its Commencement as a State in 1818 to 1847*, 2 vols. (1854; Ann Arbor: University Microfilms, 1968) I, p. 279. Ford (1800–1850) was governor of Illinois from 1842 to 1846. His *History of Illinois* was published four years after his death.

4. Norman Dwight Harris, *The History of Negro Servitude in Illinois, and of the Slavery Agitation in that State, 1719–1864* (1904; Ann Arbor: University Microfilms, 1968), pp. 1–2. Without a doubt, Harris's book is the single most important study of the status of African Americans and the abolition movement in antebellum Illinois. The Jesuit missionaries at Kaskaskia probably were the first owners of black slaves in the Illinois Country and, in 1720, owned more slaves than anyone else there. Carl J. Ekberg, *French Roots in the Illinois Country: The Mississippi Frontier in Colonial Times* (Urbana: University of Illinois Press, 1998), p. 146.

5. Harris, *Negro Servitude in Illinois*, p. 5.

6. Quoted in *Jarrot v. Jarrot*, 7 Ill. 1, 18 (1845) (Young, J., concurring). See also Robert P. Howard, *Illinois: A History of the Prairie State* (Grand Rapids: William B. Eerdmans Publishing Company, 1972), p. 62; Harris, *Negro Servitude in Illinois*, p. 6.

7. The Northwest Ordinance preserved to French and Canadian inhabitants "who have heretofore professed themselves citizens of Virginia, their laws and customs now in force among them, relative to the descent and conveyance, of property," which, arguably, protected the ownership of slaves as "property."

8. Ninian Edwards, *History of Illinois from 1778 to 1833 and Life and Times of Ninian Edwards* (Springfield: Illinois State Journal Company, 1870), pp. 181–83; Paul Finkelman, *Slavery and the Founders: Race and Liberty in the Age of Jefferson* (Armonk, New York: M.E. Sharpe, 1996), pp. 57–79; Solon J. Buck, *Illinois in 1818* (1917; Champaign: University of Illinois Press, 1967), pp. 183–85.

9. Francis S. Philbrick, ed., *The Laws of Indiana Territory, 1801–1809*, Collections of the Illinois State Historical Library 21 (1930), pp. 136–39, 523–26 (Act of 1805), (Act of 1807). See also Buck, *Illinois in 1818*, pp. 183–85; Harris, *Negro Servitude in Illinois*, pp. 7–9. According to Allen, "Slavery and Negro Servitude in Pope County, Illinois," in a majority of the indentures recorded in Pope County, Illinois, the black servant

acknowledged receipt of a sum of money, but Allen concludes that "[i]t is to be seriously doubted whether Negroes actually received the money." Ibid., p. 106. The 1805 act had been preceded by "A Law concerning servants," adopted in 1803, which "assumed that all blacks who came into the territory were indentured servants who had *voluntarily* contracted with their masters before entering Indiana" and required that they specifically perform their contracts in full. Finkelman, *Slavery and the Founders*, pp. 68–69. Of course, most of the blacks in question were slaves and the statute a recognition of de facto slavery. Ibid., p. 36.

In 1814, the Illinois territorial legislature legalized the ongoing practice of leasing slaves from Kentucky and Tennessee to perform the backbreaking, labor-intensive work of extracting salt from the salt-rich streams in the Salines in southwestern Illinois. "An Act concerning Negroes and Mulattoes, Approved December 22, 1814," Illinois Acts, in Stephen Middleton, *The Black Laws of the Old Northwest* (Westport: Greenwood Press, 1993), pp. 285–86; Francis S. Philbrick, ed., *The Laws of Illinois Territory, 1809–1818*, Collections of the Illinois State Historical Library 25 (1950), pp. 157–58. See also Howard, *History of the Prairie State*, p. 132; Harris, *Negro Servitude in Illinois*, p. 15; Morris Birkbeck and George Flower, *History of the English Settlement in Edwards County, Illinois, Founded in 1817 and 1818 by Morris Birkbeck and George Flower* (1882; Ann Arbor: University Microfilms, 1968), p. 198.

10. *Harry v. Jarrot*, 6 Ill. 119, 125, 1844 Ill. LEXIS 18, 8 (1844)(emphasis added).

11. Buck, *Illinois in 1818*, p. 140; Howard, *History of the Prairie State*, pp. 130–31. Madison County records for the years 1815–1818 reveal that a servant named Willis, who was sixteen years old, was indentured for fifty years; Sarah, who was nineteen, was indentured for ninety years; and Peter, who was seventeen when he was indentured in 1817, could look forward to the end of his term of service in 1916, ninety-nine years later when he was 116 years old. Harris, *Negro Servitude in Illinois*, p. 11 n.3.

12. Harris, *Negro Servitude in Illinois*, pp. 12–14.

13. Buck, *Illinois in 1818*, p. 215.

14. Indiana repealed its black indenture act in 1810. Louis Ewbank and Dorothy Riker, eds., *The Laws of Indiana Territory, 1809–1816* (Indianapolis: Indiana Historical Bureau, 1934), pp. 138–39.

15. Section 1 of Article VI of the Illinois Constitution of 1818 read as follows:

Neither slavery nor involuntary servitude shall *hereinafter* be introduced into this state otherwise than for the punishment of crimes whereof the party shall have been duly convicted [emphasis added].

In contrast, Article 11, section 7 of the Indiana Constitution read as follows:

There shall be neither slavery nor involuntary servitude in this State, otherwise than for the punishment of crimes, hereof the party shall have been duly convicted.

In *State v. Lasselle*, the Indiana Supreme Court ruled that "the framers of our Constitution intended a total and entire prohibition of slavery in this State," including preexisting master-slave relationships. 1 Blackford (Indiana) 60, 62 (1820). See Sandra Boyd Williams, "The Indiana Supreme Court and the Struggle Against Slavery," in John R.

McKivigan, ed., *Abolitionism and American Law* (New York: Garland Publishing, Inc., 1999), pp. 159–71, for an interesting discussion of this and later cases dealing with African Americans in Indiana.

16. Illinois Constitution of 1818, Art. VI, section 1. This provision borrowed language from the Ohio Constitution of 1802. Buck, *Illinois in 1818*, pp. 278–79. Article VIII, section 2 of the Ohio Constitution of 1802, read in pertinent part:

... nor shall any male person, arrived at the age of twenty-one years, or female person arrived at the age of eighteen years, be held to serve any person as a servant, under the pretense of indenture or otherwise, unless such person shall enter into such indenture while in a state of perfect freedom, and on a condition of a bona fide consideration, received or to be received, for their service, except as before excepted.

17. Illinois Constitution of 1818, Art. VI, section 1. The provision made an exception for indentures "given in cases of apprenticeship." The section also borrowed language from the Ohio Constitution of 1802.

18. Illinois Constitution of 1818, Art. VI, section 3. The new constitution permitted the use of leased slaves in the Salines until 1825, provided that a slave could work there only "one year at any one time." Illinois Constitution of 1818, Art. VI, section 2. The salt works were the only exception. Otherwise, according to the constitution, "[n]o person bound to labor in any other state, shall be bound to labor in this state" and any violation ... shall effect the emancipation of such person from his obligation of service." Ibid.

19. Illinois Constitution of 1818, Art. VI, section 1; Harris, *Negro Servitude in Illinois*, pp. 22 n.3, 23.

20. Harris, *Negro Servitude in Illinois*, p. 23.

21. Ibid., pp. 24–26.

22. An Act respecting Free Negroes, Mullatoes, Servants, and Slaves, Approved March 30, 1819, Illinois Session Laws, 1819, p. 354; Finkelman, *Slavery and the Founders*, p. 77.

23. Finkelman, *Slavery and the Founders*, p. 77. Finkelman points out that this statute created a presumption of servitude for all blacks in Illinois and, "along with the constitution, provided no hope that slavery in Illinois would end soon." Ibid.

24. Howard, *History of the Prairie State*, p. 137. The vote was 6,640 to 4,972. Ibid. In Gallatin County, just across the Ohio River from Kentucky, 82 percent of the vote was in favor of the convention. Neighboring Hamilton, Franklin, and Pope Counties were 67 percent, 60 percent, and 69 percent, respectively, in favor. An average of 91 percent of the voters in the state's northernmost counties—Pike, Morgan, Fulton, Sangamon, and Edgar—voted against the convention. "Voting for the 1824 constitutional convention Arranged by County," Elijah Lovejoy Site, found at http//www.state.Il.us/hpa/love joy/county.htm (November 15, 2005). It should be noted that in 1824 the four northern counties of Illinois were considerably larger than they are today. See James Simeone, *Democracy and Slavery in Frontier Illinois* (DeKalb: Northern Illinois Press, 2000), for a different take on the convention controversy. Simeone contends that the movement for a convention was "an egalitarian social revolution in full bloom." Ibid., p. 4.

25. *Nance v. Howard*, 1 Ill. 242, 245–46 (1828)(did not address legality of black indentured servitude, but held that the Illinois legislature always regarded indentured

servants "as property which might be seized or sold"); *Phoebe v. Jay*, 1 Ill. 207, 211 (1828) ("registered and indentured servants are bound to serve").

26. *Phoebe v. Jay*, 1 Ill. at 209.

27. *Nance v. Howard*, 1 Ill. at 246. Justice Lockwood, who wrote the opinion for the court, clearly was not happy that he had to equate indentured servitude with slavery. Early in his opinion, he made his personal views clear:

> Are registered servants goods or chattels, within the meaning of the [execution] statute? This is a question of mere dry law, and does not involve in its investigation and decision, any thing relative to the humanity, policy or legality of the laws and constitution, authorizing and recognizing the registering and indenturing of negroes and mulattoes.

28. Northwest Ordinance (July 13, 1787).

29. *Phoebe v. Jay*, 1 Ill. at 210–11.

30. *Cornelius v. Cohen*, 1 Ill. 131 (1825).

31. *Phoebe v. Jay*, 1 Ill. 207 (1828).

32. *Choisser v. Hargrave*, 2 Ill. 317, 1836 Ill. LEXIS 29 (1836).

33. 2 Ill. 258, 1836 Ill. LEXIS 8, 9 (1836).

34. 4 Ill. 232, 1841 Ill. LEXIS 80 (1841).

35. Ibid. at 233, 1841 Ill. LEXIS 80, p. 2.

36. Ibid., 1841 Ill. LEXIS 80, p. 3.

37. Ibid., 1841 Ill. LEXIS 80, pp. 3–4.

38. *Jarrot v. Jarrot*, 7 Ill. 1 (1845). The supreme court distinguished between indentured servants whose status was provided for in the Illinois Constitution of 1818 and French slaves whose status was not. The majority held that because the plaintiff had been born after the passage of the Northwest Ordinance, which forbade slavery in the Illinois Territory, he was a free man. Ibid. at p. 22. Concurring Justice Wilson maintained that Jarrot was free because he was born after the adoption of the Illinois Constitution in 1818. Ibid. at 32 (Wilson, C. J., concurring). Three of the nine justices dissented. Ibid.

39. *Sarah v. Borders*, 5 Ill. 341 (1843).

40. Illinois law defined "mulatto" as every person with "one-fourth part or more negro blood." "Who may be witnesses in criminal cases," Approved March 3, 1845, Revised Statutes, in Middleton, *Black Laws of the Old Northwest*, p.315.

41. Ill. Rev. Stat., ch. LXXIV, sec. 1 (1845). (No "black or mulatto person" is permitted to reside in Illinois "until such person shall have given bond, with sufficient security, to the people of this State, for the use of the proper county, in the penal sum of one thousand dollars, conditioned that such person will not, at any time, become a charge to said county, or any other county of this State, as a poor person, and that such person shall, at all times demean himself or herself, in strict conformity with the laws of this State").

42. Ibid., sec. 8 (1845).

43. Ibid., sec. 1 (1845).

44. Ibid., sec. 2 (1845).

45. Constitution of Illinois of 1818, Article V, section 1 ["The militia of the state shall consist of all free male able bodied persons, (negroes, mulattoes and Indians excepted,) resident of the state. . . ."]. See also "Militia," Section 1, Approved March 3, 1845, Revised Statutes, in Middleton, *Black Laws of the Old Northwest*, p. 280 (requires enrollment of

all "free white male inhabitants" resident in Illinois, between eighteen and forty-five years of age).

46. Constitution of Illinois of 1818, Article II, section 27 (right to vote limited to "all white male inhabitants").

47. "Who may be Witnesses in criminal cases," Approved March 3, 1845, Revised Statutes, in Middleton, *Black Laws of the Old Northwest*, p. 315 (cannot testify in criminal cases on behalf of or against whites); "Evidence and Depositories," Approved March 3, 1845, Revised Statutes, in Middleton, *Black Laws of the Old Northwest*, p. 318 (cannot testify in "any court" or in "any case against a white person").

48. "White and colored persons committing adultery and fornication together," Approved December 3, 1844, Session Laws, in Middleton, *Black Laws of the Old Northwest*, pp. 323–24. Upon conviction, mixed couples who lived together "in an open state of adultery or fornication" could be fined up to five hundred dollars and imprisoned up to one year. The punishment increased proportionately with each offense. Ibid. Illinois statutes also criminalized interracial marriage and punished clerks who issued marriage licenses to interracial couples. "Marriages," Approved March 3, 1845, Revised Statutes, in Middleton, *Black Laws of the Old Northwest,* pp. 324–25.

49. Harris, *Negro Servitude in Illinois*, pp. 226–29; Howard, *History of the Prairie State*, p. 131.

50. Ill. Rev. Stat., ch. LXXIV, sec. 4 (1845).

51. Ibid., sec. 5 (1845). For an example of an application for a certificate of freedom by a suspected runaway slave who had served his twelve-month term, see Application for Certificate of Freedom (September 20, 1844), Hayes Miscellaneous Document No.18440920, Sparta [Illinois] Public Library, found at http://www.eliillinois .org/30626_00/main/18440920.jpg (April 27, 2005).

52. Ill. Rev. Stat., ch. LXXIV, sec. 4 (1845).

53. Ibid., secs. 2, 5 (1845). Occasionally, in egregious cases, free blacks found relief in the state's courthouses. For example, in 1831, the Illinois Supreme Court upheld a judgment against two white men who the jury found had forced a free Negro to work for them. *Littleton v. Moses*, 1 Ill. 393, 1831 Ill. LEXIS 4 (1831). Similarly, in *Nixon v. People*, the state supreme court affirmed the conviction of Absalom Nixon, who had thrown Adam, a "deformed," nearly mute "man of color," from his wagon and abandoned him to die on the frozen ground, a crime "of a very atrocious character." 3 Ill. 267, 270, 1840 Ill. LEXIS 24, pp. 24–25.

54. Petition for Writ of Habeas Corpus, *Ex parte Warman*, Menard County Circuit Court (June 9, 1845), LPAL, File ID L05867, Document No. 136133.

55. Ibid. Warman was fortunate. He connected with an attorney named Aquilla Parker, who filed a petition for his release. Supreme Court Justice Samuel Hubbell Treat, sitting as a circuit judge, granted the petition, and Warman was released from custody. Writ of Habeas Corpus, *Ex parte Warman*, Menard County Circuit Court (June 10, 1845), LPAL, File ID L05867, Document No. 136138; Order, *Ex parte Warman*, Menard County Circuit Court (June 10, 1845), LPAL, File ID l05867, Document No. 136143.

56. The convention had been called to deal with the relationship between the governor and the legislature, the structure of the state's supreme court, the problem of the state's banks (or lack of banks), and the voting rights of aliens. Willard L. King, *Lincoln's Manager, David Davis* (Cambridge: Harvard University Press, 1960), p. 55; Arvarh E. Strickland, "Illinois Background of Lincoln's Attitude Toward Slavery and the Negro,"

Journal of the Illinois State Historical Library 56 (1963), p. 483; Howard, *History of the Prairie State*, p. 232.

57. Illinois Constitution of 1818, Art. VI. See pp. 9—10 supra.

58. Arthur C. Cole, ed., *The Constitutional Debates of 1847*, Collections of the Illinois State Historical Library 14 (Springfield, 1919), pp. 83, 86–87. The provision, as adopted, reads as follows: "There shall be neither slavery nor involuntary servitude in this state, except as punishment for crime whereof the party shall have been duly convicted." Illinois Constitution of 1848, Art. XIII, sec. 16.

59. *Constitutional Debates of 1847*, pp. 104–5.

60. Ibid., p. 170.

61. Ibid., pp. 47, 870, 871.

62. Ibid., p. xxvii.

63. Ibid., pp. 201–2. Bond was the youngest son of Shadrach Bond, the first governor of Illinois. In 1862, he was arrested for his antiwar views. Ibid., p. 951.

64. Quoted in King, *Lincoln's Manager*, p. 55. J. H. Buckingham, a Boston newspaperman, did not necessarily disagree with Davis as to the delegates' merit, but was put off by their style: "As for discipline and etiquette, I cannot say much for them. Every member who spoke, rose and put one foot in his chair, and one hand in his breeches pocket, and more than half of the whole sat with their feet on the desks before them, tilting up in their chairs. They looked like sensible men, but they want training from the President down." Henry E. Pratt, ed., "Illinois As Lincoln Knew It: A Boston Reporter's Record of a Trip in 1847," *Papers in Illinois History 1937* (Springfield: The Illinois State Historical Society, 1938), p. 38.

65. *Constitutional Debates of 1847*, p. 202.

66. Ibid., pp. 223 (Singleton), 227 (Geddes). Singleton was born in Virginia and "[h]is own feelings had always been upon the side of slavery." Ibid., p. 223. During the Civil War, he was a leader in the Illinois peace party. Ibid., p. 977. Geddes, a Whig, was a farmer from Hancock County. Ibid., p. 960.

67. Ibid., p. 221 (Alexander Jenkins). Jenkins, a Democrat, had been lieutenant governor from 1834 to 1836. Ibid., p. 965. Singleton claimed that exclusion was "a matter of self-defense." Ibid., p. 225.

68. Ibid., p. 221.

69. Ibid., pp. 208, 216, 218.

70. Ibid., pp. 208, 216.

71. Ibid., p. 202.

72. Ibid.

73. Ibid., p. 203.

74. Ibid., p. 212. A Whig, Davis later became a Democrat and a "violent" opponent of Lincoln's war policies. Ibid., pp. 956–57.

75. Ibid., pp. 223, 226–27.

76. Ibid., p. 220.

77. Ibid., p. 217.

78. Ibid., p. 228.

79. Ibid., p. 206. Pinkney was only thirty years old in 1847. He was the principal of the Rock River Seminary. Later, he became a member of the state legislature where he served in both the house and the senate. Ibid., p. 974.

80. Ibid., pp. 204–5 (Church), 210 (Norton). Church was from New York and Norton was from Vermont. Both were Whigs who later became Republicans.

81. King, *Lincoln's Manager*, p. 56; Strickland, "Illinois Background of Lincoln's Attitude Toward Slavery," p. 486.

82. *Constitutional Debates of 1847*, pp. 218–19. Stephen T. Logan, whom David Davis described as "the influential man of the body," declared that "[h]e was opposed to making this provision the all absorbing topic that was to influence the people's votes upon the adoption of the constitution." Ibid., p. 219; Strickland, "Illinois Background of Lincoln's Attitude Toward Slavery," p. 496.

83. *Constitutional Debates of 1847*, p. 855. James Singleton, who strongly supported exclusion, kept the pressure on by presenting another petition "for a provision in the constitution to prevent the emigration of negroes to, and the emancipation of, slaves in this State." The petition gave him the opportunity to rail against abolitionists and to raise the specter of miscegenation, race war, and black domination:

> The odious doctrine of abolition will 'divide and conquer,' and too much reliance on the strength of our government exposes us to a weaker power; broad, deep and firm as the government may be in its foundation, bold and commanding in its superstructure, it is not beyond the reach of such odious steps as have been allowed to abolitionists on this floor. And when the time comes, sir, who will sympathize with Illinois, when the hideous shouts of exhalation rise from a victorious negro population in Illinois? What sound but the death shrieks of Liberty? Shall we hear it?

Ibid., p. 238.

84. Among other things, the statute passed pursuant to this resolution made it a misdemeanor for "any negro, or mulatto, bond or free," to enter Illinois "and remain ten days, with the evident intention of residing in the same." "An act to prevent the migration of free Negroes into this state," Section 3, Approved February 12, 1853, Laws of Illinois, in Middleton, *Black Laws of the Old Northwest*, p. 300. Speaking or voting against the proposal could be politically dangerous. John M. Palmer, a delegate from Macoupin County in south-central Illinois, voted against it "on account of which I was, at the election which occurred in the month of August, defeated for reelection to the office of probate justice of the peace." John M.Palmer, *The Bench and Bar of Illinois*, 2 vols. (Chicago: The Lewis Publishing Company, 1899), I, p.4.

85. *Constitutional Debates of 1847*, pp. 856–63; Theodore Calvin Pease, *Illinois Election Returns, 1818–1848*, Collections of the Illinois State Historical Library 18 (1923), p. 176; Strickland, "Illinois Background of Lincoln's Attitude Toward Slavery," p. 487. The exclusion provision received strong support in the southern and central counties that overwhelmed the opposition to it in the northeastern part of the state. Strickland, "Illinois Background of Lincoln's Attitude Toward Slavery," p. 487.

86. Harris, *Negro Servitude in Illinois*, p. 161.

87. See Merton L. Dillon, *Elijah P. Lovejoy: Abolitionist Editor* (Urbana: University of Illinois, 1961), pp. 94–95.

88. Alice Felt Tyler, *Freedom's Ferment: Phases of American Social History from the Colonial Period to the Outbreak of the Civil War* (1944; New York: Harper & Row, 1962),

p. 501; Russell B. Nye, *Fettered Freedom: Civil Liberties and the Slavery Controversy, 1830–1860* (East Lansing: Michigan State College Press, 1949), p. 15.

89. Nye, *Fettered Freedom*, pp. 12–13.

90. Ibid., p. 17. For example, James M. Davis, who railed against blacks at the 1847 Illinois constitutional convention, had little doubt "that the object of the Abolitionists was to dissolve the union." *Constitutional Debates of 1847*, p. 212.

91. John Brewer Stewart, *Holy Warriors: The Abolitionists and American Slavery* (New York: Hill & Wang, 1976), pp. 61–62.

92. Quoted in Nye, *Fettered Freedom*, p. 157.

93. *Constitutional Debates of 1847*, pp. 205–6.

94. John Dean Caton, *Early Bench and Bar of Illinois* (Chicago: The Chicago Legal News Company, 1893), p. 122.

95. "Preamble and Constitution of the Adams County Antislavery Society" (August 25, 1835). Historical Society of Quincy and Adams Counties, Illinois, found at history. alliancelibrarysystem.com/IllinoisAlive/files/qh/htm2/qh000077.cfm (March 3, 2005) ("awful sin"); *Constitutional Debates of 1847*, p. 212 ("demons").

96. Nye, *Fettered Freedom*, p. 173.

97. Quoted in ibid.

98. D. W. Lusk, *Eighty Years of Illinois: Politics and Politicians, Anecdotes and Incidents, A Succinct History of the State, 1809–1889*, 3d rev. ed. (Springfield: H. W. Rokker, 1889), p. 143.

99. Henry Tanner, *History of the rise and progress of the Alton Riots* (Buffalo: Printing House of J.D. Warren, 1878), p. 12. Tanner, who was one of the defenders of Lovejoy's press, maintains that he was "amid all the scenes" that he writes about. Ibid., p. 6.

100. Ibid., p. 11.

101. One nineteenth-century Illinois historian understated it this way: "Outbreaks of the mob spirit—local revolts against the constituted authorities have, indeed been of rather frequent occurrence in Illinois." John Moses, *Illinois Historical and Statistical*, 2d rev. ed., 2 vols. (1887; Chicago: Chicago Printing Company, 1895), I, p. 512. In his *Frontier Illinois* (Bloomington: Indiana University Press, 1998), James E. Davis argues that in its frontier stage, Illinois enjoyed a general consensus in basic values and assumptions that acted to limit violence, but as population increased and the frontier disappeared, this consensus broke down and violence increased.

102. Richard Maxwell Brown, *Strain of Violence: Historical Studies of American Violence and Vigilantism* (New York: Oxford University Press, 1975), pp. 119, 305–19.

103. *Charleston Courier* (July 10, 1841), ALPL.

104. For example, in June 1841, a man named Bridge, who was known as "a notorious confederate and harborer of horsethieves and counterfeiters," received notice from "a certain association" that he must leave Ogle County before June 17 or "he would be looked upon as a proper subject for Lynch law." William Cullen Bryant, *Letters of a Traveler or Notes of Things Seen in Europe and America* (New York: George P. Putnam, 1851), p. 55.

105. When two hundred armed Regulators descended on an accused outlaw's home, the county sheriff and the district attorney "hastened to the scene of the action," but apparently did nothing. *Charleston Courier* (July 10, 1841), ALPL. On another occasion, the sheriff attempted to persuade a group of about five hundred Regulators to release some accused murderers into his custody, but to no avail and they were executed. *Ogle County*

Republican (October 20, 1904), ALPL; Robert Huhn Jones, "Three Days of Violence: The Regulators of the Rock River Valley," *Journal of the Illinois State Historical Society* 49 (Summer 1966), p. 138; Ford, *History of Illinois*, II, p. 37.

106. Galena *Gazette* (July 3, 22, 1841), quoted in Rodney D. Davis, "Judge Ford and the Regulators, 1841–1842," *Selected Papers in Illinois History 1981* (Springfield: Illinois State Historical Society, 1982), p. 29. See also the Ottawa *Free Trader* (July 9, 1841)("A more respectable assemblage of individuals could hardly be convened in the northern part of Illinois" than the vigilantes); Peoria *Democratic* Press (July 21, 1841)(Ogle County was a "peaceful, quiet, moral; community" driven by necessity to vigilante action). Both quoted in ibid.

107. Jones, "Three Days of Violence," p. 140.

108. Moses, *Illinois Historical and Statistical*, I, p. 513; Ford, *History of Illinois*, II, p. 344.

109. James A. Rose, "The Regulators and Flatheads in Southern Illinois," *Transactions of the Illinois State Historical Society* 9 (1906), pp. 112–13. According to Thomas Ford, who was governor of Illinois at the time, the Regulators tortured suspected criminals by holding their heads under water or wrapping them with ropes and then twisting the ropes with a stick to crush the suspect's ribs. Ford, *History of Illinois*, II, p. 348.

The term "Flatheads" may have been taken from the name given to a species of catfish found in the Ohio River. Nicole Etcheson, "Good Men and Notorious Rogues: Vigilantism in Massac County, Illinois 1846–1850," in Michael A. Bellesiles, ed., *Lethal Imagination: Violence and Brutality in American History* (New York: New York University Press, 1999), p. 150. It is used as a derogatory term in *Huckleberry Finn*. See, e.g., Mark Twain, *Adventures of Huckleberry Finn* (1884; New York: Washington Square Press, 1998), pp. 196, 213.

110. Patrick B. Nolan, *Vigilantes on the Middle Border: A Study of Self-Appointed Law Enforcement in the States of the Upper Mississippi from 1840 to 1880* (New York: Garland Publishing, Inc., 1987), p. 174.

111. Rose, "Regulators and Flatheads," pp. 114–16; Etcheson, "Good Men and Notorious Rogues," p. 152. In his *History of Illinois*, Ford maintains that he acted in a somewhat restrained manner because his term as governor was about to expire and he was loath to act in a way which might not be approved or adopted by his successor. He also asserts that it would have been useless to order out the state militia because no one would turn out to protect "horse thieves." Ford, *History of Illinois*, II, pp. 350–51.

112. N. H. Purple, ed., *Compilation of the Statutes of the State of Illinois . . . In Force January 1, 1856* (Chicago: Kein & Lee, 1856), Part II, pp. 1268–69.

113. Ibid., p. 1268.

114. Augustus C. French to William A. Denning (March 27, 1847), in Evarts Boutell Greene and Charles Manfred Thompson, eds., *Governors' Letter Books, 1840–1853*, Collections of the Illinois Historical Library 7 (1911), pp. 141–42; Etcheson, "Good Men and Notarious Rogues," p. 157.

115. Greene and Thompson, *Governors' Letter Books*, p. 141 n.3.

116. Rose, "Regulators and Flatheads," pp. 116, 119–21; Ford, *History of Illinois*, II, pp. 355–56; Brown, *Strain of Violence*, p. 309; Etcheson, "Good Men and Notorious Rogues," pp. 158–62. By its terms, the Riot Act of 1847 was to expire after two years, but the continuing violence led to it being made permanent on January 25, 1848. Purple, *Compilation of Statutes* (1856), p. 1269.

117. Robert Bruce Flanders, *Nauvoo: Kingdom on the Mississippi* (Urbana: University of Illinois Press, 1965), p. 309; John E. Hallwas and Roger D. Launius, *Cultures in Conflict: A Documentary History of the Mormon War in Illinois* (Logan: Utah University Press, 1995), pp. 176–77, 244–45; Howard, *History of the Prairie State*, pp. 218–19; Ford, *History of Illinois*, II, p. 304.

118. "Thomas Ford to the People of Warsaw in Hancock County, July 25, 1844," *Nauvoo Neighbor* (July 31, 1844), in Hallwas and Launius, *Cultures in Conflict*, pp. 254–55.

119. Howard, *History of the Prairie State*, p. 219; Hallwas and Launius, *Cultures in Conflict*, pp. 244–45.

120. Ford, *History of Illinois*, II, pp. 308–09.

121. Ibid., pp. 311–15, 319–20. See also Annette P. Hampshire, *Mormonism in Conflict: The Nauvoo Years* (Lewiston, N.Y.: The Edwin Mellon Press, 1985), p. 255.

122. Ibid.

123. "Nauvoo—Then and Now," *Carthage Gazette* (January 19, 1876), in Hallwas and Launius, *Cultures in Conflict*, p. 331; ibid., pp. 329–30; Hampshire, *Mormonism in Conflict*, p. 255.

124. "Nauvoo—Then and Now," *Carthage Gazette* (January 19, 1876), in Hallwas and Launius, *Cultures in Conflict*, p. 330; ibid., pp. 334–35.

Chapter Two

1. See, e.g., Jesse W. Weik, "Lincoln and the Matson Negroes," *Arena* 17 (April 1897), p. 73; Albert J. Beveridge, *Abraham Lincoln*, 2 vols. (Boston: Houghton Mifflin Company, 1928), I, p. 392; Quarles, *Lincoln and the Negro*, pp. 23–24; Albert A. Woldman, *Lawyer Lincoln* (Boston: Houghton Mifflin Company, 1936), p. 59; Anton-Hermann Chroust, "Abraham Lincoln Argues a Pro-Slavery Case," *American Journal of Legal History* 5 (1961), p. 297; Steiner, *An Honest Calling*, pp. 105–6.

2. Notice, *Matson v. Bryant* (August 23, 1847), Coles County Circuit Court, copy in Herndon-Weik Collection: Group III, Document Nos. 1968–69, LOC, Manuscript Division; LPAL, File ID L00714, Doc. No. 5509.

3. D. T. McIntyre, "History of the Matson Slave Trial in 1847," typewritten manuscript, Albert J. Beveridge Papers, Container 404, LOC, Manuscript Division. Duncan T. McIntyre, who wrote several articles about the Matson case, was a Coles County lawyer who lived in Matoon, Illinois. Apparently, he was a friend of Hiram Rutherford. Hendrick, *On the Illinois Frontier*, p. 133. McIntyre's articles, while interesting and colorful, are not altogether reliable in some respects, such as the reported dialogues between some of the participants.

4. Notice, *Matson v. Bryant* (August 23, 1847), Coles County Circuit Court, copy in Herndon-Weik Collection: Group III, Document Nos. 1968–69, LOC, Manuscript Division; LPAL, File ID L00714, Doc. No. 5509.

5. D. T. McIntyre, "History of the Matson Slave Trial in 1847."

6. Weik, "Lincoln and the Matson Negroes," p. 753. As a young man, Weik (1857–1930) collaborated with William H. Herndon on his biography of Lincoln. See William H. Herndon and Jesse W. Weik, *Herndon's Life of Lincoln*, introduction by Henry Steele Commager (1889; New York: Da Capo Press, 1983), pp. xxxiii–xxxiv. Apparently, most of Weik's information about the Matson case was based upon one or more interviews in 1892 with Hiram Rutherford. See "Notes—Oakland Apr. 4th 1892," Weik MSS, ALPL.

7. Notice, *Matson v. Bryant* (August 23, 1847), Coles County Circuit Court, copy in Herndon-Weik Collection: Group III, Document Nos. 1968–69, LOC, Manuscript Division; LPAL, File ID L00714, Doc. No. 5509.

8. Ibid.

9. Orlando Ficklin's account of the Matson trial, first published on January 15, 1885, reprinted as "A Pioneer Lawyer in the *Tuscola Review* (September 7, 1922) (hereinafter cited as Ficklin, "A Pioneer Lawyer"); D. T. McIntyre, "History of the Matson Slave Trial in 1847."

10. D. T. McIntyre, "Matson Slave Trial," *Oakland Weekly Ledger* (July 17, 1896), Albert J. Beveridge Papers, File No. 728, LOC, Manuscript Division.

11. Beveridge, *Abraham Lincoln*, I, p. 392.

12. Duff, *A. Lincoln: Prairie Lawyer*, p. 130.

13. Woldman, *Lawyer Lincoln*, p. 59.

14. Robert MATSON ID 1317, "Talley Family," Family Trees, found at www.rootsweb .com (May 1, 2003).

15. Quoted in D. T. McIntyre, "History of the Matson Slave Trial in 1847."

16. Ibid.

17. Ficklin, "A Pioneer Lawyer."

18. E-mail from genealogist Dorothy Burditt to author (December 4, 2001).

19. Ibid.; "Re: James MATSON, b. Ca. 1740's, d. 1826," posted on Matson Family Genealogy Forum, GENFORM, found at www.genealogy.com (October 15, 2002), "James MATSON" ID: 1657, "Talley Family," Family Trees, found at www.rootsweb.com (May 1, 2003).

20. E-mail from Dorothy Burditt to author (December 4, 2001).

21. "Richard MATSON," ID: 1665, Talley Family, Family Trees, found at www .rootsweb.com (May 1, 2003); C. Edward Skeen, *Citizen Soldiers in the War of 1812* (Lexington: The University Press of Kentucky, 1999), p. 85; Bruce Catton, *Michigan: A Bicentennial History* (New York: W.W. Norton & Company, Inc., 1976), p. 63.

22. "Enoch MATSON," ID: 1665, Talley Family, Family Trees, found at www.rootsweb .com (May 1, 2003).

23. E-mail from Dorothy Burditt to author (December 4, 2001); "Peyton MATSON," ID: 1666, "Talley Family," Family Trees, found at www.rootsweb.com (May 1, 2003).

24. *Louisville Public Advertiser* (April 6, 1830).

25. E-mail from Dorothy Burditt to author (December 4, 2001).

26. "Re: Ky Militia in War of 1812," posted on War of 1812 Genealogy Forum, GENFORUM, found at www.genealogy.com (November 27, 2001).

27. "Thomas Matson," ID: 1663, "Talley Family," Family Trees, found at www.rootsweb .com (May 1, 2003).

28. Order, *Robert Matson v. Thomas Matson* (August 16, 1823), Case No. 12003, BCCCR.

29. Ibid.

30. Bill, *James Matson v. Thomas Matson* (April 29, 1826), Case No. 13625, BCCCR; Bill, Robert Matson & Nicholas Talbott, Executors v. Thomas Matson (May 29, 1826), Case No. 13625), BCCCR.

31. Answer and Cross Bill, *Robert Matson & Nicholas Talbott, Executors v. Thomas Matson* (November 29, 1836), Case No. 13625, BCCCR.

32. Complaint, *Robert Matson V. Thomas Matson* (March 17, 1827), Case No. 15625.2, BCCCR.

33. "Thomas Matson," ID 1663, Talley Family, Family Trees, found at www.rootsweb .com (May 1, 2003).

34. Quoted in "LaFayette in Kentucky," *Register of the Kentucky State Historical Society* 34 (1936), p. 153.

35. Lewis Collins, *History of Kentucky*, 2 vols. (Covington: Collins & Co., 1878, 1882), II, p. 772.

36. "Re: James MATSON, b. Ca. 1740's, d. 1826," posted on Matson Family Genealogy Forum, GENFORUM, found at www.genealogy.com (October 15, 2002). The number of slaves that Robert Matson inherited may have been one of the reasons that his brother, Thomas, accused him of undue influence over their father. Thomas inherited only one. Ibid.

37. Bill, *Robert Matson v. Jesse* Todd (April 18, 1827), Case No. 13625.3, BCCCR.

38. Ibid.

39. Ficklin, "A Pioneer Lawyer"; Charles H. Coleman, *Abraham Lincoln and Coles County* (New Brunswick: Scarecrow Press, 1955), p. 104 n.5; "A Story of Long Ago," *Matton Sunday Sun* (August 24, 1884), ALPL.

40. *The History of Coles County, Illinois* (Chicago: William Le Baron, Jr. & Co.. 1879), p. 216; Charles Edward Wilson, *Encyclopedia of Illinois and History of Coles County* (Chicago: Munsell Publishing Company, 1906), pp. 663, 683.

41. Ficklin, "A Pioneer Lawyer."

42. Wilson, *Encyclopedia of Illinois and History of Coles County*, p. 663.

43. Pease, "Illinois Election Returns," p. 176.

44. "In the Matter of Jane," *Western Law Journal* 5 (1848), pp. 203, 204 ; Weik, "Lincoln and the Matson Negroes," p. 753.

45. Ficklin, "A Pioneer Lawyer."

46. Accounts differ as to when Matson brought Jane Bryant and her children into Illinois. Some secondary sources state that it was in 1847, but the primary sources and most contemporaneous secondary materials give the year as 1845. See, e.g., "In the Matter of Jane," *Western Law Journal* 5 (1848), pp. 202, 203 ("In 1845 he brought Jane and her children to this State"); Hiram Rutherford to John Bowman (October 25, 1847), Lincoln Collection, ALPL ("About 2 years ago Matson brought with him from Kentucky a free man and his wife & five children who were his slaves").

47. Writ of capias ad respondendum, *Matson v. Bryant* (August 17, 1847), Coles County Circuit Court, copy in Herndon-Weik Collection: Group III, Document Nos. 1970–71, LOC, Manuscript Division; LPAL, File ID L00714, Doc. No. 5510. McIntyre maintains that Matson was "pressed for debt" in Kentucky and brought the Bryants to Illinois "in order to save them from being taken and sold for his debts." D. T. McIntyre, "History of the Matson Slave Trial in 1847."

A "writ of capias ad respondendum" is a document commonly used to commence actions by which the sheriff is commanded to seize and safely keep the defendant so that he may appear before the court on a given day and answer the plaintiff's allegations. *Blacks Law Dictionary* (1891; 4th ed., St. Paul: West Publishing Co., 1951), p. 262.

48. D. T. McIntyre ,"Matson Slave Trial."

49. Quoted in Weik, "Lincoln and the Matson Negroes," p. 153.

50. Mattoon (Illinois) *Sunday Sun* (August 24, 1884), Albert J. Beveridge Papers, File No. 728, Library of Congress, Manuscript Division. This article probably was written by McIntyre. It uses much of the phraseology of his other writings on the subject.

51. Weik, "Lincoln and the Matson Negroes," p. 753. Orlando Ficklin was a bit more circumspect, describing Mary Corbin as "[i]n temper . . . not the most gentle and amiable of her sex." Ficklin, "Pioneer Lawyer."

52. Duff, A. Lincoln: Prairie Lawyer, p. 131.

53. 1850 Census, Fulton County, Kentucky, Reel No. M432–200, p. 134B. US GenWeb Archives, found at www.rootsweb.com/genweb/ky/fulton/1850census.html (April 29, 2003).

54. Ficklin, "Pioneer Lawyer."

55. Ibid.

56. Ibid.

57. Ibid.

58. At the time, Independence consisted of "1 tavern, 1 grocery, 3 stores, 1 Blacksmith, 1 waggonmaker [sic], 2 carpenters, 1 lawyer, and two doctors." Hiram Rutherford to John Bowman (November 30, 1846), in Hendrick, On the Illinois Frontier, p. 57.

59. Harris, Negro Servitude in Illinois, pp. 118–19.

60. Essay by Hiram Rutherford (undated) in Hendrick, On the Illinois Frontier, pp. 80–81; Weik, "Lincoln and the Matson Negroes," p. 754; Wilson, Encyclopedia of Illinois and History of Coles County, p. 680; "Re: Gideon M. Ashmore Tenn, II, Wi" posted on Ashmore Family Genealogy Forum, found at Genforum, Genealogy.com (August 14, 2001). Gideon M. Ashmore was the son of Samuel C. Ashmore, who moved to Coles County in 1829. Gideon had at least sixteen siblings, one of whom was an older brother named Samuel Claburn Ashmore who may have played a role in this matter. See p. 28 infra. "Samuel Ashmore," found at home.earthlink.netlloash/ashmore_samuel_c.html (October 8, 2005). According to Rutherford, it was Ashmore's belief in "high-sounding" names that led him to name his new town Independence, but, again according to Rutherford, the name "was too long, too many syllables, and malice and spite soon found it a nickname in 'Pinhook,' which name stuck like a burr, and for a long time it was generally known by that alias." Article by Rutherford (undated) in Hendrick, On the Illinois Frontier, pp. 81–82. The name was changed to Oakland in 1851 by an act of the Illinois legislature. Ibid, p. 82.

61. Ficklin, "A Pioneer Lawyer."

62. History of Coles County, pp. 576–77.

63. Coleman, Lincoln in Coles County, p. 104 n.3.

64. Hendrick, On the Illinois Frontier, p. 131.

65. "Notes–Oakland Apr. 4th 1892," Weik MSS, ALPL.

66. Rutherford quoted in Weik, "Lincoln and the Matson Negroes," p. 754.

67. Ibid.

68. Duncan T. McIntyre, "Lincoln and the Matson Slave Case," Illinois Law Review 1 (1907), p. 388 ("infamous"); Ficklin, "A Pioneer Lawyer" ("poor white trash"); Weik, "Lincoln and the Matson Negroes," p. 756 ("ignorant and worthless fellow").

69. Hendrick, On the Illinois Frontier, p. 136.

70. Writ of capias ad respondendum, Matson v. Bryant (August 17, 1847), Coles County Circuit Court, copy in Herndon-Weik Collection: Group III: Document Nos. 1970–71, LOC, Manuscript Division; LPAL, File ID L00714, Doc. No. 5510.

71. Writ of capias ad respondendum, Matson v. Bryant (August 17, 1847), Coles County Circuit Court, copy in Herndon-Weik Collection: Group III: Document Nos. 1970–71, LOC, Manuscript Division; LPAL, File ID L00714, Doc. No. 5510.

72. Weik, "Lincoln and the Matson Negroes," p. 754.

73. Quoted in Weik, "Lincoln and the Matson Negroes," p. 754.

74. Hiram Rutherford to John Bowman (October 25, 1847), Lincoln Collection, ALPL.

75. D. T. McIntyre, "History of the Matson Slave Trial in 1847," p. 3.

76. Hendrick, *On the Illinois Frontier*, p. 134. Eastin's name sometimes appears as "Easton." In 1844, he was elected a vice president of the Charleston Clay Club, a local Whig organization. Sheriff Lewis R. Hutchason also was a member of the club. "Politics in Coles County," found at iltrails.org/coles/politics.htlm (September 27, 2005). Eastin and Hutchason also were officers of the Charleston Masonic Lodge in the early 1850s as was Usher Linder. "One Hundred Years of Freemasonry in Charleston, Illinois, 1845–1995," found at Iltrails.org/coles/masons150.html (October 8, 2005).

77. D. T. McIntyre, "History of the Matson Slave Trial in 1847," p. 3. Dean's testimony may have been entered into evidence by deposition or affidavit. McIntyre states that Dean "had sworn" to certain facts. Ibid.

78. England abolished the rule in 1843. In 1846, Michigan became the first American jurisdiction to do so and the other states followed. Lawrence M. Friedman, *A History of American Law* (New York: Simon & Schuster, 1973), pp. 136, 350. Although the rule has been long gone from Illinois juriprudence, as late as the 1860s it apparently was alive and well. See, e.g., *Marks v. Butler*, 24 Ill. 568–69, 1860 Ill. LEXIS 139, pp. 1–2 (1860) (individual who is a beneficial party to a case "is incompetent as a witness at trial"); *Babcock v. Smith,* 31 Ill. 57, 61–62, 1863 Ill. LEXIS 162, pp. 7–9 (1863)(individual whose interest was in favor of the party calling him as a witness was incompetent to testify).

79. "Competency of witness," Approved March 3, 1845, Illinois Revised Statutes, in Middleton, *Black Laws of the Old Northwest*, p. 316; "Who may be witnesses in Criminal cases," Approved March 3, 1845, Illinois Revised Statutes, in ibid., p. 315.

80. Duncan T. McIntyre, "Lincoln and the Matson Case," p. 388.

81. Quoted in McIntyre, "History of the Matson Slave Trial in 1847," p. 3.

82. Ibid.

83. McIntyre, "Lincoln and the Matson Slave Case," p. 383.

84. Ibid.

85. Weik, "Lincoln and the Matson Negroes," p. 754.

86. Hiram Rutherford quoted in ibid.

87. Ibid.

88. Ibid.

89. Writ of capias ad satisfaciendum, *Matson v. Bryant* (August 20, 1847), Coles County Circuit Court, copy in Herndon-Weik Collection: Group III, Document Nos. 1974–75, LOC, Manuscript Division; LPAL, File ID L00714, Doc. No. 5512; "Notes–Oakland Apr. 4th 1892," Weik MSS, ALPL.

90. Ibid.

91. Transcript, *People v. Matson* (August 24, 1847), Coles County Circuit Court, copy in Herndon-Weik Collection: Group III, Document No. 1952, LOC Manuscript Divsion; LPAL, File ID L00714, Doc. No. 5512.

92. Ibid. Samuel Ashmore, together with Gideon Ashmore and Rutherford, later put up bond for the Bryants. Bond (October 17, 1847), Coles County Circuit Court, copy in Herndon-Weik Collection: Group III. Document Nos. 1959–60, LOC, Manuscript Division; LPAL, File ID L00714, Doc. No. 5505.

93. Complaint, *Matson v. Rutherford* (September 1, 1847), Coles County Circuit Court, copy in Herndon-Weik Collection: Group III, Document Nos. 1950–51, LOC; LPAL, File ID L00715, Doc. No. 36865. See also Orders, *Matson v. Rutherford, Matson v. Ashmore* (May 1848), Coles County Circuit Court, LPAL, File ID L00715, Doc. No. 36865; Hiram Rutherford to John Bowman (October 25, 1847), Lincoln Collection, ALPL.

94. Petition, In re Bryant (October 16, 1847), copy in Herndon-Weik Collection: Group III, Document Nos. 1954–56, LOC, Manuscript Division; LPAL, File ID L00714, Doc. No. 5506.

95. Ibid.

96. Ibid.

97. Petition, In re Bryant (October 16, 1847), Coles County Circuit Court, copy in Herndon-Weik Collection: Group III, Document Nos. 1961–63, LOC Manuscript Division; LPAL, File No. L00714, Doc. No. 5504.

98. Ibid.

99. Ibid.

100. Hiram Rutherford to John Bowman (October 25, 1847), Lincoln Collection, ALPL.

101. See, e.g., Beveridge, *Abraham Lincoln*, I, pp. 394–95.

102. Caton, *Early Bench and Bar of Illinois*, pp. 50–51; Coleman, *Lincoln and Coles County*, p. 113; Donald, *Lincoln*, p. 105; Frank, *Lincoln as a Lawyer*, pp. 22–23.

103. McIntyre, "Lincoln and the Matson Slave Case," p. 387.

104. Bond, *Matson v. Rutherford* (September 27, 1847), Coles County Circuit Court, copy in Herndon-Weik Collection: Group III, Document N. 1972, LOC, Manuscript Division; LPAL, File ID L00715,Doc. No. 5511.

105. Earl Shenk Miers, *Lincoln Day by Day: A Chronology*, 3 vols. (Dayton: Morningside, 1991) I, p. 293; Duff, *A. Lincoln: Prairie Lawyer*, p. 134.

106. "Notes–Oakland Apr. 4th 1892," Weik MSS, ALPL.

107. Quoted in Weik, "Lincoln and the Matson Negroes," p. 755.

108. Summons, *Alexander v. Affleck & Rutherford* (May 5, 1843), Coles County Circuit Court, LPAL, File ID L00702, Doc. No. 36645; Injunction Bond, *Alexander v. Affleck & Rutherford* (May 9, 1843), Coles County Circuit Court, LPAL, File ID L0072, Doc. No. 36646; Separate Answer (October 25, 1843), *Alexander v. Affleck & Rutherford*, Coles County Circuit Court, LPAL, File ID L00702, Doc. No. 1945.

109. Decree, *Alexander v. Affleck & Rutherford* (October 15, 1846), Coles County Circuit Court, LPAL, File ID L00702, Doc. No. 36652.

110. The plaintiff's complaint is missing from the court file as is whatever answer Rutherford may have filed. Therefore, the allegations against Rutherford must be gleaned from Affleck's answer. Apparently, Rutherford had purchased land from McClelland and paid for it with notes which ended up in Affleck's possession. Rutherford may have been joined as a party defendant because of his interest in the realty involved. Separate Answer (October 25, 1843), *Alexander v. Affleck & Rutherford*, Coles County Circuit Court, LPAL, File ID L00702, Doc. No. 1945.

111. Quoted in Weik, "Lincoln and the Matson Negroes," p. 755.

112. Ibid.

113. Ibid.

114. Ibid.

115. Ibid.

116. Ibid.
117. Ibid.
118. Ibid.

Chapter Three

1. Herndon and Weik, *Herndon's Life of Lincoln*, p. 471; Gibson William Harris, "My Recollections of Abraham Lincoln," *The Farm and Fireside* (December 15, 1904), p. 24. Much of Lincoln's height was in his legs. His junior law partner and biographer, William H. Herndon, was struck by this fact: "In sitting down on a common chair, he was no taller than ordinary men. His legs and arms were abnormally, unnaturally long, and in undue proportion to the remainder of his body. It was only when he stood up that he loomed above other men." Herndon and Weik, *Herndon's Life of Lincoln*, p. 472.

2. Herndon and Weik, *Herndon's Life of Lincoln*, p. 471. Lincoln's apparent scrawniness was deceptive. He was "wiry, sinewy," and "very powerful." Ibid. Usher Linder recalled Lincoln "as a man of great physical powers," and Herndon maintained that Lincoln could lift "with ease four hundred, and in one case six hundred pounds." Usher Linder, *Reminiscences of the Early Bench and Bar of Illinois* (Chicago: The Chicago Legal News Company, 1879), p. 59; Herndon and Weik, *Herndon's Life of Lincoln*, p. 471.

3. Donn Piatt, a journalist who first met Lincoln when he was president-elect, described him as "the homeliest man I ever saw." Donn Piatt in Allen Thorndike Rice, ed., *Reminiscences of Abraham Lincoln by Distinguished Men of His Time* (New York: North American Review, 1888), p. 16.

4. Herndon and Weik, *Herndon's Life of Lincoln*, pp. 280, 472. Gibson William Harris, Lincoln's law clerk in the mid-1840s, writes of Lincoln's "indifference regarding dress." Harris, "My Recollections of Abraham Lincoln," *The Farm and Fireside* (December 15, 1904), p. 25. Donald, *Lincoln*, pp. 258–59, has an interesting and amusing analysis of why Lincoln decided to grow a beard.

5. Thomas, *Abraham Lincoln*, p. 117; Donald, *Lincoln*, p. 115. Those in attendance included Horace Greeley (1811–1872), the antislavery editor of the *New York Tribune*; Thurlow Weed (1797–1882), Whig lawyer and newspaper editor; Daniel Webster (1782–1852), U.S. senator from Massachusetts; and Thomas Hart Benton (1782–1858), U.S. senator from Missouri. Thomas, *Abraham Lincoln*, pp. 117–18.

6. Elihu B. Washburne in Rice, ed., *Reminiscences of Abraham Lincoln*, p. 16. Washburne was one of Lincoln's greatest admirers.

7. Lincoln often told a story about meeting a stranger who pulled a gun on him with the explanation that he had sworn to shoot any man he found uglier than himself. Lincoln took a good look at his adversary's face and replied, "If I am uglier than you are, I don't want to live. Go ahead and shoot." Quoted in Saul Sigelschiffer, *The American Conscience: The Drama of the Lincoln-Douglas Debates* (New York: Horizon Press, 1973), p. 144.

8. Letter from Usher Linder to Joseph Gillespie (August 8, 1867), Joseph Gillespie Papers, CHS.

9. Donald, *Lincoln*, p. 39; Duff, *A. Lincoln: Prairie Lawyer*, p. 101. Usher Linder claimed that, in this respect, Lincoln took after his uncle, Mordecai Lincoln, whom Linder had known since boyhood. According to Linder, "Uncle Mord . . . was quite a

story-teller, and they were generally on the smutty side and in this Abe resembled his Uncle. . . . No one ever took offense at Uncle Mord's stories—not even the ladies." Linder, *Reminiscences*, p. 38.

10. Pratt, "Illinois As Lincoln Knew It," p. 30.

11. Quoted in Herndon and Weik, *Herndon's Life of Lincoln*, p. 256.

12. Interview with Judge Anthony Thornton at Shelbyville, Illinois (June 18, 1895). Weik MSS, ALPL. See also Bateman, Selby, and Curry, *Historical Encyclopedia of Illinois*, p. 522. According to Herndon, Lincoln said that "[i]f it were not for these stories, jokes, jests, I should die; they give vent—are the vents—of my moods and gloom." Don E. Fehrenbacher and Virginia Fehrenbacher, eds., *Recollected Words of Abraham Lincoln* (Stanford: Stanford University Press, 1996), p. 252. When James M. Ashley, an Ohio congressman, became visibly impatient with one of his anecdotes, President Lincoln told him that "if I couldn't tell these stories, I would die." Ibid., p. 19.

13. Gibson Wilson Harris, "My Recollections of Abraham Lincoln," *The Farm and Fireside* (January 1, 1905), p. 25.

14. Duff, *A. Lincoln: Prairie Lawyer*, p. 103; Donald, *Lincoln*, p. 102.

15. Samuel C. Parks to William H. Herndon (March 25, 1866), in Douglas L. Wilson and Rodney O. Davis, *Herndon's Informants: Letters, Interviews, and Statements About Abraham Lincoln* (Urbana: University of Illinois Press, 1998), p. 239.

16. "Stephen T. Logan Talks About Lincoln," *Lincoln Centennial Association Bulletin*, No. 12 (September 1, 1928), pp. 2–3. This is a reproduction of a document dated July 6, 1875, apparently in the handwriting of William H. Herndon.

17. Herndon and Weik, *Herndon's Life of Lincoln*, p. 473.

18. Henry C. Whitney to William H. Herndon (June 23, 1887) (Nancy Hanks's "constant trepidation and frequent affrights . . . while she was pregnant . . . made a maternal *ante* natal impression" on Lincoln), in Wilson and Davis, *Herndon's Informants*, p. 617; Sigelschiffer, *The American Conscience*, pp. 145–46; "Blue No More," University of Minnesota–Twin Cities, Researchers and Scholars at http://www1.umn.edu/twincities/research/february2002.html (April 27, 2003). According to Herndon, Lincoln took the "blue-mass pills" at Stuart's suggestion. Herndon and Weik, *Herndon's Life of Lincoln*, p. 473. See Doris Kearns Goodwin, *Team of Rivals: The Political Genius Of Abraham Lincoln* (New York: Simon & Schuster, 2005), pp. 102–4, and Joshua Wolfe Shenk, *Lincoln's Melancholy: How Depression Challenged a President and Fueled His Greatness* (Boston: Houghton Mifflin Company, 2005).

19. William H. Herndon, quoted in John P. Frank, *Lincoln as a Lawyer* (Urbana: University of Illinois, 1961), pp. 14–15. Herndon maintained that Lincoln "never had a confidant, and therefore never unbosomed himself to others." Herndon and Weik, *Herndon's Life of Lincoln*, p. 348.

20. See David Herbert Donald, *"We Are Lincoln Men": Abraham Lincoln and His Friends* (New York: Simon & Schuster, 2003), for a useful study of this aspect of Lincoln's personality.

21. Frank, *Lincoln as a Lawyer*, p. 14. To Lincoln, Herndon always was "Billy." Ibid.

22. Donald, *Lincoln*, p. 95.

23. Mary Lincoln to Josiah G. Holland (December 4, 1865), in Justin G. Turner and Linda Levitt Turner, *Mary Todd Lincoln: Her Life and Letters* (New York: Alfred A. Knopf, 1972), p. 293. Mrs. Lincoln went on to write that '[e]ven between ourselves, when our deep & touching sorrows, were *one* & the same, his expressions were few." Ibid.

24. Hazel Felleman, *The Best Loved Poems of the American People* (New York: Doubleday, 1936), pp. 632–33; Herndon and Weik, *Herndon's Life of Lincoln*, pp. 114, 257–58. John T. Stuart, one of Lincoln's early law partners, maintained that Lincoln "loved the Raven" and "read Poe because it was gloomy." John T. Stuart interview with William Herndon (December 20, 1866), in Wilson and Davis, *Herndon's Informants*, p. 519. Lincoln's efforts at poetry often reeked of melancholy, such as the closing line of the first canto of his "My Childhood-Home I See Again":

> *I range the fields with pensive tread,*
> *And pace the hollow rooms,*
> *And feel (companion of the dead)*
> *I'm living in the tombs.*

Roy P. Basler, ed. *The Collected Works of Abraham Lincoln*, 8 vols. (New Brunswick, Rutgers University Press, 1953), I, pp. 378–79.

25. Harris, "My Recollections of Abraham Lincoln," *The Farm and Fireside* (January 1, 1905), p. 25.

26. Charles B. Strozier, *Lincoln's Quest for Union: A Psychological Portrait* (1982; 2d rev. ed., Philadelphia: Paul Dry Books, Inc., 2001), p. 139; Donald, *Lincoln*, p. 94.

27. See Donald, *Lincoln*, chaps. 1–4. In 1837, Lincoln engineered the breakup of his somewhat informal engagement with Mary Owens, a girl Herndon describes as "polished in manners, pleasing in her address, and attractive in many ways." Herndon and Weik, *Herndon's Life of Lincoln*, p. 117. He also broke off his first engagement to Mary Todd. Donald, *Lincoln*, pp. 86–87.

28. Donald, *Lincoln*, p. 84.

29. Harris, "My Recollections of Abraham Lincoln," *The Farm and Fireside* (December 12, 1904), p. 23.

30. Sale Contract by Charles Dresser and Abraham Lincoln, *Lincoln Collected Works*, I, p. 331.

31. Donald, *Lincoln*, p. 96.

32. Duff, *A. Lincoln: Prairie Lawyer*, p. 28.

33. Donald, *Lincoln*, p. 53.

34. Linder, *Reminiscences*, pp. 37, 39–40.

35. See Speech in the Illinois Legislature Concerning the State Bank (January 11, 1837), *Lincoln Collected Works*, I, pp. 61–69.

36. The expression "power to hurt" was used by Lincoln in a speech to the United States House of Representatives in defense of Zachary Taylor, the Whig candidate for president in 1844, in which Lincoln warned Democrats against taking the low road in political debate. *Lincoln Collected Works*, I, p. 509. See Robert Bray, "The Power to Hurt: Lincoln's Early Use of Satire and Invective," *Journal of the Abraham Lincoln Association* 16 (Winter 1995), pp. 1–36, for a useful analysis of Lincoln's ability in this regard.

37. Quoted in William E. Baringer, *Lincoln's Vandalia* (New Brunswick: Rutgers University Press, 1949), p. 96.

38. Speech in the Illinois Legislature Concerning the State Bank (January 11, 1837), *Lincoln's Collected Works*, I, p. 62.

39. *Journal of the House of Representatives of the Tenth General Assembly of the State of Illinois* (Vandalia: William Waters), p. 589, Illinois Historical Digitalization Projects, found at lincoln.lib.niu.edu (September 24, 2005).

40. Linder, *Reminiscences,* p. 62. Sangamon County's two state senators and seven representatives in the Illinois legislature were known as the "Long Nine" because they averaged about six feet in height in an era when a six-footer was a rather rare commodity. Donald, *Lincoln,* p. 60.

41. Linder, *Reminiscences*, p. 62.

42. Ibid.

43. Ibid., p. 63.

44. Ibid., pp. 62–63.

45. Duff, *A. Lincoln: Prairie Lawyer*, p. 28.

46. Donald, *Lincoln*, pp. 60–62, 75–78, 86.

47. Strickland, "Illinois Background of Lincoln's Attitude Toward Slavery," p. 480.

48. Donald, *Lincoln*, p. 16.

49. Quoted in Strickland, "Illinois Background of Lincoln's Attitude Toward Slavery," p. 481.

50. Donald, *Lincoln*, p. 63.

51. Carl Sandberg, *Abraham Lincoln* (1925; New York: Harcourt, Brace and Company, 1954), p. 53; Strickland, "Illinois Background of Lincoln's Attitude Toward Slavery," p. 481.

52. Protest in the Illinois Legislature on Slavery (March 3, 1837), *Lincoln Collected Works*, I, pp. 74–75.

53. Ibid., p. 75.

54. Remarks in the Illinois Legislature Concerning Resolutions in Relation to Fugitive Slaves (January 5, 1839), Ibid., I, p. 126.

55. Harris, "My Recollections of Abraham Lincoln," *The Farm and Fireside* (January 1, 1905), p. 25; Donald W. Riddle, *Congressman Abraham Lincoln* (Urbana: University of Illinois Press, 1957), pp. 5–6; Donald, *Lincoln*, pp. 111–15. Although congressional elections usually were held in even-numbered years, the reapportionment after the 1840 census was delayed so long that the 1842 election had to be held in 1843. When Lincoln's turn came, Hardin did not abide by the agreement and announced his intention to run for Congress. Lincoln shamed him into withdrawing. In the election, Lincoln defeated Democrat Peter Cartwright, a circuit-riding preacher, and Elihu Walcott, the Liberty Party candidate. Riddle, *Congressman Abraham Lincoln*, p. 6; Donald, *Lincoln*, pp. 113–115.

56. Herndon and Weik, *Herndon's Life of Lincoln*, p. 304.

57. Quoted in Emanual Hertz, *The Hidden Lincoln* (New York: The Viking Press, 1938), pp. 415, 417.

58. Donald, *Lincoln*, p. 110.

59. Herndon and Weik, *Herndon's Life of Lincoln*, p. 304.

60. Donald, *Lincoln*, p. 103.

61. LPAL, File ID No5553.

62. Mark E. Steiner, *An Honest Calling: The Law Practice of Abraham Lincoln* (DeKalb: Northern Illinois Press, 2006), p. 37; Brian Dirck, *Lincoln the Lawyer* (Urbana: University of Illinois, 2007), pp. 14–22; Frank, *Lincoln as a Lawyer*, pp. 10–11; Duff, *A. Lincoln: Prairie Lawyer*, pp. 31–32.

63. Frank, *Lincoln as a Lawyer*, p. 10; Dirck, *Lincoln the Lawyer*, pp. 40–43.

64. Donald, *Lincoln*, p. 64; Duff, *A. Lincoln: Prairie Lawyer*, p. 31; Frank, *Lincoln as a Lawyer*, p. 12; Dirck, *Lincoln the Lawyer*, p. 27.

65. "Stephen T. Logan Talks About Lincoln," p. 5; Frank, *Lincoln as a Lawyer*, pp. 12–13; Donald, *Lincoln*, p. 100.

66. Donald, *Lincoln*, pp. 100–101. Apparently, Lincoln's stature still had a way to go in 1843, when Julius A. Willard and his son, Samuel, were looking for a lawyer to defend them on charges of harboring a fugitive slave. See p. 72 infra. They consulted Luther N. Ransom, a noted abolitionist, for advice. He mentioned Lincoln and then "dimist [*sic*] him with the remark that he had not any reputation, and wanted a man of note." Mark E. Steiner, "Abolitionists and Escaped Slaves in Jacksonville: Samuel Willard's 'My First Adventure with a Fugitive Slave: The Story of It and How It Failed,'" *Illinois Historical Journal* 84 (Winter 1996), p. 227.

67. See, e.g., Frank, *Lincoln as a Lawyer*, p. 14; Duff, *A. Lincoln: Prairie Lawyer*, pp. 97, 101–2.

68. Duff, *A. Lincoln: Prairie Lawyer*, p. 97. See also Dirck, *Lincoln the Lawyer*, p. 30 (Herndon "had a loose-cannon quality").

69. Donald, *Lincoln*, pp. 96, 101. See also Dirck, *Lincoln the Lawyer*, pp. 30–31.

70. Duff, *A. Lincoln: Prairie Lawyer*, p. 111. See also Dirck, Lincoln the Lawyer, pp. 37–38 (office was an "epic mess"); John A. Lupton, "A. Lincoln, Esquire: The Evolution of a Lawyer," in Allen D. Spiegel, *A. Lincoln, Esquire: A Shrewd, Sophisticated Lawyer in His Time* (Macon: Mercer University Press, 2002), p. 30.

71. Harris, "My Recollections of Abraham Lincoln," *The Farm and Fireside* (January 1, 2005), p. 24.

72. Frank, *Lincoln as a Lawyer*, pp. 38–39. According to the monetary conversion table found in LPAL, a dollar in the 1840s was equal, on average, to about 5 percent of a 1999 dollar. In the 1840s, a male mill hand or laborer made from seventy-five cents to a dollar for a twelve-to-thirteen-hour work day. Back then a dollar would buy about ten pounds of meat, several gallons of whiskey, or almost an acre of public land. Don E. Fehrenbacher, *The Era of Expansion* (New York: John Wiley & Sons, 1969), p. 73.

73. Harry E. Pratt, *The Personal Finances of Abraham Lincoln* (Springfield: The Abraham Lincoln Association, 1943), p. 36; Duff, *A. Lincoln: Prairie Lawyer*, pp. 113–14; Donald, *Lincoln*, p. 104; Frank, *Lincoln as a Lawyer*, p. 39; Lupton, "A. Lincoln, Esquire," p. 34 ("standard $10 to $20 fee").

74. William H. Herndon to Jesse W. Weik (January 27, 1888), LPAL, File ID Nonlit 05456, Doc. No. 131175; Duff, *A. Lincoln: Prairie Lawyer*, pp. 97, 114; Donald, *Lincoln*, p. 104; Lupton, "A. Lincoln, Esquire," p. 57.

75. Years later, in a letter to Lincoln biographer Jesse W. Weik, Herndon described Lincoln's somewhat unique protocol:

> If I were not on the circuit—was at the office attending to our affairs at home, Lincoln would collect monies due us & our fees on the circuit & divide, putting his half in his pocket-book & using it as he wanted to: he would wrap my half up in a roll, putting my name on a slip of paper and then wrapping it, the slip, around the roll of money and then putting it in his pocket book and when he came home he would come to the office and hand me the money.

William H. Herndon to Jesse W. Weik (January 27, 1888), LPAL, File ID Nonlit 05456, Doc. No. 131175. Herndon was intrigued by Lincoln's system and asked him why he was "so particular in this matter." Lincoln explained:

Well Billy, I do it for various reasons—1st unless I did as I do I might forget that I collected money or had money belonging to you; 2dy I explain to you how & from whom I got it so that you know not to dun this man who paid [.] Thirdly if I were to die you would have no evidence that I had your money & you could not prove that I had it. By marking the money it becomes yours & I have not in law or morality a right to use it. I make it a practice never to use any mans money without his consent first obtained.

Ibid.

76. William H. Herndon to Jesse W. Weik (January 27, 1888), LPAL, File ID Nonlit 05456, Doc No. 131175; Harris, "My Recollections of Abraham Lincoln," *The Farm and Fireside* (December 1, 1904), p. 23; Frank, *Lincoln as a Lawyer*, p. 15. Herndon maintained that Lincoln was hopeless when it came to record keeping:

He was proverbially careless as to habits. In a letter to a fellow lawyer in another town, apologizing for failure to answer sooner, he explains: "First, I have been very busy in the United States Court; second, when I received the letter I put it in my old hat and buying a new one the next day the old one was set aside, and so the letter was lost sight of for a time." The hat of Lincoln's—a silk plug—was an extraordinary receptacle. It was his desk and memorandum book. In it he carried his bank book and the bulk of his letters. Whenever in his reading or researches he wished to preserve an idea, he jotted it down on an envelope or stray piece of paper and placed it inside the lining. Afterwards when the memorandum was needed there was only one place to look for it.

Herndon and Weik, *Herndon's Life of Lincoln*, pp. 253–54.

77. "Stephen T. Logan Talks About Lincoln," p. 3.

78. William H. Herndon quoted in Hertz, *The Hidden Lincoln*, p. 427.

79. Quoted in Donald, *Lincoln*, p. 99. Lincoln's former law partner, Stephen T. Logan, agreed with this assessment: "When he was with me, I have seen him get a case and seem to be bewildered at first, but he would go at it and after a while he would master it. He was very tenacious in his grasp of a thing that once he got hold of." "Stephen T. Logan Talks About Lincoln," p. 5.

80. Frank, *Lincoln as a Lawyer*, p. 23.

81. Lawrence Weldon quoted in Rice, *Reminiscences of Abraham Lincoln*, p. 129. Weldon rode the circuit with Lincoln in the 1850s. Ibid., p. 124.

82. Dirck, *Lincoln the Lawyer*, p. 142; Steiner, *An Honest Calling*, p. 54.

83. Dirck, *Lincoln the Lawyer*, pp. 142–44.

84. Lupton, "A. Lincoln, Esquire," p. 33.

85. Herndon and Weik, *Herndon's Life of Lincoln*, p. 247.

86. John W. Starr, Jr., *Lincoln and the Railroads* (New York: Dodd, Mead & Company, 1927), pp. 126–31.

87. Dirck, *Lincoln the Lawyer*, pp. 91–92.

88. Ibid.

89. George Rogers Taylor, *The Transportation Revolution, 1815–1860* (1951; New York: Harper & Row, 1968), p. 79.

90. Lupton, "A. Lincoln, Esquire," pp. 23, 26–27, 31.

91. Ibid., p. 22; Steiner, *An Honest Calling*, pp. 76, 83, 87.

92. 4 Ill. 71 (1841).

93. See, e.g., Harris, *Negro Servitude*, p. 105 ("established presumption of freedom"); John P. Hand, "Negro Slavery in Illinois," *Transactions of the Illinois State Historical Society* 15 (1910), p. 45 (same); Duff, *A. Lincoln: Prairie Lawyer*, p. 86 (same); Thomas, *Abraham Lincoln*, p. 118 ("won freedom for a slave girl"); Stephen P. Oates, With Malice Toward None: The Life of Abraham Lincoln (New York: Harper & Row, 1977)(same).

94. 4 Ill. 71.

95. Ibid. at 73; Donald, *Lincoln*, p. 615.

96. 4 Ill. 71, 73.

97. Indictment, *People v. Pond*, Menard County Circuit Court (June 11, 1845), LPAL, File ID L00335, Doc. No. 15040.

98. Order, *People v. Pond*, Menard County Circuit Court (November 3, 1845), LPAL, File ID L00335, Doc. No. 15043.

99. Ibid. Lincoln and Herndon received five hundred dollars for their legal services in the case. Office Fee Book, LPAL, File No. L00335, Doc. No. 126434.

100. The only evidence usually cited in support of Lincoln's involvement in the Scott and Kern cases is a sentence in William E. Baringer's *Lincoln Day by Day* which vaguely cites court records for the reference. William E. Baringer, *Lincoln Day by Day, 1809–1848*, in Earl Schenck Miers, editor-in-chief, *Lincoln Day by Day: A Chronology, 1809–1865*, 3 vols. (Washington: Lincoln Sesquicentennial Commission, 1960), I, p. 287. Because existing court documents relating to the cases make no mention of Lincoln and nothing in his papers refers to the cases, historians have been reluctant to conclude that he played some role in them. See, e.g., Steiner, *An Honest Calling*, p. 127.

While understandable, this approach seems overly cautious. It seems unlikely that Baringer had no basis for his conclusion that Lincoln appeared in the cases. The relevant court documents are incomplete and anything with Lincoln's name on it could well have been purloined by souvenir hunters. Steiner, *An Honest Calling*, p. 127 n.183. Moreover, Lincoln rarely wrote about his cases so the absence of any reference in his papers to the Scott and Kern proceedings is not unusual. In addition, there is affirmative evidence that Lincoln was in the same court during the term in which Scott and Kern were acquitted. He had at least three other cases there. *See Walker v. Livingston & Powell*, Tazewell County Circuit Court, LPAL, File ID L01135; *Phillips v. Merrium*, Tazewell County Circuit Court. LPAL, File ID L01145; *Wells v. Clark*, Tazewell County Circuit Court, LPAL, File ID L01196.

More directly, Kern and Scott family traditions have it that Lincoln defended their ancestors. See, e.g., Emma J. Scott, "Some Interesting History of the Scott Family, Who were Early Settlers," in *Early History of Washington, Illinois and Vicinity* (1929; Washington, Illinois: Washington Historical Society, 2000), p. 86 (in the possession of Linda Kern Moore); e-mail from K. Zinzer to author (July 9, 2007)(her great-grandfather George Kern was "defended by Mr. A. Lincoln"); e-mail from Linda Kern Moore to author (June 22, 2007)(same). In 1929, long before *Lincoln Day by Day* was published, Emma J. Scott wrote a reminiscence about her family. In discussing the antislavery activities of her father, J. Randolph Scott, Ms. Scott noted that "[o]n one occasion, when he and George Kern were arrested and tried, they were honored by having Abraham Lincoln, then a rising lawyer to defend them." "History of the Scott Family," p. 86. Emma Scott was born in 1854, seven years after her father's trial. It seems reasonable to assume that she learned the story from her father. By all accounts, in 1929, although seventy-five years old, Emma Scott had all of her faculties. She often repeated the account. Apparently, no one ever has challenged it. *Tazewell County Reporter and Washington Post and News* (June 4, 1942), WHS.

101. Order, *People v. Kern*, Woodford County Circuit Court (September 11, 1845), LPAL, File ID L01267, Doc. No. 46017; Indictment, *People v. Scott*, Woodford County Circuit Court (September 1845), LPAL, File ID L01266, Doc. No. 46006; Order, *People v. Scott*, Woodford County Circuit Court (September 11, 1845), LPAL, File ID L01266, Doc No. 46007. It seems likely that Lincoln also represented James Kern, who was also indicted in September 1845 in Woodford County for harboring a runaway slave. Indictment, *People v. Kern*, Woodford County Circuit Court (September 1845), LPAL File ID L01267, Doc. No. 121075.

102. *Galesburg Republican Register* (April 18, 1894), quoted in Scott, "History of the Scott Family," p. 92; ibid., p. 85.

103. Dr. J.S. Whitmire to Wilber Siebert (March 5, 1896), Siebert Papers, Ohio Historical Society.

104. Indictment, *People v. Scott*, Woodford County Circuit Court (September 1845), LPAL, File ID L01266, Doc. No. 46006.

105. Judge's Docket, *People v. Kern*, Tazewell County Circuit Court (April 1847), LPAL, File ID L01267, Doc. No. 46028; Newton Bateman and Paul Selby, *Historical Encyclopedia of Illinois and History of Champaign County* (Chicago: Munsell Publishing Company, 1905), p. 422; Scott, "History of the Scott Family," p. 92.

106. Scott, "History of the Scott Family," p. 86; Order, *People v. Kern*, Woodford County Circuit Court (April 16, 1846), LPAL. File ID L01267, Doc. No. 46022; Order, *People v. Scott*, Woodford County Circuit Court (April 16, 1846), LPAL, File ID L01266, Doc. No. 46011; Order, *People v. Scott*, Tazewell County Circuit Court (April 8, 1847), LPAL, File ID L01266, Doc. No. 46017; Order, *People v. Kern*, Tazewell County Circuit Court (April 8, 1847), LPAL, File ID L01267, Doc. No. 46029. The prosecutor's decision to enter a nolle prosequi in the Scott case probably was prompted by Scott's motion to quash the indictment on the ground that he "is named & called Randolph Scott in the indictment" but "that his name is John Randolph Scott and . . . that he hath never been called or known by the name of Randolph Scott." Plea in Abatement, *People v. Scott*, Tazewell County Court (April 8, 1847), LPAL, File ID L01266, Doc. No. 4608. Scott's plea of misnomer, having the wrong name in the indictment, if proven as a question of fact, probably would have led to his acquittal. See *Schram v. People*, Ill. 162, 1852 Ill. LEXIS 5 (1852); *Turner v. People*, 40 Ill.App. 17, 1891 Ill.App, LEXIS 8 (4th Dist. 1891). According to Emma Scott, the jury's verdict in Kern's favor stemmed from the prosecutor's failure to prove that the black in question was, in fact, a slave. Emma J. Scott, "The Underground Railroad" (1934), p. 31.

A jury also found James Kern not guilty. Order, *People v. Kern*, Tazewell County Circuit Court (April 8, 1847), LPAL, File ID L01267, File No. 46029.

Lincoln may have played a part in another fugitive slave case, but it is not clear what role he played. See Ex parte Warman, Menard County Circuit Court (June 1845), LPAL, File ID L05867.

107. John Long, *Law of Illinois*, foreword by William D. Beard (Shiloh, Illinois: The Illinois Company, 1993), I, p. ii. William H. Herndon believed that Lincoln "was greatest . . . as a lawyer in the Supreme Court of Illinois." Herndon and Weik, *Herndon's Life of*

Lincoln, p. 272. See also Steiner, *An Honest Calling*, p. 61 ("Lincoln's most impressive legal work was before the state supreme court").

108. Long, *Law of Illinois*, p. 1.

109. Ibid., p. ii.

110. In 1847, the Eighth Circuit was the largest in Illinois. Located in the center of the state, it consisted of fourteen counties. The circuit included acreage equal to about one-quarter of all of Illinois, and a trip around the circuit was a trip of about four hundred miles. Duff, *A. Lincoln: Prairie Lawyer*, pp. 175–76.

111. Ibid., p. 134; Coleman, *Lincoln and Coles County, p. 80;* Wilson, *Encyclopedia of Illinois and History of Coles County,* p. 680; King, *Davis*, p. 84. Lincoln had personal ties to Coles County. His father, Thomas, and his stepmother, Sara Bush, lived seven miles outside of Charleston, and his stepbrother, John, and two stepsisters, Matilda and Sara Elizabeth, lived nearby. His cousin and boyhood friend, Dennis Hanks, who was married to Sara Elizabeth, lived in Charleston itself. Coleman. *Lincoln and Coles County*, pp. 7, 13 n.9, 246.

112. See, e.g., *Hodges v. Vanderen* (1846–47) (Linder), LPAL, File ID L00707; *Aertson v. Ashmore & Ashmore* (1841) (Ficklin), LPAL, File ID L00697; Miller v. Munson (1842–44)(Linder, Ficklin), LPAL, File ID L00717; *Turner v. Craig* (1841–42) (Linder, Ficklin), LPAL, File ID L00731; *Pearson & Anderson v. Monroe* (1841–42) (Linder), LPAL, File ID L00739; *Nordyke v. Fleenor* (1843) (Linder, Ficklin), LPAL, File ID L00736; *Nabb v. Radley & Sawyer* (1840–41) (Linder, Ficklin), LPAL, File ID L00735; *Moore v. White* (1841–42) (Linder, Ficklin), LPAL, File ID L00719; *Miller v. Turner* (1842–44) (Linder, Ficklin), LPAL, File ID L00718; *McKibbon v. Hart* (1844–45) (Linder, Ficklin); LPAL, File ID L00717; *Eccles v. True* (1844–45) (Linder, Ficklin), LPAL, File ID L00703; *Johnson v. Lester* (1846–47) (Linder, Ficklin), LPAL, File ID L00844; *Burson v. Newman* (1846–47) (Linder, Ficklin), LPAL, File ID L00700; *Ewing v. Goodman* (1841) (Linder), LPAL, File ID L00704. See also Coleman, *Lincoln and Coles County*, p. 112.

Chapter Four

1. See p. 26 supra.

2. Coleman, *Lincoln in Coles County,* p. 113.

3. Ibid. Ficklin served one term as a representative from Wabash County and two terms as a representative from Coles County. Ibid.

4. Ibid.

5. *History of Coles County*, p. 519.

6. Coleman, *Lincoln and Coles County*, p. 113.

7. Linder, *Reminiscences*, p. 112.

8. Ibid., p. 111.

9. Coleman, *Lincoln and Coles County*, p. 113.

10. Hiram Rutherford quoted in Weik, "Lincoln and the Matson Negroes," p. 754.

11. Gustave Koerner, *Memoirs of Gustave Koerner, 1809–1896*, 2 vols. (Cedar Rapids: The Torch Press, 1909), I, p. 481.

12. Usher Linder to John Hardin (February 21, 1844), CHS. As noted earlier in the text, many years later Linder had good things to say about Ficklin. In his memoirs, Linder described Ficklin as "an old friend" and a "prince of good fellows." Linder, *Reminiscences*, pp. 110, 112.

13. See pp. 26–27 supra.

14. Quoted in Hendrick, *Life on the Frontier*, p. 142.

15. Letter from Hon. Jacob W. Wilkin to [?] (September 24, 1895), Albert J. Beveridge Papers, File No. 728, LOC, Manuscript Division; *Constitutional Debates of 1847*, p. 1018 (foldout).

16. Weik, "Lincoln and the Matson Negroes," p. 756; Beveridge, *Abraham Lincoln*, I, p. 395 n.2.

17. Quoted in Weik, "Lincoln and the Matson Negroes," p. 755.

18. Linder, *Reminiscences*, p. 282. Linder was quite taken with Constable's looks. At another point in his *Reminiscences*, he describes his first meeting with Constable and another attorney, Anthony Thornton, which took place in 1839 or 1840: "I was introduced to them both at the same time, and thought then, and I still think, they were two of the finest, most imposing and handsome men that my eyes ever looked upon. They were both over six feet in height, well shaped and symmetrical in form, and it would have troubled the most tasteful young lady to have given preference to either of them." Ibid., p. 109. Constable's fastidiousness left a lasting impression. Writing years after the fact, John M. Palmer remembered Constable as "a good lawyer" who "was remarkable for his personal neatness." Palmer, *Bench and Bar*, I, p. 5. A fellow delegate to the 1847 constitutional convention sarcastically remarked: "I hope Charlie Constable will be put in jail for twenty-four hours and kept without a looking-glass, a hair-brush or a toothbrush." Ibid., p. 3.

19. Linder, *Reminiscences*, p. 282. It was "through the kindness of our then State Senator, Mr. Constable" that Gibson W. Harris went to study law at the offices of Lincoln and Herndon in 1845 as their first law clerk. Gibson William Harris, "My Recollections of Abraham Lincoln," *The Farm and Fireside* (December 1, 1904), p. 23.

20. Linder, *Reminiscences*, p. 21.

21. Ibid., p. 24; E. B. Linder to Jesse Weik (September 3, 1895), Herndon-Weik Papers, Manuscript Division, LOC; George K. Holbert, "Lincoln and Linder in Kentucky," *Lincoln Herald* 44 (June 1942), pp. 3, 11.

22. Linder, *Reminiscences*, pp. 35–37: George K. Holbert, "Lincoln and Linder in Illinois," *Lincoln Herald* 44 (October–December 1942), pp. 2–3; Pease, *Illinois Election Returns*, p. 293.

23. Linder, *Reminiscences*, p. 261.

24. Newton Bateman, Paul Selby, and J. Seymour Curry, *Historical Encyclopedia of Illinois and History of Coles County* (Chicago: Munsell Pub. Co., 1921), p. 489; Ford, *History of Illinois*, I, pp. 61, 63.

25. Linder, *Reminiscences*, p. 260.

26. Clarence W. Alvord, *Governor Edward Coles*, Collections of the Illinois State Historical Library 15 (1930), p. 137. Smith misjudged his opponent when he took on Hooper Warren. Failing to whip Warren into submission, Smith pulled a knife on him. Warren responded with a pistol, but the two were separated before either was seriously injured. Ibid.

27. Linder, *Reminiscences*, p. 260.

28. Baringer, *Lincoln's Vandalia*, p. 32.

29. *Memoirs of Gustave Koerner*, I, 374.

30. Ford, *History of Illinois*, I, pp. 340–41.

31. Ibid., p. 254.

32. Ibid., pp. 254–55.

33. Ibid., pp. 255–56. As soon as it was clear that Smith would survive the impeachment vote, the Illinois House of Representatives passed a resolution by a two-thirds vote to remove him by a request to the governor called an "address," but the measure failed in the senate. Ford, *History of Illinois*, I, p. 256; Alexander Davidson and Bernard Stuve, *A Complete History of Illinois from 1673 to 1873* (Springfield: Illinois Journal Company, 1874), p. 369. Thomas Ford, whose *History* has few good things to say about Smith, was one of his defense lawyers in the impeachment proceedings.

34. Linder, *Reminiscences*, p. 261.

35. Ibid.

36. Ford, *History of Illinois*, I, pp. 268–69, 275; Baringer, *Lincoln's Vandalia*, pp. 98–99.

37. Linder, *Reminiscences*, p. 261.

38. Ibid.

39. Ibid.

40. In his memoirs, Linder claims that when the debate on the bank question was over, "we carried the resolutions by a large majority." Linder, *Reminiscences*, p. 261. Actually, his resolutions, though popular with many antibank Democrats, met with opposition from the Whigs and from more conservative members of his own party. Linder was compelled to submit a modified resolution which called for a more limited investigation. Although the house adopted this resolution, it later was "sidetracked in favor of a similar Senate resolution." Baringer, *Lincoln's Vandalia*, p. 99.

41. Linder, *Reminiscences*, p. 261. Linder was elected attorney general of the state of Illinois on February 11, 1837, on a joint ballot of the two houses of the legislature.

42. Linder, *Reminiscences*, p. 13 (introduction by Joseph Gillespie). See also Palmer, *Bench and Bar of Illinois*, I, p. 658 ("a great stump orator"); Beveridge, *Abraham Lincoln*, I, p. 180 ("a terror on the stump"); Duff, *A. Lincoln: Prairie Lawyer*, p. 132 ("fine orator"); Coleman, *Lincoln and Coles County*, p. 123 ("a notable orator"); Baringer, *Lincoln's Vandalia*, p. 82 ("powerful speaker").

43. Baringer, *Lincoln's Vandalia*, p. 82.

44. Of course, in this respect, Linder's appeal was far from unique. In 1840, William Henry Harrison won the presidency as a Whig, the self-proclaimed "party of hard cider and log cabins." Arthur M. Schlesinger, Jr., *The Age of Jackson* (Boston: Little, Brown and Company, 1945), p. 91.

45. *Missouri Republican* (February 15, 1837), MHS.

46. Ibid.

47. Ibid.

48. In his *Reminiscences* (pp. 221–23), Linder makes light of the incident. He does not mention that he had shot Reiley (whom he describes as "a very desperate man") or that the dispute was resolved when he made "a full and sufficient written apology" to Reiley. *Missouri Republican* (February 15, 1837), MHS.

49. Linder, *Reminiscences*, p. 395. Writing years later, Linder discussed his move to Alton: "As the law then stood, it required the Attorney-General to reside at the seat of government, which I am sorry to say I did not obey, but took my family to Alton." Ibid.

50. *Daily Missouri Republican* (April 28, 1837), MHS; *Illinois State Register and People's Advocate* (June 9, 1837), ALPL.

51. *Illinois State Register and People's Advocate* (June 9, 1837), ALPL.

52. Ibid.

53. Ibid.

54. Ibid.

55. *Daily Missouri Republican* (August 23, 1837), MHS.

56. Ibid.

57. *Sangamon Journal* (September 2, 1837), ALPL.

58. Linder, *Reminiscences*, p. 223.

59. "Being a man of strong Southern proclivities, [Linder] believed that the abolition of slavery would be ruinous to the South . . . ." Linder, *Reminiscences*, p. 19 (introduction by Joseph Gillespie).

60. Revenge also might have played a part in Linder's motivation. It probably is just a coincidence, but Benjamin Godfrey and Winthrop C. Gilman, two of Lovejoy's supporters, were involved in the group which won control of the Illinois State Bank from Theophilus Smith, Linder's mentor. Ford, *History*, I, p. 269.

61. Edward Beecher, *Narrative of the Riots at Alton* (1838; New York: E. P. Dutton & Co., 1965), pp. 16–20; Linder, *Reminiscences*, pp. 103–4; Duff, *A. Lincoln: Prairie Lawyer*, p. 110.

62. Quoted in Beecher, *Narrative of the Alton Riots*, p. 20 ("no right to abolish slavery"); quoted in Dillon, *Elijah P. Lovejoy*, p. 138 ("ought to be discountenanced").

63. Beecher, *Narrative of the Alton Riots*, p. 57 ("vindictive spirit"). According to Beecher, the "leading individuals" included some prominent merchants, professionals, and clergy. Beecher, *Narrative of the Alton Riots*, p. 32. For two different versions of Lovejoy's speech, see ibid. and "Final Public Speech of Elijah Parish Lovejoy," ISHL, found at www.state.il.us/hpa/lovejoy/speech.htm (October 3, 2004).

64. Tanner, *History of the Alton Riots*, pp. 7–8.

65. Ibid., p. 6.

66. Quoted in Paul Simon, *Elijah Lovejoy: Freedom's Champion* (Carbondale: Southern Illinois Press, 1994), p. 122.

67. Linder allegedly made the statement on November 3, 1837. Lovejoy was murdered on November 7, 1837.

68. According to his memoirs, Linder had left Alton "to attend the Green County Circuit Court." Linder, *Reminiscences*, p. 105.

69. Henry Tanner, *The Martyrdom of Lovejoy* (1881; New York: Augustus M. Kelley, 1971), p. 190; William S. Lincoln, *Alton Trials* (New York: John F. Trow, 1838), pp. 13–15. Gilman and the others who defended Lovejoy's press were charged with breaching the peace by "unlawfully, riotously, and routously [tumultuously], and in a violent manner" resisting the efforts of the mob to "force open and enter the storehouse" and "to break and destroy a printing press." Quoted in Tanner, *Martyrdom of Lovejoy*, pp. 188–89. When Gilman was acquitted after only fifteen minutes of jury deliberation, the charges against the other warehouse defenders were dropped. Lincoln, *Alton Trials*, p. 81.

70. None of the accused rioters went to jail.

71. Lincoln, *Alton Trials* (Linder's closing argument), p. 77. Linder went on to argue: "I might portray to you the scenes which would exist in our neighbor states from the influence of [Lovejoy's] press: the father aroused to see the last gasp of his dying child, as it lays in the cradle, weltering in its blood; and the husband awakened from his last sleep by the shrieks of his wife as she is brained to the earth. I might paint to you a picture which would cause a demon to start back with affright, and still fall short of the awful reality which would be caused by the promulgation of the doctrines which the press was intended to disseminate." Ibid.

72. *The Liberator* (October 5, 1838).

73. *Western Citizen* (September 16, 1842), ALPL.

74. Linder, *Reminiscences*, p. 371.

75. *Lacon Herald* (July 28, 1838), ALPL; George Thompson, *Prison Life and Reflections* (1847; Freeport: Books for Libraries Press, 1971), pp. 224–25. See also *The Liberator* (October 5, 1838) (Linder was "one of the foremost in urging on the blood-thirsty mobocrats of Alton"). In his memoirs, Linder argues that he in no way "stole into" the abolitionist convention in Upper Alton in 1837, and that he was not "in complicity with the mob that killed Lovejoy." He maintains that "[i]nstead of participating in the riot that resulted in the death of Lovejoy, I, for weeks and weeks before its occurrence, did all that I could to prevent such a catastrophe and bring about a compromise." Linder, *Reminiscences*, pp. 103–5.

76. Linder, *Reminiscences*, p. 395; Coleman, *Lincoln in Coles County*, p. 114.

77. Daniel W. Linder to Jesse Weik (September 3, 1895), Albert Beveridge Papers, File No. 728, LOC, Manuscript Division.

78. Ibid.

79. George K. Holbert, "Lincoln and Linder in Illinois," *Lincoln Herald* 44 (October–December 1942), p. 3.

80. *Lacon Herald* (July 28, 1838), ALPL.

81. Ibid.

82. Ibid.

83. Linder, *Reminiscences*, pp. 305–6. Linder put it this way: "In 1838, we returned to Coles county, Illinois, and from that time up to 1860 led a career of proud legal success on the Wabash circuit which makes my heart now swell with pride when I think of it." Ibid.

84. *Charleston Courier* (April 15, 1843) (emphasis in original), ALPL.

85. Coles County went Whig in the presidential election of 1836 despite the fact that the county could not agree on any particular Whig candidate. Michael J. Dubin, *United States Presidential Elections, 1788–1860: The Official Results by County and State* (Jefferson, S.C.: McFarland & Company, Inc., 2002), p.63.

86. Pease, *Illinois Election Returns*, p. 316.

87. Ibid.

88. Ibid., p. 374. The number of representatives for each county varied from year to year as population increased and as territory was lopped off to form new counties.

89. George K. Holbert, "Lincoln and Linder in Illinois," p. 4 n. 15. See, e.g., *Charleston Courier* (April 15, 1843), ALPL.

90. Michael J. Dubin, *United States Congressional Elections, 1788–1997: The Official Results of the Elections of the 1st Through 105th Congresses* (Jefferson, N.C.: McFarland & Company, Inc., 1998), p. 133.

91. Linder to John J. Hardin (January 2, 1844), CHS; Linder, *Reminiscences*, pp. 118–19.

92. Linder, *Reminiscences*, p. 42. Ficklin had defeated Harlan with about 53.8 percent of the vote. Dubin, *United States Congressional Elections*, p. 133.

93. Linder to John J. Hardin (February 21, 1844), CHS.

94. Ibid.

95. Ibid. In his letter to Hardin, Linder stated that if he saw "Henry Clay the president, and Illinois resurrected, . . . so help me God I am contented to go into retirement, and quit politicks [*sic*] forever."

96. Ibid.

97. Ibid.

98. Ibid.

99. Daniel W. Linder to Jesse Weik (September 3, 1895), Albert Beveridge Papers, File No. 728, LOC, Manuscript Division.

100. Ibid.

101. Ficklin won over 56.6 percent of the vote in 1844 as compared with about 53.8 percent in 1843. Linder received about 39.3 percent and a second Democrat, Wickliff Kitchell, garnered about 3 percent. Dubin, *United States Congressional Elections, 1788–1997*, pp. 133, 139.

102. Linder received 636 (49.3 percent) votes in Coles County. Ficklin received 568 (44.1 percent) and Kitchell received 85 (6.6 percent). Pease, *Illinois Election Returns*, p. 144. How much of Linder's success in Coles County was due to Whig presidential candidate Henry Clay's coattails is difficult to determine. Clay ran stronger in Coles County than Linder did. He won 776 votes (57.1 percent) in Coles County. Dubin, *United States Presidential Elections*, p. 85.

103. Linder received 50 percent more votes than the second-place finisher, William D. Watson, another Whig who won the second house seat. Linder received almost twice as many votes as the leading Democrat. Pease, *Illinois Election Returns, 1818–1848*, p. 428.

104. Baringer, *Lincoln's Vandalia*, p. 82. See also Beveridge, *Abraham Lincoln*, I, p. 180 (Linder was "more than six feet in stature, slender, raw-boned. . . .").

105. *Peoria Democratic Press* (February 10, 1847), Peoria Public Library.

106. Ibid. A description about four years later painted a remarkably similar picture of Linder: "Then comes Linder, with his short neck, his curly pate, his brilliant eye of genius that looks like a diamond set in a pork ham, his voice like the softest tones of a flute, or the trumpet tones of a bugle. . . ." Brattleboro (Vermont) *Weekly Eagle* (December 8, 1851).

107. Charleston *Republican* (June 5, 1846), found at www.itrails.Org/coles/mexvolunteers.html (December 8, 2005).

108. Palmer, *The Bench and Bar of Illinois*, p. 33.

109. See p. 35 supra.

110. Linder, *Reminiscences*, pp. 248–49.

111. Ibid., pp. 240–41.

112. Ibid., p. 241.

113. Ibid.

114. Ibid.

115. *Peoria Democratic Press* (February 10, 1847), Peoria Public Library.

116. Palmer, *The Bench and Bar of Illinois*, p. 34.

117. Linder, *Reminiscences*, p. 113.

118. Ibid. Typical in this regard is the story told by Linder's cousin about the time, probably a few years after the Matson case, when Lincoln and Linder were riding the judicial circuit together and had arrived at the house of Usher Linder's cousin, Elisha Linder, in western Coles County:

Usher Linder was drunk. They dismounted from their horses and when they reached the house, Lincoln said: "Lish, we are going over to Shelbyville to plead some cases and Ursh has been drinking heavy and is so drunk we can't go any further. Help me sober him up." Grandmother asked Lincoln if they had any dinner.

He replied "No, Becky we haven't eaten anything since breakfast." Grandmother killed a chicken and fried it for dinner while Grandfather gave Usher strong coffee to sober him up. He thought he had succeeded, so they sat down to dinner. Usher reached for the plate of chicken, poured it out on his own plate, and then handed Lincoln the empty plate, saying "Abe, have some chicken." Abe and my grandfather had to pour Ursh more strong coffee. After the meal, they proceeded on their way to Shelbyville.

Coleman, *Lincoln in Coles County*, p. 115.
    119. King, *Davis*, p. 83.
    120. Ibid.
    121. Linder, *Reminiscences*, p. 119.
    122. Quoted in Hendrick, *On the Illinois Frontier*, p. 142.
    123. See p. 51 supra.

Chapter Five

    1. Act of February 12, 1793, Ch. 7, 1 Stat. 302 (1793); 41 U.S. 39 (1842).
    2. Act of February 12, 1793, Ch. 7, 1 Stat. 302 (1793). Section 3 of the act read, in pertinent part:

[T]he person to whom such labor or service may be due . . . is hereby empowered to seize or arrest such fugitive from labor, and to take him or her before any Judge of the Circuit or District Courts of the United States, residing or being within the State, or before any magistrate of a county, city, or town corporate . . . and upon proof to the satisfaction of such Judge or magistrate, either by oral testimony or affidavit taken before and certified by a magistrate of such State or Territory, that the person so seized or arrested doth, under the laws of the State or Territory from which he or she fled, owe service or labor to the person claiming him or her, it shall be the duty of such Judge or magistrate to give a certificate thereof to such claimant . . . which shall be sufficient warrant for removing the said fugitive from labor to the State or Territory from which he or she fled.

    3. Ibid. (". . . it shall be the duty of such Judge or magistrate to give a certificate thereof to such claimant. . . ."). The law was enacted in reaction to the indictment under a Pennsylvania antikidnapping statute of some slave catchers who had seized a black in Pennsylvania and forcibly removed him to Virginia. Robert A. Burt, *The Constitution in Conflict* (Cambridge: Harvard University Press, 1992), p. 176.
    4. Robert M. Cover, *Justice Accused: Antislavery and the Judicial Process* (New Haven: Yale University Press, 1975), p. 87.
    5. Friedman, *A History of American Law*, p. 98.
    6. 20 Howell's State Trials 82, 98 Eng. Rep. 510. See Paul Finkelman, *An Imperfect Union: Slavery, Federalism, and Comity* (Chapel Hill: The University of North Carolina Press, 1981), pp. 38–40; William M. Wiecek, *Sources of Antislavery Constitutionalism in America, 1760–1848* (Ithaca: Cornell University Press, 1977), pp. 20–39; Cover, *Justice Accused*, pp. 16–17, for discussions of the case and its impact on American law.

7. David Brian Davis, *The Problem of Slavery in the Age of Revolution, 1770–1823* (Ithaca: Cornell University Press, 1975), pp. 480–81. Black slaves were a fact of life in England beginning in the reign of Elizabeth I. There may have been as many as fifteen thousand slaves residing in the British Isles in 1770. They were openly advertised for sale through most of the eighteenth century and were bequeathed in wills until the 1820s. Wiecek, *Sources of Antislavery Constitutionalism in America,* p. 25; Cover, *Justice Accused,* p. 472.

8. Davis, *The Problem of Slavery,* p. 473 n.8.

9. Don E. Fehrenbacher, *The Dred Scott Case: Its Significance in American Law and Politics* (New York: Oxford University Press, 1978), p. 53 n.13.

10. Quoted in Wiecek, *Sources of Antislavery Constitutionalism in America,* pp. 31–32. See also Cover, *Justice Accused,* p. 17; Davis, *Problem of Slavery,* p. 473.

11. Cover, *Justice Accused,* p. 17.

12. Ibid., 87.

13. For an interesting discussion of the broader aspects of this dilemma, see Cover, *Justice Accused.*

14. 1845 Ohio Misc. LEXIS 19, pp. 17–19, 10 Ohio Dec. Reprint 279, 285–86 (1845). Samuel Watson, the accused runaway slave, was represented by a team of antislavery lawyers led by Salmon P. Chase, who later became governor of Ohio, secretary of the treasury, and chief justice of the United States Supreme Court. Their arguments were to no avail. Despite his deep "regret . . . that slavery exists," the judge held that the Fugitive Slave Law was valid and, therefore, Samuel Watson was "subject to recapture." Ibid., p. 18, 10 Ohio Dec. Reprint, pp. 2, 292.

15. U.S. Constitution, Art. IV.

16. Thomas D. Morris, *Free Men All: The Personal Liberty Laws of the North, 1780–1861* (Baltimore: The Johns Hopkins University Press, 1974), pp. 221–22.

17. Under the terms of the act, only a local sheriff or constable could seize an alleged runaway slave and then only pursuant to a lawful warrant, *Prigg v. Pennsylvania,* 41 U.S. 539, 551 (1842) [Act, section 3]. To obtain such a warrant, the master or the master's agent had to go before a judicial officer and convince him by "oath or affirmation . . . that said fugitive hath escaped from service." Ibid. The accused was entitled to a hearing, and at that hearing, the claimant had to prove his case under the same rules as any other litigant and, unlike the federal procedure, could not rely on his affidavit. The accused fugitive could present evidence in his or her defense. Ibid. at 553–53 [Act, sections 4, 6]. The act forbade most state officials from jurisdiction or cognizance under the federal Fugitive Slave Act. Ibid. at 553 [Act, section 5], 555 [Act, section 9]. A slave catcher who failed to obtain a judicial certificate to remove an alleged slave from Pennsylvania and, nonetheless, did so could be found guilty of a felony. Ibid. at 550–51 [Act, section 1].

18. Morris, *Free Men All,* pp. 71–72.

19. Ibid., pp. 219–21.

20. Cover, *Justice Accused,* p. 162.

21. 41 U.S. 539 (1842). See Paul Finkelman, "*Prigg v. Pennsylvania* and Northern Courts: Anti-Slavery Use of a Pro-Slavery Decision," in John R. McKivigan, ed., *Abolitionism and American Law* (New York: Garland Publishing, Inc., 1999), pp. 199–229, for a first-rate discussion of the background of *Prigg* and the decision's ramifications. Most likely, Mr. Prigg was not a professional slave catcher, but merely a neighbor of the slave's owner.

22. 41 U.S. at 611.

23. 41 U.S. at 611–12.

24. Ibid. at 626. The Supreme Court reaffirmed the constitutionality of the 1793 Act in *Jones v. Van Zandt*, 46 U.S. 215 (1847).

25. Burt, *Constitution in Conflict*, pp. 177–79.

26. 41 U.S. at 622.

27. Ibid. at 625.

28. Ibid. at 622 (emphasis added).

29. Morris, *Free Men All*, pp. 109–14; Stanley W. Campbell, *The Slave Catchers: Enforcement of the Fugitive Slave Act* (1968; New York: W.W. Norton Company, Inc., 1972), p. 14.

30. Morris, *Free Men All*, p. 109.

31. An Act to Further Protect Personal Liberty (March 24, 1843). Massachusetts Archives.

32. Writ of capias ad respondendum, *Matson v. Bryant*, Coles County Circuit Court (August 17, 1847), copy in Herndon-Weik Collection: Group III, Document Nos. 1970–71, LOC, Manuscript Division; LPAL, File ID L00714, Doc. No. 5510.

33. Act of February 12, 1793, Ch. 7, 1 Stat. 302 (1793), section 3.

34. Finkelman, *An Imperfect Union*, p. 148.

35. 41 U.S. at 628 (Taney, J., concurring).

36. 4 Fed. Cas. 904 (1806).

37. Ibid.; Fehrenbacher, *Dred Scott*, p. 54.

38. *Western Law Journal* 3, p. 65, 28 Fed. Cas. 1115 (C.C.D. 1845).

39. Ibid. at pp. 68–69.

40. Ibid. at p. 69.

41. Ibid.

42. Ibid.

43. Ibid. at p. 71.

44. *Winney v. Whitesides*, 1 Mo. 472, 476, 1824 Mo. LEXIS 21, p. 7 (1824).

45. 9 Ky. 467, 1820 Ky. LEXIS 122 (1820).

46. Ibid. at 467–68, 1820 Ky. LEXIS 122, p. 1.

47. Ibid. at 470–71, 1829 Ky. LEXIS 122, pp. 7–8.

48. Ibid. at 471, 1820 Ky. LEXIS 122, pp. 8–9.

49. Ibid. at 471–72, 1820 Ky. LEXIS 122, p. 9.

50. Ibid. at 472, 1820 Ky. LEXIS 122, pp. 10–11.

51. 2 Martin (n.s.) 401, 408, 1824 La. LEXIS 75, p. 7 (1824). In *Forsyth v. Nash*, 4 Martin (o.s.)(La.) 183, 1816 La. LEXIS 47 (1826), the Louisiana Supreme Court had affirmed the freedom of an alleged slave because the claimant failed to prove that the man ever had been a slave and because he always had lived in free territories, thus implying that residence in a free state might free a slave. See Finkelman, *An Imperfect Union*, p. 207.

52. Fehrenbacher, *Dred Scott*, pp. 54–55.

53. 9 Ky. 467, 478, 1820 Ky. LEXIS 122, p. 22 (1820).

54. 44 Ky. 173, 1844 Ky. LEXIS 103 (1844).

55. Ibid. at p. 183, 1844 Ky. LEXIS 103, pp. 20–21.

56. *Strader v. Graham*, 46 Ky. 633, 645, 1847 Ky. LEXIS 89, p. 5 (1847).

57. Ibid. The case was appealed to the United States Supreme Court where it was dismissed for want of jurisdiction. In his opinion for the court, Chief Justice Taney

maintained that neither the United States Constitution nor the Ordinance of 1787 gave the court jurisdiction to interfere with Kentucky's right to determine the status of individuals within its territory. In the Court's view, there was nothing in the Constitution "that could in any degree control the law of Kentucky on this subject," and that the Ordinance of 1787 "is not in force." *Strader v. Graham*, 51 U.S. 82, 93–95 (1851). See Finkelman, *An Imperfect Union*, pp. 196–200.

58. 1 Mo. 472, 476, 1824 Mo. LEXIS 21, p. 7 (1824).

59. Ibid.

60. 2 Mo. 214, 1830 Mo. LEXIS 17 (1830).

61. Ibid. at 216, 1830 Mo. LEXIS 17, p. 4.

62. Ibid.

63. Ibid.

64. Finkelman, *An Imperfect Union*, p. 220.

65. Ibid.

66. 3 Mo. 270, 1833 Mo. LEXIS 32 (1833).

67. Ibid. at 274, 1833 Mo. LEXIS 32, p. 8.

68. Ibid. at 275, 1833 Mo. LEXIS 32, pp. 8–9.

69. Ibid. at 274, 1833 Mo. LEXIS 32, pp. 7–8. In *Ralph v. Duncan*, the Missouri Supreme Court used the "introduction of slavery" test to free a slave whose master had allowed him to hire himself out in Illinois. 3 Mo. 194, 195, 1833 Mo. LEXIS 2, p. 22 (1833). Later, in *Nat v. Huddle*, the court ruled that a slave who, against his master's wishes, visited his master in Illinois and hired himself out there was not emancipated. 3 Mo. 400, 401–02, 1834 Mo. LEXIS 37, pp. 3–4 (1834).

70. Fehrenbacher, *Dred Scott*, p. 54.

71. Ibid., p. 54 n.7.

72. Ibid.

73. 7 Serg. & Rawle 378, 383–84, 1821 Pa. LEXIS 114, pp. 10–11 (Pa. Sup. Ct. 1821).

74. 35 Mass. 193, 1836 Mass. LEXIS 38 (Mass. Sup. Ct. 1836).

75. Ibid., 1836 Mass. LEXIS 38, pp. 1–4.

76. Ibid. at pp. 217, 224, 1836 Mass LEXIS 38, pp. 46, 60–61.

77. Ibid. at p. 202, 1836 Mass, LEXIS 38, p. 28.

78. Harold M. Hyman and William Wiecek, *Equal Justice Under Law: Constitutional Development, 1835–1875* (New York: Harper & Row, 1982), p. 99. In recognition of this fact, Med was renamed "Med Maria Sommersett." Ibid. See also Finkelman, *An Imperfect Union*, p. 113 ("Shaw's decision was virtually a total application of Somerset to Massachusetts").

79. 12 Conn. 38, 49, 1837 Conn. LEXIS 4, p. 22 (1837).

80. Ibid. at p. 52, 1837 Conn. LEXIS 4, pp. 26–27. The court did not go so far as to free any slave who had been voluntarily brought into Connecticut. It excluded those accompanying a master who was a "traveler" merely "passing through the state." Ibid. at p. 51, 1837 Conn. LEXIS 4, p. 24. See Finkelman, *An Imperfect Union*, pp. 127–29

81. Finkelman, *An Imperfect Union*, pp. 130–45; Fehrenbacher, *Dred Scott*, pp. 55 n.18, 57.

82. Fehrenbacher, *Dred Scott*, p. 55, n.18.

83. In 1819, Illinois passed a law which required anyone who "shall forcibly take out of this State a negro or mulatto having gained a legal settlement in this State" to pay "the sum of $1000 to the party injured." Davidson and Struve, *Complete History of Illinois*, pp. 318–19.

In 1825, punishment replaced restitution. A defendant convicted of kidnapping "any negro, mulatto or person of color" with an intent to enslave them faced twenty to a hundred lashes, two to four hours in the pillory, and a fine of one thousand dollars. "An Act to more effectively prevent kidnapping and for other purposes," Approved January 17, 1825, Laws of Illinois, in Middleton, *Black Laws of the Old Northwest*, pp. 310–11.

Section 56 of the 1845 version of the criminal code made it a felony, with a penalty of one to seven years in prison, to "forcibly" take, or seize with intent to take, "any man, woman, or child, whether white, black or colored," out of Illinois "without having established a claim according to the laws of the United States [i.e., Fugitive Slave Act of 1793]." Illinois Revised Statutes, Criminal Code, sec. 56.

Section 57 of the 1845 criminal code extended the punishment under Section 56 to

[e]very person who shall hire, persuade, entice, decoy, or seduce by false promises, misrepresentations and the like, any negro, mulatto or colored person, not being a slave, to go out of the State, or to be taken or removed therefrom, for the purpose and with the intent to sell such negro, mulatto or colored person into slavery or involuntary servitude, or otherwise employ him or her for his own use, or to the use of another, without the free will and consent or to such negro, mulatto or colored person. . . .

Ibid. All of these prohibitions had the same basic problem—enforcement. Often the kidnapped victim was long gone before the crime was reported. If there were witnesses, many times they were people of color and, as such, prohibited from testifying against whites in court. Whites often were too uninterested, intimidated, or antagonistic to become involved. Such impediments left Section 56 with little or no deterrent effect. See Jon Musgrave, "Black Kidnappings in the Wabash and Ohio Valleys of Illinois," Hickory Hill Plantation–Old Slave House Preservation Project, found at www.illinoishistory. com/blackkidnappings.html (October 8, 2005); Jon Musgrave, "History Comes Out of Hiding Atop Hickory Hill," *Springhouse Magazine* (December 1996), Hickory Hill Plantation–Old Slave House Preservation Project, found at www.illinoishistory.com/ osharticle.htm (October 8, 2005).

84. Cong. Globe, 36th Cong., 2d Sess. 52 (December 11, 1860). An example of this was the Illinois statute against kidnapping discussed supra. Although the law mandated prison time for persons convicted of forcibly removing blacks from Illinois, it specifically excepted those who "established a claim according to the Laws of the United States." Criminal Code, Section 56, Illinois Revised Statutes (1856).

85. Criminal Code of Illinois, Section 149, Statutes of Illinois, 1833–1834, pp. 206–7.

86. *Western Citizen* (October 26, 1843), ALPL. Owen Lovejoy was the pastor of the Hampshire Congregational Church in Princeton, Illinois, which had the largest membership in Bureau County. The word was that all of Lovejoy's congregation were "pronounced abolitionists" and that he himself "was the most prominent abolitionist in the northern part of the state." Caton, *Early Bench and Bar of Illinois*, p. 122; Edward Magdol, *Owen Lovejoy: Abolitionist in Congress* (New Brunswick: Rutgers University Press, 1967), p. 35. He was, in the words of one who knew him well, a man of "unflinching" courage who was "thoroughly in earnest if not fanatical in his politics." Lisk, *Eighty Years of Illinois Politics*, p. 531.

87. *Western Citizen* (October 26, 1843), ALPL; Harris, *Negro Servitude in Illinois*, p. 110; Lusk, *Eighty Years of Illinois Politics*, p. 538. In the late 1850s, Purple compiled a

collection of the laws of the state of Illinois which became known as the "Purple Statutes." Bateman, Selby, aand Curry, *Historical Encyclopedia of Illinois*, p. 436.

88. *Western Citizen* (October 26, 1843), ALAP. James H. Collins earned a reputation as a "most violent and extreme Abolitionist." Speech by Isaac N. Arnold before the Bar Association of Illinois at Springfield, January 1881, quoted in Lusk, *Eighty Years of Illinois Politics*, p. 530. Collins had once been a law partner of John D. Caton, the presiding judge at the Owen Lovejoy trial. Caton, *Early Bench and Bar of Illinois*, p. 124.

89. Quoted in Lusk, *Eighty Years of Illinois Politics*, pp. 530–31.

90. Ibid.

91. Caton, *Early Bench and Bar of Illinois*, p. 125; Lusk, *Eighty Years of Illinois Politics*, p. 530.

92. Caton, *Early Bench and Bar of Illinois*, p. 125.

93. Ibid., pp. 125–26.

94. Harris, *Negro Servitude in Illinois*, p. 111; Lusk, *Eighty Years of Illinois Politics*, pp. 531–32.

95. Caton, *Early Bench and Bar of Illinois*, pp. 143–44; quoted in Lusk, *Eighty Years of Illinois Politics*, pp. 531–32.

96. *Western Citizen* (October 26, 1843), ALPL. See also Lusk, *Eighty Years of Illinois Politics*, p. 532; Caton, *Early Bench and Bar of Illinois*, p. 143. Caton distinguished the situation before him from one in which the slave escaped into Illinois: "If the slave come within the state without the consent of the master, he is nevertheless still his slave. . . . under the Constitution of the U. States, the free states cannot be made the asylum of the fugitive slave, and no matter how he may fly, or how long he may be concealed, if, within the jurisdiction of the United States, the title of the master to his slave remains unimpaired." *Western Citizen* (October 26, 1843), ALPL. Years later, in writing about this case, Caton did not recall giving this instruction to the jury. When Owen Lovejoy's son brought it to his attention, Caton gracefully conceded that he must have done so despite the fact that he subsequently had taken a different position while sitting on the state supreme court in *Willard v. People*, 5 Ill. 461 (1843). Caton, *Early Bench and Bar of Illinois*, pp. 142–44. See pp. 71–73 infra. It should be noted that at the time of the trial, Caton was, by his own admission, in "feeble health." *Western Citizen* (October 26, 1843), ALPL.

97. *Western Citizen* (October 26, 1843), ALPL; Hand, "Negro Slavery in Illinois," p. 46. Fourteen years later, Findley's prediction came true—Lovejoy was elected to Congress.

98. 5 Ill. 498 (1843), *aff'd*, *Moore v. People*, 55 U.S. 13 (1852).

99. *Eells v. People*, 5 Ill. at 511–14. Eells was an ardent abolitionist who helped form the Adams County Antislavery Society. "Preamble and Constitution of the Adams County Antislavery Society" (August 25, 1835), Historical Society of Quincy and Adams Counties, Illinois, found at history.alliancecelibraries/stem.com/IllinoisAlive/files/qh/htm2/qh000077.cfm (March 3, 2005). He was on the faculty of the antislavery Mission Institute in Quincy, Illinois. He and his wife often assisted escaping slaves, and the doctor was a defendant in several cases stemming from these efforts. Terrell Dempsey, *Searching for Jim: Slavery in Sam Clemens's World* (Columbia: University of Missouri Press, 2003), p. 25; Palmyra *Missouri Whig* (December 9, 1843), State Historical Society of Missouri.

According to Stephen Douglas, who sat as the trial judge, the case first came to his attention in a somewhat unusual manner: "One morning, just after I had opened court, Captain Pitman, the constable, marched into the court-room, holding a physician by the collar, and said, 'If your honor please, I caught this Dr. Eells running off a fugitive slave this morning, contrary to the Statute of Illinois; and I have brought him and the slave into court to know what I shall do with them.' I said, 'Captain Pitman, you will hand the slave over to the sheriff, and go to the grand jury and state the facts.'" Con. Globe, 36th Cong., 2d Sess. 54 (December 11, 1860).

100. 5 Ill. at 518 (Lockwood, J., dissenting)(emphasis added).

101. 3 Mo. 270, 1833 Mo. LEXIS 32 (1833). See pp. 66–67 supra.

102. Ibid. at pp. 273–75, 1833 Mo. LEXIS 32, pp. 6–9.

103. 5 Ill. at 461 (1843). See Finkleman, *An Imperfect Union*, pp. 97–98.

104. Julius Willard, "The Jacksonville Slave Case," *Western Citizen* (August 24, 1843), ALPL; Steiner, "Abolitionists and Escaped Slaves in Jacksonville: Samuel Willard's 'My First Adventure with a Fugitive Slave: The Story of It and How It Failed,'" *Illinois Historical Journal* 89 (1996), p. 219. The Willards spelled Sarah's last name "Lisle," while the Illinois Supreme Court spelled it "Liles."

105. 5 Ill. at 468. According to Julius Willard, Julia had told him that her name was Judy Green but that Sarah Lisle had changed it to "Julia." Steiner, "Abolitionists and Escaped Slaves in Jacksonville," p. 219 n.31.

106. 5 Ill. at 468–69.

107. Ibid. at 469. See Steiner, "Abolitionists and Escaped Slaves in Jacksonville," p. 217, for an excellent discussion of this point.

108. The senior Willard was tried first. He hired the local firm of Henry B. McClure and William Brown to represent him. Willard was acquainted with Edward D. Baker, a prominent Whig and friend of Lincoln whom Willard described as "perhaps the most eloquent man that I have ever heard." Baker refused the case for "political reasons." He sent the Willards to Stephen T. Logan, who declined the case as soon as he heard the facts. Lincoln's name was mentioned by a friend, who, as noted earlier, dismissed him with the remark that "he has not any reputation, and we wanted a man of note." Willard finally settled upon a personal friend, Alfred Cowles of Alton, who had represented the defenders of Lovejoy's press and prosecuted the rioters. Steiner, "Abolitionists and Escaped Slaves in Jacksonville," pp. 227–28.

109. 5 Ill. at p. 471.

110. Steiner, "Abolitionists and Escaped Slaves in Jacksonville," pp. 230–31.

111. Ibid., p. 231. Samuel Willard concluded that it "would plainly be of no use" to go to trial. Ibid. This may have been because the facts clearly were against Willard, or because, as Steiner suggests, the trial would have been before a "proslavery jury," or both. Ibid., 217.

112. Ibid., p. 230.

113. Speech by Isaac N. Arnold before the Bar Association of Illinois at Springfield, Illinois, in January 1881, quoted in Lusk, *Eighty Years of Illinois Politics*, p. 530.

114. 5 Ill. at 452.

115. Ibid. at 465.

116. Ibid. at 469–70.

117. Ibid. at 472.

118. Ibid.

119. Ibid. In a concurring opinion, joined in by Chief Justice Wilson, Justice Lockwood maintained that it was up to the courts, not the legislature, to determine "the extent and force of this law of comity . . . [and] to determine how far the laws of other nations shall be recognized and carried into effect." He concluded that although Illinois

had no obligation to do so, the right of slave owners to freely traverse Illinois with their slaves should be recognized because the owners of slaves had been doing so for more than thirty years to the "advantage" of the slaveholding states and to Illinois, and because a refusal to permit slave owners to do so might "engender feelings on their part not favorable to a continuance of our happy Union." Ibid. at pp. 476–77. (Lockwood, J., concurring).

120. Finkelman, *An Imperfect Union*, p. 99.

121. Quoted in Harris, *Negro Servitude in Illinois*, p. 118.

Chapter Six

1. Duff, *A. Lincoln: Prairie Lawyer*, p. 137; *History of Coles County*, pp. 335–36. During the "winter of the deep snow," it snowed almost continually from November 1830 until late January 1831. In many places in northern Illinois, the snow cover was more than four feet deep. *History of Coles County*, p. 335. Meteor showers were responsible for "the night of the falling stars" in 1833. Ibid. The "sudden freeze" followed an early thaw in December 1836. Cattle, hogs, birds, and other animals were frozen fast to the ground. Ibid., p. 339; Davis, *Frontier Illinois*, pp. 244–45; Sigelschiffer, *The American Conscience*, p. 54.

2. Writ of capias ad satisfactum, *Matson v. Bryant*, Coles County Circuit Court (August 20, 1847), copy in Herndon-Weik Collection: Group III, Document Nos. 1974–75, LOC, Manuscript Division; LPAL, File ID L00714, Document No. 5509; Notice, *Matson v. Bryant*, Coles County Circuit Court (August 23, 1847), copy in Herndon-Weik Collection: Group III, Document Nos. 1968–1969, LOC, Manuscript Division; LPAL, File ID L00714, Document No.5509.

3. Notice, *Matson v. Bryant*, Coles County Circuit Court (October 8, 1847), copy in Herndon-Weik Collection: Group III, Document No. 1964, LOC, Manuscript Division; LPAL, File ID L00714, Doc. No. 5507.

4. McIntyre, "Lincoln and the Matson Slave Case," p. 390.

5. *History of Coles County*, pp. 313–14.

6. Ibid., p. 314.

7. *History of Coles County*, pp. 245, 313–14; Wilson, *Encyclopedia of Illinois and History of Coles County*, p. 671.

8. Ficklin, "A Pioneer Lawyer."

9. Ibid.

10. Wilson was appointed to complete the term of William P. Foster, "a great rascal," who, after taking a year's salary without ever taking the bench, resigned in disgrace. Ford, *History of Illinois*, I, p. 29; William Coffin, *Life and Times of Samuel D. Lockwood* (Chicago: Knight & Leonard, 1889), p. 44.

11. Duff, *A. Lincoln: Prairie Lawyer*, pp. 141–42; Bateman, Selby, and Curry, *Historical Encyclopedia of Illinois*, p. 595; Bannister, *Lincoln and the Illinois Supreme Court*, p. 19; Coffin, *Lockwood*, p. 45, Birkbeck and Flower, *History of the English Settlement in Edwards County*, p. 142 n.

12. Bateman, Selby, and Curry, *Historical Encyclopedia of Illinois*, p. 595; Bannister, *Lincoln and the Illinois Supreme Court*, p. 19.

13. Caton, *Early Bench and Bar of Illinois*, p. 167.

14. Ibid., p. 168.

15. Koerner, *Memoirs*, I, p. 373.

16. Ibid.

17. Linder, *Reminiscences,* p. 73. *Nisi prius* courts are held for the trial of issues before a judge or a judge and jury as distinguished from appellate courts. *Blacks Law Dictionary* (1951), p. 1197.

18. Caton, *Early Bench and Bar of Illinois*, p. 168.

19. Bateman, Selby, and Curry, *Historical Encyclopedia of Illinois*, p. 528; Duff, *A. Lincoln: Prairie Lawyer*, pp. 141–42.

20. Linder, *Reminiscences*, p. 388.

21. Palmer, *The Bench and Bar of Illinois*, p. 22.

22. See p. 10 supra.

23. See pp. 10–11, 41–42 supra.

24. See p. 11 supra.

25. *Willard v. People*, 5 Ill. 461 (1843).

26. Ibid. at 472.

27. 5 Ill. 498 (1843), *aff'd, Moore v. People*, 55 U.S. 13 (1852).

28. Ibid. at p. 518 (Lockwood, J., dissenting). See pp. 70–71 supra.

29. See p. 12 supra.

30. *Sangamon Journal* (February 18, 1842), ALPL; *Genius of Liberty* (February 26, 1842), ALPL.

31. *Sangamon Journal* (February 18, 1842), ALPL; *Genius of Liberty* (February 26, 1842), ALPL.

32. "In the Matter of Jane," *Western Law Journal* 5 (1848), p. 202.

33. See, e.g., *Ex parte Thatcher,* 7 Ill. 167, 1845 LEXIS 22 (1845); *Ex rel Birch,* 8 Ill. 134, 1846 Ill. LEXIS 23 (1846); *Application of Klepper,* 26 Ill. 532, 1862 Ill. LEXIS 374 (1862).

34. See *In re Bryant et al.*, File ID: L00714, LPAL.

35. D. T. McIntyre, "Matson Slave Trial," *Oakland Weekly Ledger* (July 17, 1896).

36. See p. 27 supra.

37. Ficklin, "A Pioneer Lawyer"; Weik, "Lincoln and the Matson Negroes," p. 756.

38. Ficklin, "A Pioneer Lawyer."

39. Ibid. Linder might not have been offended by this reference. He named one of his sons John Calhoun Linder no doubt after the outspoken states' rights senator from South Carolina.

40. Ibid.

41. Ibid.

42. See p. 58 supra.

43. Ficklin, "A Pioneer Lawyer." John Philpot Curran (1750–1817), an Irish Protestant, was a lawyer, politician, and judge who became famous for his speeches on behalf of defendants in criminal trials. One of these defendants was Archibald Hamilton Rowan (1751–1834), a member of the nationalist United Irishmen, who was tried for sedition in 1794. Despite Curran's famous speech, Rowan was sentenced to two years in prison. He escaped to France and then to the United States. Rowan was pardoned in 1803 and returned to Ireland where he died in 1834. Henry Boylan, *A Dictionary of Irish Biography* (New York: Barnes & Noble Books, 1978), pp. 77, 314.

44. Quoted in Weik, "Lincoln and the Matson Negroes," p. 757.

45. See, e.g., Beveridge, *Abraham Lincoln*, I, p. 397; Woldman, *Lawyer Lincoln*, p. 62; Chroust, "Abraham Lincoln Argues A Pro-Slavery Case," pp. 303–4; Coleman, *Lincoln and Coles County*, p. 107.

46. Weik, "Lincoln and the Matson Negroes," p. 757.

47. Ficklin, "A Pioneer Lawyer."

48. Ibid.

49. Ibid.

50. Ibid.

51. Ibid.

52. Although there is no indication that he did so, Lincoln might have argued that because Jane had requested to come to Illinois, she was not entitled to her freedom. There was some authority for this contention. An 1840 Louisiana case, *Thomas v. Generis*, 16 La. 483, 1840 La. LEXIS 429 (1840), involved a slave who had been allowed, at her request, to go to Illinois to receive medical treatment and had stayed five years. Testifying as an expert on the Illinois Constitution, Judge Walter B. Scates, later an Illinois Supreme Court justice (1841–47), opined that "a residence by a slave from another state, in Illinois, with the consent of the owner and slave, would never operate an emancipation of the slave." Ibid. at p. 487, 1840 La. LEXIS 429, p. 7. The Louisiana Supreme Court disagreed. It held that the slave's five-year residence in Illinois freed her, and the fact that she had consented was irrelevant because "by our laws . . . A slave has no will and cannot give consent." Ibid. at p. 489, 1840 La. LEXIS 429, p. 10.

53. Ficklin, "A Pioneer Lawyer."

54. Ibid.

55. Order, *In re Bryant*, Coles County Circuit Court (October 16, 1847), Docket Book, Coles County Circuit Court, p. 191, ALPL; LPAL, File ID, Document No. 36857.

56. Ibid.

57. Ibid.

58. Quoted in Weik, "Lincoln and the Matson Negroes," pp. 756–57. See also Ficklin, "A Pioneer Lawyer."

59. Duff, *A. Lincoln: Prairie Lawyer*, p. 137.

60. Elmer Gertz, "The Black Laws of Illinois," *Journal of the Illinois State Historical Society* 46 (1963), p. 470 ("feeble"), Weik, "Lincoln and the Matson Negroes," p. 756 ("pitiably weak"); Woldman, *Lawyer Lincoln*, p. 64 ("spiritless, half–hearted," etc.).

61. Ficklin, "A Pioneer Lawyer."

62. Weik, "Lincoln and the Matson Negroes," p. 756 (emphasis in original).

63. Ibid.

64. Burchard, *Lincoln and Slavery*, p. 32.

65. Duff, *A. Lincoln: Prairie Lawyer*, p. 140. See also Chroust, "Lincoln Argues a Pro-Slavery Case," pp. 306–7 (Lincoln "seized upon the only arguable point in favor of his client").

66. 5 Ill. 461, 472 (1843).

67. 35 Mass. (18 Pick.) 193 (1836). See pp. 67–68 supra.

68. See pp. 64–67 supra. As noted earlier, however, there was a line of cases from Missouri which held, generally, that a slave who worked in a free state was liberated. See pp. 65–66 supra.

69. See pp. 64–68 supra.

70. Ficklin had exactly the same understanding of what was at issue: "It was therefore of the highest importance to ascertain 'the true intent and meaning' of Matson in placing his slaves upon the Black Grove farm." Ficklin, "A Pioneer Lawyer." Ficklin's identification of intent as the critical issue in the case would seem to indicate that neither he nor Constable had argued the *Julia v. McKinney*, 3 Mo. 270, 1833 Mo. LEXIS 32 (1833), line

of cases that held that the factual question of whether a slave owner actually introduced slavery into a free state, not intention, was the most significant factor in determining whether time spent in a free state liberated a slave. In this respect, *Vincent v. Duncan*, 2 Mo. 214, 216, 1830 Mo. LEXIS 17, p. 4 (1830), probably would have been helpful because, using this test, the Missouri Supreme Court held that a slave who had been sent to work in Illinois was, in consequence, a free man. See pp. 65–66 supra.

71. Ficklin, "A Pioneer Lawyer."

72. Ibid.

73. Duff, *A. Lincoln: Prairie Lawyer*, p. 140.

74. Chroust, "Lincoln Argues A Pro-Slavery Case," p. 303.

75. *Bailey v. Cromwell*, 4 Ill. 71 (1841).

76. Ibid. at 73.

77. Ibid.

78. Ficklin, "A Pioneer Lawyer."

79. Ibid.

80. Ibid. In using the words "local habitation," Ficklin may have been quoting from Shakespeare's *A Midsummer Night's Dream* (V, i, 7):

> *And, as imagination bodies forth*
> *The forms of things unknown, the poet's pen*
> *Turns them to shapes, and gives to airy nothing*
> *A local habitation and a name.*

81. Ficklin, "A Pioneer Lawyer."

82. Ibid.

83. "In the Matter of Jane," *Western Law Journal* 5, pp. 203–4.

84. Ibid. at pp. 204–5.

85. Ibid. at p. 205.

86. Ibid. at p. 203.

87. Ibid. at pp. 205–6.

88. Paul Finkelman, "Slavery, the 'More Perfect Union,' and the Prairie State," p. 256. This also was the incorrect conclusion of Chicago's antislavery newspaper, the *Western Citizen*: "[*In the Matter of Jane*] may be considered an important decision in Illinois' jurisprudence—but only reaffirming decisions made in all parts of the country, even in the slave states. It is so plain a case that we wonder it was brought into court. There is no plainer principle laid down than that if an owner of a slave carries his slave beyond the jurisdiction or dominion of the state law, he by that act frees his slave,—This is not only just, in accordance with common sense, but according to law." *Western Citizen* (November 16, 1847), ALPL.

89. "In the Matter of Jane," *Western Law Journal* 5, p. 203.

90. Ibid. at pp. 205–6. In 1853, in response to the voters' authorization to do so pursuant to the compromise reached at the 1847 state constitutional convention, the Illinois legislature passed "An Act to prevent the immigration of free negroes into this State," Act of February 12, 1853, Laws of Illinois, 18 G.A. 57–60. Among other things, the act addressed blacks who, like Jane Bryant and her children, were voluntarily brought into Illinois. Section 1 made it a crime for anyone "to bring, or cause to be brought into this state, any negro or mulatto slave, whether said slave is set free or not." Ibid., sec. 1. There

was, however, an important caveat: "[T]his section shall not be construed so as to affect persons or slaves, bona fide traveling through this state from and to any other state in the United States." Ibid.

91. Ibid. at p. 206. In support of his ruling, Wilson cited *Ex parte Simmons*, 22 F. Cas. 151 (Cir. Ct. E.D. Pa. 1823) and *Vaughn v. Williams*, 28 F. Cas. 1115 (Cir. Ct. D. Ind. 1845). With regard to *Simmons*, Wilson's characterization is correct. That case stands for the proposition that the Fugitive Slave Act did not apply to slaves "voluntarily carried by his master into another state." 22 F. Cas. at 151. *Vaughn* is less on point. While the court in that case held that three slaves were entitled to their freedom because their master had taken them to Illinois, the facts in *Vaughn* were significantly different from those in the Matson case. In *Vaughn*, the master had openly declared that he intended to become a citizen of Illinois and had "actually exercised the rights of a citizen by voting." 28 F. Cas. at 1118.

Chapter Seven

1. Ficklin, "A Pioneer Lawyer."

2. Duff, *A. Lincoln: Prairie Lawyer*, p.143.

3. Weik, "Lincoln and the Matson Negroes," p. 756 (emphasis in original).

4. Beveridge, *Abraham Lincoln*, I, p. 396.

5. Ibid.

6. Sigelschiffer, *The American Conscience*, p. 109.

7. Thomas, *Abraham Lincoln*, p. 118.

8. Woldman, *Lawyer Lincoln*, p. 64.

9. David Davis interview with William H. Herndon (September 19, 1866), in Wilson and Davis, *Herndon's Informants*, p. 347.

10. Samuel C. Parks to William H. Herndon (March 25, 1866), in Wilson and Davis, *Herndon's Informants*, p. 238.

11. Henry C. Whitney interview with Jesse W. Weik (1887–89), in Wilson and Davis, *Herndon's Informants*, p. 733. See also Henry C. Whitney to William H. Herndon (August 27, 1887) ("Swett made a first rate speech: & Lincoln who closed our case a very poor one for us"), in Wilson and Davis, *Herndon's Informants*, p. 633; John G. Nicolay and John Hay, *Abraham Lincoln: A History*, 10 vols. (New York: The Century Co., 1890), I, p. 303 ("Such was the transparent candor and integrity of his nature, that he could not well or strongly argue a side or cause he thought wrong"—quoting Judge Thomas Drummond, a Lincoln contemporary).

12. See, e.g., Weik, "Lincoln and the Matson Negroes," p. 756; Beveridge, *Abraham Lincoln*, I, p. 396; Coleman, *Lincoln and Coles County*, p. 108.

13. See pp. 82–83 supra.

14. Daniel Walker Howe, "Why Abraham Lincoln Was a Whig," *Journal of the Abraham Lincoln Association* 16 (1995), p. 33; Daniel Walker Howe, *The Political Culture of the American Whigs* (Chicago: The University of Chicago Press, 1979), pp. 205, 269; Kenneth M. Stampp, *The Era of Reconstruction, 1865–1877* (New York: Alfred A. Knopf, 1965), pp. 31–32; Richard Carwardine, *Lincoln: A Life of Purpose and Power* (New York: Alfred A. Knopf, 2006), pp. 30–31; Steiner, *An Honest Calling*, pp. 26–74, 136.

15. Daniel Walker Howe, "Why Abraham Lincoln Was a Whig," p. 33.

16. Ibid.

17. Steiner, *An Honest Calling*, p. 177.

18. Allen C. Guelzo, *Abraham Lincoln: Redeemer President* (Grand Rapids: William B. Eerdmans Publishing Company, 1999), p. 129.

19. Ibid., pp. 129–30; Steiner, *An Honest Calling*, pp. 126–27.

20. Howe, *The Political Culture of the American Whigs*, p. 64; Steiner, *An Honest Calling*, pp. 126–27; Guelzo, *Abraham Lincoln: Redeemer President*, pp. 129–30. Justice Joseph Story, a Jeffersonian Republican turned Whig, made what he saw as the importance of the Constitution's fugitive slave clause a foundation block of his opinion in *Prigg v. Pennsylvania*. In that opinion, he maintained that the clause "constituted a fundamental article without the adoption of which the Union could not have been formed." He contended that it was "designed to guard against the doctrines and principles prevalent in the non-slaveholding States" from abolishing the rights of the owners of slaves which, if permitted to occur, "would have engendered perpetual strife between the different States." 41 U.S. 534, 611–12 (1842).

21. Steiner, *An Honest Calling*, pp. 126–27.

22. Donald, *Lincoln*, p. 83.

23. See pp. 17–19 supra.

24. Speech in the Illinois Legislature Concerning the State Bank (January 11, 1837), *Lincoln Collected Works*, I, p. 69.

25. Address before the Young Men's Lyceum of Springfield, Illinois (January 27, 1838), *Lincoln Collected Works*, I, p. 109.

26. Ibid., p. 111.

27. Eulogy to Henry Clay, Springfield, Illinois (July 6, 1852), *Lincoln Collected Works*, I, p. 130.

28. Address before the Young Men's Lyceum of Springfield, Illinois (January 27, 1838), *Lincoln Collected Works*, I, p. 109.

29. Quoted in Donald, *Lincoln*, p. 82. See Address before Springfield Temperance Society (February 22, 1842), *Lincoln Collected Works*, I, p. 273.

30. Address before the Young Men's Lyceum of Springfield, Illinois (January 27, 1838), *Lincoln Collected Works*, I, p. 112.

31. Ibid.

32. Lincoln to William Durley (October 31, 1845), *Lincoln Collected Works*, I, p. 348. See Carwardine, *Lincoln: A Life of Purpose and Power*, p. 23.

33. Protest in the Illinois Legislature on Slavery (March 3, 1837), *Lincoln Collected Works*, I, p. 75.

34. Lincoln to William Durley (October 31, 1845), *Lincoln Collected Works*, I, p. 348.

35. Interview with John W. Bunn (October 15, 1914), Weik MSS, ALPL. John Bunn and his brother Jacob were grocery merchants and bankers in Springfield, Illinois, in the mid-nineteenth century. *Historical Encyclopedia*, p. 66. Bunn also recalled that Lincoln said that the way to deal with the fugitive slave problem was "to . . . repeal the [fugitive slave] law." According to Bunn, "in more than one [fugitive slave] case," Lincoln "suggested that a few dollars be paid to those who were holding the negro." Interview with John Bunn (October 15, 1914), Weik MM, ALPL.

36. See pp. 42–43 supra.

37. See p. 37 supra.

38. Steiner, *An Honest Calling*, p. 177. See also Carwardine, *Lincoln: A Life of Purpose and Power*, pp. 30–31 (representing Matson was part of Lincoln's "conservative Whiggery").

39. Steiner, *An Honest Calling*, p. 177.

40. Ibid., p. 136. See also Steven P. Oates, *With Malice Toward None: The Life of Abraham Lincoln* (New York: Harper & Row, 1977), p. 101 (the Matson case demonstrated "how attorney Lincoln could set aside his personal convictions").

41. Thomas, *Abraham Lincoln*, p. 118. See also Donald, *Lincoln*, pp. 103–4 (Lincoln's "business was law, not morality"); Dirck, *Lincoln the Lawyer*, p. 149 (same).

42. Guelzo, *Abraham Lincoln: Redeemer President*, p. 126. It could be argued that the fact that Lincoln said all but nothing about the Matson case demonstrates that the case was of little importance to him. His silence is not indicative of anything. Apparently, Lincoln rarely commented on his cases. Duff, *A. Lincoln: Prairie Lawyer*, p. 143.

43. Phillip Shaw Paludan, "Lincoln and Negro Slavery: I Haven't Got Time for the Pain," *Journal of the Abraham Lincoln Association* 27 (Summer 2006), p. 1, found at www.historycooperative.org (December 12, 2006).

44. Ibid., p. 3. In general, this also is the position of two far more polemical (and far less convincing) Lincoln studies. See Lerone Bennett, Jr., *Forced Into Glory: Abraham Lincoln's White Dream* (Chicago: Johnson Publishing Company, 2000), pp. 280–81, and Thomas J. Dilorenzo, *The Real Lincoln: A New Look at Abraham Lincoln, His Agenda, and an Unnecessary War* (Roseville, California: Prima Publishing, 2002), pp. 15–16. See George M. Fredrickson, *Big Enough to Be Inconsistent: Abraham Lincoln Confronts Slavery and Race* (Cambridge: Harvard University Press, 2008), pp. 1–41, for an insightful discussion of this subject.

45. Paludan, "Lincoln and Negro Slavery," pp. 6–7.

46. Ibid., p. 9; Guelzo, *Abraham Lincoln: Redeemer President*, p. 125. Guelzo argues, as have Richard Hofstadter and others, that Lincoln delayed his protest for over a month after the proslavery resolutions, "long enough for Lincoln to slide the relocation of the state capital through the Assembly. . . ." Ibid. See Richard Hofstadter, *The American Political Tradition and the Men Who Made It* (New York: Vintage Books, 1948), pp. 108–9. See also Donald, *Lincoln*, p. 63 (a "cautious, limited dissent"); critics discussed in Michael Burlingame, "The Lincoln-Stone Protest Against Slavery Reconsidered," *Papers from the Thirteenth and Fourteenth Annual Lincoln Colloquia* (1998–99), pp. 57–65. See also Bennett, Jr., *Forced Into Glory*, p. 255 (Lincoln took a "safe position").

47. Lincoln to A.G. Hodges (April 4, 1864), *Lincoln Collected Works*, VII, p. 281. Hodges was the editor of the Frankfort, Kentucky, *Commonwealth*. Ibid., n.1. In his *Lincoln's Virtues: An Ethical Biography* (New York: Alfred A. Knopf, 2002), pp. 284–85, William Lee Miller provides a detailed chronology of Lincoln's public statements on the immorality of slavery.

48. Protest in the Illinois Legislature on Slavery (March 3, 1837), *Lincoln Collected Works*, I, p. 75.

49. Guelzo, *Abraham Lincoln: Redeemer President*, p. 128. Burlingame, who argues that Lincoln deserves a great deal of credit for his protest, labels it "a remarkably bold statement for 1837." Burlingame, "The 1837 Lincoln-Stone Protest," p. 57.

50. The resolutions were passed by the Illinois Legislature "by the rousing vote of 77 to 6." Donald, *Lincoln*, p. 63.

51. See pp. 8–10 supra.

52. According to the federal census of 1840, there were 115 blacks living in Springfield, 6 of whom were slaves. Richard E. Hart, "Springfield's African Americans as a Part of the Lincoln Community," *Journal of the Abraham Lincoln Association* 20 (Winter 1999), found at jala.press.uici.edu/20.1/hart.html (October 17, 2004).

53. See Burlingame, "The 1837 Lincoln-Stone Protest," pp. 57–59.

54. See pp. 16–17 supra.

55. See p. 90 supra. See also Carwardine, *Lincoln: A Life of Purpose and Power*, p. 21 (not a "direct assault on abolitionist teaching itself").

56. Fragments of an Answer to John Hill (September 1860), *Lincoln Collected Works*, IV, p. 108. In an autobiography written in 1860 as guidance for the author of a campaign biography, Lincoln stated that his 1837 protest "briefly defined his position on the slavery question; and so far as it goes, it was the same as it is now." Autobiography Written for John L. Scripps (c. June 1860), *Lincoln Collected Works*, IV, p. 65.

57. Fragments of an Answer to John Hill (September 1860), *Lincoln Collected Works*, IV, p. 108.

58. Address before the Springfield Washington Temperance Society (February 22, 1842), *Lincoln Collected Works*, I, p. 279.

59. Lincoln to William Durley (October 31, 1845), *Lincoln Collected Works*, I, p. 348.

60. Quoted in Francis Marion Van Natter, *Lincoln's Boyhood: A Chronicle of His Indiana Years* (Washington, D.C.: Public Affairs Press, 1963), p. 145.

61. John Hanks interview with William H. Herndon (1865–66), in Wilson and Davis, *Herndon's Informants*, p. 457. His experiences in New Orleans may have been on his mind when, in speaking of slavery, Lincoln purportedly told Robert H. Brown, an office boy in Bloomington, Illinois, in the 1850s: "I saw it myself when I was only a little older than you are now, and the horrid pictures are in my mind yet." Fehrenbacher and Fehrenbacher, *Recollected Words of Abraham Lincoln*, p. 61.

62. *See* Guelzo, *Abraham Lincoln: Redeemer President*, p. 128; Paludan, "Lincoln and Negro Slavery," pp. 5–6.

63. Lincoln to Mary Speed (September 27, 1841*)*, *Lincoln Collected Works*, I, p. 260. Mary Speed was a half-sister to Joshua F. Speed, one of Lincoln's closest friends. She lived on a slave plantation in Kentucky from which Lincoln was returning when he observed the slaves on the riverboat. Donald, *Lincoln*, p. 88.

64. Carwardine, *Life of Purpose and Power*, p. 21; Guelzo, *Abraham Lincoln: Redeemer President*, p. 127; Paludan, "Lincoln and Negro Slavery," p. 7; Bennett, Jr., *Forced Into Glory*, p. 256.

65. Lincoln to Mary Speed (September 27, 1841), *Lincoln Collected Works*, I, p. 260.

66. Ibid.

67. Mary Lincoln to Josiah G. Holland (December 4, 1865), in Turner and Levitt, *Mary Todd Lincoln*, p. 293.

68. Lincoln to Joshua F. Speed (August 24, 1855), *Lincoln Collected Works*, II, p. 320.

69. Ibid. Even Bennett, Jr., concedes that Lincoln's 1855 letter "is strong testimony indicating what seems to be repugnance over 'a thing which has, and continually exercises, the power of making me miserable.'" *Forced into Glory*, p. 258. Fredrickson concludes that "there is no reason to doubt the sincerity of Lincoln's numerous statements, public and private, to the effect that he detested slavery and opposed it in principle." *Big Enough to Be Inconsistent*, p. 81.

70. Steiner, "Abolitionists and Escaped Slaves in Jacksonville," pp. 227–28 (quoting Illinois abolitionist Luther N. Ransom); quoted in Weik, "Lincoln and the Matson Negroes," p. 755.

71. Quoted in Weik, "Lincoln and the Matson Negroes," p. 755.

72. Ibid.

73. Ibid. "[A] peculiarly troubled look came over his face . . . , his eyes appeared to be fixed in the distance . . . , and he shook his head several times as if debating with himself some question of grave import." Ibid.

74. Ibid.

75. Steiner, *An Honest Calling,* p. 70.

76. See p. 40 supra.

77. Joseph Gillespie to William H. Herndon (January 31, 1866), in Wilson and Davis, *Herndon's Informants,* p. 181; Herndon and Weik, *Herndon's Lincoln,* p. 279.

78. One of Lincoln's fellow circuit riders described "the business on the circuit" as "meagre and uninteresting." Whitney, *Life on the Circuit,* p. 63. Lincoln's practice often reflected the predominantly agrarian character of the counties in which he practiced. In the year or so before the Matson case, he was involved in about a dozen cases involving livestock. They ranged from *Borson v. Newman,* in which he represented a man accused of slander for calling another a hog thief, to *Page v. Boyd & Boyd,* in which his clients were sued for negligence in the death of a horse, to *Strader v. Harris,* in which his client was sued for wrongful possession of a horse and a cow. *Borson v. Newman,* Coles County Circuit Court (1846–47), LPAL, File ID L00700; *Page v. Boyd & Boyd,* Menard County Circuit Court (1847), LPAL, File ID L00254; *Strader v. Harris,* Coles County Circuit Court (1847–48), LPAL, File ID L00730.

79. Rutherford quoted in Weik, *Lincoln and the Matson Negroes,* p. 755.

80. Ibid.

81. Ficklin, "A Pioneer Lawyer."

82. See Complaint, *Robert Matson v. Hiram Rutherford,* Coles County Circuit Court (October Term, 1847), Herndon-Weik Collection: Group III, Document Nos. 1949–1953, LOC, Manuscript Division.

83. Wilson, *Encyclopedia pf Illinois and History of Coles County,* p. 648; Coleman, *Lincoln and Coles County,* p. 168.

84. Coleman, *Lincoln and Coles County,* pp. 177, 185, 191–95.

85. Ibid., pp. 234–37. See, e.g., Thomas A. Marshall to Lincoln (February 10, 1861) (preventing the border states from seceding); Thomas A. Marshall to Lincoln (July 27, 1862) (emancipation), The Abraham Lincoln Papers at the Library of Congress, Series I, General Correspondence, 1833–1916, American Memory, found at memory.loc.gov (May 19, 2003).

86. Ibid., p. 168; *History of Coles County,* p. 296; Wilson, *Encyclopedia of Illinois and History of Coles County,* p. 648. Thomas A. Marshall's father, Thomas Alexander Marshall, a justice on the Kentucky Court of Appeals, wrote the opinions in *Strader v. Graham,* 44 Ky. 173, 1844 Ky. LEXIS 103 (1844), and 46 Ky. 633, 1847 Ky. LEXIS 89 (1847). See pp. 83–84 supra.

87. See *Nordyke v. Fleenor,* Coles County Circuit Court (1843), LPAL, File ID L00736; *Frost v. Gillenwaters,* Coles County Circuit Court (1845), LPAL, File ID L00705.

88. Collins, *History of Kentucky,* II, p. 72.

89. Donald, *Lincoln,* pp. 42, 109.

90. Coleman, *Lincoln and Coles County*, p. 168.

91. David Herbert Donald, *"We Are Lincoln Men."*

92. Richard J. Oglesby to William H. Herndon (January 5, 1866), in Wilson and Davis, *Herndon's Informants*, p. 153.

93. Joseph Gillespie to William H. Herndon (December 8, 1866), in Wilson and Davis, *Herndon's Informants*, p. 507.

94. Ninian W. Edwards, interview with William H. Herndon (1865–66), in Wilson and Davis, *Herndon's Informants*, p. 446.

95. Ibid.

96. John T. Stuart, interview with William H. Herndon (late June 1865), in Wilson and Davis, *Herndon's Informants*, p. 63.

97. Ficklin, "A Pioneer Lawyer."

98. Richard J. Oglesby to William H. Herndon (January 5, 1866), in Wilson and Davis, *Herndon's Informants*, p. 153.

99. Coleman, *Lincoln and Coles County*, p. 117. See, e.g., Lincoln to Usher F. Linder (March 8, 1853) and Lincoln to Usher F. Linder (January 13, 1858), *Lincoln Collected Works*, II, pp. 191, 431.

100. Lincoln to Usher F. Linder (February 20, 1848), *Lincoln Collected Works*, I, pp. 453.

101. Lincoln to Usher F. Linder (March 22, 1848), *Lincoln Collected Works*, I, pp. 457–58.

102. Linder, *Reminiscences*, pp. 248–50. Like Ficklin when Lincoln praised his speech in the Matson case, Linder saw Lincoln's comment as "no ordinary compliment coming from Mr. Lincoln, for he was no flatterer." Ibid., p. 249.

103. William A. Bishop and Alexander Dunbar to Lincoln (June 6, 1849), The Abraham Lincoln Papers at the Library of Congress, Series I, General Correspondence, 1833–1916, American Memory, found at memory.loc.gov (January 7, 2009). Dunbar was a Whig who represented Coles County in the Illinois House of Representatives in 1837–38 and 1845–47. Bishop, a Whig, served as a captain in the Mexican War and was the editor of the Charleston *Courier*.

104. Ibid.

105. Lincoln requested "the papers on file" at the department of the Interior that related to his quest for the General Land Office position. Among these was a letter from Cyrus Edwards, whom Lincoln had once supported for the job. The letter, in Lincoln's words, was "against me." Apparently, no such correspondence from Linder turned up. Lincoln to Thomas Ewing (June 22, 1849), *Lincoln Collected Works*, II, p. 55; Lincoln to Joseph Gillespie (July 13, 1849), ibid., p. 57.

106. Quoted in John G. Nicolay and John Hay, eds., *The Complete Works of Abraham Lincoln*, 12 vols. (New York: Francis D. Tandy Company, 1894), II, p. 132, found at Abraham Lincoln Historical Digitization Project, Northern Illinois University Libraries, Northern Illinois University, at http:lincoln.lib.niu.edu (October 19, 2004). Apparently, Lincoln was quite embarrassed by Linder's diatribe. In a letter to the editor of the *Chicago Journal*, he praised the man who received the land office position and described Secretary Ewing as "an able and faithful officer." Lincoln explained that he had been absent from the legislature the day that Linder blasted Ewing and had "the intention of any Whig to deliver such a speech been known to me, I should, to the utmost of my ability, have endeavored to prevent it." Lincoln to editor of *Chicago Journal* (November

21, 1849), Nicolay and Hay, found at *Complete Works of Abraham Lincoln*, II, pp. 131–32, Abraham Lincoln Digitilzation Project, Northern Illinois University Libraries, Northern Illinois, at http://lincoln.lib.niu.edu (October 19, 2004).

107. Quoted in *Lincoln Collected Works*, I, p. 62 n.2.

108. *Chicago Times* (April 19, 1865).

109. Ibid. See also Coleman, *Lincoln and Coles County*, pp. 117–18.

110. Linder, *Reminisences*, p. 79.

111. Ibid.

112. Ibid.

113. Ibid. The appellation became so identified with Linder that his obituary in the *Milwaukee Daily Sentinel* (June 9, 1876) was entitled "For God's Sake Linder." Linder's efforts on behalf of Douglas may not have been motivated solely by political loyalty. He intimated to others that he was "handsomely remunerated or paid for his services." Compton to Lincoln (September 7, 1858), The Abraham Lincoln Papers at the Library of Congress, Series I, General Correspondence, 1833–1916, American Memory, found at memory.loc.gov (February 5, 2009).

114. Coleman, *Lincoln and Coles County*, p. 113.

115. Ibid., p. 120.

116. Linder, *Reminiscences*, introduction by Joseph Gillespie, p. 19.

117. Usher F. Linder to Lincoln (March 26, 1864), The Abraham Lincoln Papers at the Library of Congress, Series 1, General Correspondence, 1836–1916, American Memory, found at memory.loc.gov (May 19, 2003).

118. Lincoln to Edwin M. Stanton (December 26, 1863), *Lincoln Collected Works*, VII, p. 95.

119. *Chicago Times* (April 19, 1865); Lincoln to Usher F. Linder (December 26, 1863), *Lincoln Collected Works*, VII, p. 95.

120. Entry in diary of Edward Bates (December 24, 1863), *Lincoln Collected Works*, XII, p. 91 n. 1. Lincoln did a similar favor for Alexander H. Stephens, vice president of the Confederacy and a man Lincoln admired when the two were Whigs in Congress together. At the ill-fated Hampton Roads peace conference on February 3, 1865, Lincoln promised Stephens that he would parole Stephens's nephew, who was incarcerated in a Union prison camp. The next day, Lincoln made good on his promise. Lincoln to officer in command at Johnson's Island, Ohio (February 4, 1865), *Lincoln Collected Works*, VII, p. 259; Lincoln to Alexander H. Stephens (February 10, 1865), *Lincoln Collected Works*, VII, p. 287.

121. Henry C. Whitney to William H. Herndon (January 23, 1887), in Wilson and Davis, *Herndon's Informants*, p. 617.

122. Coleman, *Lincoln and Coles County*, p. 113.

123. *Chicago Times* (April 19, 1865), ALPL.

124. Henry C. Whitney to William H. Herndon (August 27, 1887), in Wilson and Davis, *Herndon's Informants*, p. 631 (Lincoln "did not drink at all").

125. Linder, *Reminiscences*, p. 396. See also Baringer, *Lincoln's Vandalia*, p. 82; Beveridge, *Abraham Lincoln*, I, p. 180.

126. Linder, *Reminiscences*, introduction by Joseph Gillespie, p. 19.

127. Brattleboro, Vermont, *Weekly Eagle* (December 8, 1851).

128. Linder, *Reminiscences*, introduction by Joseph Gillespie, p. 19.

129. Ibid., p. 18. According to Gillespie, in his introduction to Linder's *Reminiscences*, Lincoln thought Linder "was inimitable in his capacity to talk about everything and

nothing, by the hour." Ibid. Lincoln was bemused by Linder's audacity. John Hay, one of Lincoln's secretaries, in a diary entry dated July 18, 1863, recorded that the president "told one devilish good story about U. F. Linder, getting a fellow off who had stolen a hog, by advising him to go & get a drink suggesting that the water was better in Tennessee...." Michael Burlingame and John R. Turner Ettinger, *Inside Lincoln's White House: The Complete Civil War Diary of John Hay* (Carbondale: Southern Illinois University Press, 1997), p. 64.

130. Dirck, *Lincoln the Lawyer*, pp. 30–31.

131. See p. 39 supra. See also Donald, *"We Are Lincoln Men,"* pp. 73–74, 91; Donald, *Lincoln*, pp. 101–2; Donald, *Lincoln's Herndon*, pp. 65–66; Dirck, *Lincoln the Lawyer*, pp. 30–31.

132. Jesse Weik, *The Real Lincoln: A Portrait* (Boston: Houghton Mifflin Company, 1922), p. 301.

133. Donald, *"We Are Lincoln Men,"* p. 91.

134. See p. 55 supra.

135. Linder, *Reminiscences*, pp. 248–50.

136. Weik, "Lincoln and the Matson Negroes," p. 755.

137. Autobiography written for John L. Scripps (c. June 1861), *Lincoln Collected Works*, IV, p. 67.

138. LPAL, *passim*.

139. The Fugitive Slave Act of 1850 removed state officials from the slave rendition process by providing for federal commissioners to hear fugitive slave cases. In the "summary" proceedings established by the statute, a person claiming a runaway could prove his or her claim to a certificate of removal either by court testimony under oath or by an affidavit sworn to before the claimant's hometown magistrate. The Fugitive Slave Act (September 18, 1850), secs. 1, 5, 6, 10, found at www.yale.edu/lawweb/avalon/fugitive .htm (January 4, 2003).

The strengthened act was a part of the Compromise of 1850, an attempt by the United States Congress to deal with the differences between the North and the South over the place of slavery in the nation. Other statutes passed as part of the compromise provided that Texas, a slave state, receive $10 million to relinquish its claims to part of New Mexico; that the slave trade be abolished in the District of Columbia; that California enter the union as a free state; and that Utah and New Mexico be organized as territories with the question of slavery left open. See David Potter, *The Impending Crisis, 1848–1861* (New York: Harper & Row, 1976), pp. 90–120; Cover, *Justice Accused*, p. 175; Burt, *The Constitution in Crisis*, p. 186.

140. Steiner, *An Honest Calling*, p. 127.

141. Donald, *Lincoln's Herndon*, pp. 48, 106, 134.

142. See, e.g., Carwardine, *Lincoln: A Life of Purpose and Power*, pp. 20–21; Benjamin Quarles, *Lincoln and the Negro* (New York: Oxford University Press, 1962), pp. 30–31; Barry Schwartz, *Abraham Lincoln and the Forge of National Memory* (Chicago: University of Chicago Press, 2000), p. 28.

143. Carwardine, *Lincoln: A Life of Purpose and Power*, p. 20; see also Strickland, "Illinois Background of Lincoln's Attitude Toward Slavery," p. 490; Frederickson, *Big Enough to Be Inconsistent*, p. 43

144. Letter to Joshua F. Speed (August 24, 1855), *Lincoln Collected Works*, II, p. 320. Apparently, Lincoln's representation of Matson never became generally known or grist

for the mill of his enemies. Even the abolitionist Wendell Phillips, who publicly hammered Lincoln as the "slave-Hound of Illinois" for what Phillips saw as Lincoln's support
of the Fugitive Slave Act, never mentioned the case. Liberator (June 22, 1860); Max Skid-
more, "Prominent Abolitionists on Abraham Lincoln," *For the People*, Abraham Lincoln
Association, v. 6 (2004); Donald, *Lincoln*, pp. 137–38.

Post Trial Briefs

1. Bond, *In re Bryant* (October 17, 1847), Coles County Circuit Court, copy in Herndon-Weik Collection: Group III, Document Nos. 1959–1960, LOC, Manuscript Division; LPAL, File ID L00714, Doc. No. 5505.

2. D. T. McIntyre, "History of the Matson Slave Trial in 1847." Weik maintains that
Anthony Bryant, "determined to leave the scene of his troubles," made the decision to
leave for Africa. Weik, "Lincoln and the Matson Negroes," pp. 757–58.

3. Weik, "Lincoln and the Matson Negroes," p. 758. See also "Notes—Oakland (April
4, 1892)," Weik MSS, ALPL.

4. S. S. Ball, *Report on the Condition and Prospects of the Republic of Liberia* (Alton:
Printed at the "Telegraph" Office, 1848), p. 13. Samuel S. Ball was a thirty-five-year-old
barber from Springfield when he made his four-month trip to Liberia. In 1851, he drew
up a bill for the Illinois Legislature proposing that the state support those free blacks
who wished to emigrate to Liberia. Nothing came of his efforts. Hart, "Springfield's African Americans," paragraphs 53–61.

5. Ball, *Report on Liberia*, p. 13

6. Ibid., pp. 13–14. Mary Bryant's brother, Sim Wilmoth, remained in Coles County.
Apparently, he died in about 1890. "Notes—Oakland (April 4, 1892)," Weik MSS, ALPL.

7. "In the Matter of Jane," *Western Law Journal* 5, pp. 202, 203.

8. Quoted in Coleman, *Lincoln and Coles County*, p. 109.

9. ROBERT MATSON ID 1317, "Talley Family," Family Trees, found at www.rootsweb
.com (May 1, 2003).

10. 1850 Census, Fulton County, Kentucky, Reel No. M432-200, p. 1348. U.S. Gen-
Web Archives, found at www.rootsweb.com/genweb/ky/fulton/1850census.htm/ (April
29, 2003).

11. Ibid.

12. "Re Robert Matson c. 1845 Bourbon Co. Ky." posted on Matson Family Genealogy
Forum, GENFORUM, found at www.genealogy.com. (April 29, 2003).

13. ROBERT MATSON ID 1317, "Talley Family," Family Trees, found at www
.rootsweb.com (May 1, 2003). Matson's original headstone, which bears this epitaph, has
been replaced by one apparently obtained from the Veterans Administration. The original, which is damaged, is kept indoors. See www.rootsweb.com/~kyfulton/cemeteries/
matson.html (October 7, 2004).

14. Ibid.

15. Orders, *Matson v. Rutherford* and *Matson v. Ashmore*, Coles County Circuit Court
(May Term 1848), LPAL, File ID L00715, Coc. No. 36865.

16. Coleman, *Lincoln and Coles County*, p. 109.

17. Phoebe Ashmore Barth to Jesse W. Weik (November 20, 1895), Albert J. Beveridge
Papers, No. 728, LOC, Manuscript Division. Mrs. Barth was Ashmore's daughter.

18. Shonna Bercaw, "Dr. Rutherford and the Underground Railroad," found at www
.colescounty.net (October 10, 2002).

19. Ibid.

20. Ibid.; *History of Coles County*, p. 576.

21. Charles H. Constable to Lincoln (May 5, 1849), The Abraham Lincoln Papers at
the Library of Congress, Series 1, General Correspondence, 1833–1916, American Memory, found at memory.loc.gov (May 23, 2003).

22. Quoted in King, *David Davis*, p. 83. Constable also pressed mutual friends into
service on behalf of his search for a place in government. *See* Justin Harlan to Lincoln
(May 3, 1849), The Abraham Lincoln Papers at the Library of Congress, Series 1, General Correspondence, 1833–1916, American Memory, found at memory.loc.gov (May 23,
2003). Harlan was a lawyer who rode the circuit with Lincoln. According to his letter, Constable was "very solicitous to receive an appointment of some kind from which
some money and the more the better, is to follow." Ibid.

23. Lincoln to John M. Clayton (May 13, 1849), *Lincoln Collected Works*, II, p. 48.

24. See Lincoln to James A. Pearce (January 13, 1851), *Lincoln Collected Works*, II, p.
97. Pearce was a United States senator from Maryland. Lincoln's letter was enclosed with
one from David Davis bearing the same date. Ibid., p. 97 n.1.

25. Josiah G. Holland, *Holland's Life of Abraham Lincoln* (1866; Lincoln: University of
Nebraska Press, 1998), pp. 97–98.

26. Quoted in ibid.

27. Quoted in King, *David Davis*, p. 83; Lincoln to Lyman Trumbull (June 7, 1856),
Lincoln Collected Works, II, p. 342.

28. *Historical Encyclopedia of Illinois*, p. 117.

29. Anthony Thornton quoted in Linder, *Reminiscences*, p. 238. See also *Historical
Encyclopedia of Illinois*, p. 117.

30. Davidson and Stuve, *Complete History of Illinois*, p. 891; Frank L. Klement, *The
Copperheads in the Middle West* (Chicago: University of Chicago Press, 1960), p. 69.

31. *Historical Encyclopedia of Illinois*, p. 117

32. Davidson and Stuve, *Complete History of Illinois*, p. 891.

33. Ibid.; Klement, *The Copperheads in the Middle West*, p. 70.

34. Moses, *Illinois Historical and Statistical*, II, pp. 687–88; Charles H. Coleman and
Paul Spence, "The Charleston Riot, March 28, 1864," *Journal of the Illinois State Historical Society* 33 (1940), p. 4.

35. Coleman and Spence, "The Charleston Riot," p. 15.

36. Ibid., pp. 18–20; Coleman, *Lincoln and Coles County*, p. 226. The soldiers may
have been looking for trouble. Reportedly, some of them had said that they planned to
pay a visit to Charleston to "clean up that Butternut [southern sympathizing] court."
Coleman and Spence, "The Charleston Riot," p. 18.

37. Coleman and Spence, "The Charleston Riot," p. 24; Coleman, *Lincoln and Coles
County*, p. 226. Constable took no part in the melee. He merely tried to get out of the
way, seeking refuge in an alley on the east side of the town square. "[W]hite and trem-
bling," he was spotted by two small boys who, until their dying days, remained amazed
"how a man of his portly form" could have departed the bench, exited the courtroom,
and deposited himself in the alley so quickly. Coleman and Spence, "The Charleston
Riot," p. 26.

38. Coleman and Spence, "The Charleston Riot," pp. 44–45.

39. Coleman, *Lincoln and Coles County*, p. 157. In his memoirs, Linder is very mysterious about the circumstances of Constable's death: "He departed this life some years ago, and the manner of his departure I shall not dwell upon. It was sad, but not dishonorable; and I do not believe that he left a single stain, blemish or blot." Linder, *Reminiscences,* p. 283.

40. Ficklin, "A Pioneer Lawyer."

41. Coleman, *Lincoln and Coles County,* p. 113; *History of Coles County*, p. 520; Bateman, Selby, and Curry, *Historical Encyclopedia of Illinois*, p. 164.

42. *History of Coles County*, p. 286.

43. Ibid.

44. Ficklin had a bit part in the Lincoln-Douglas debates. Douglas stayed at his house to prepare for the debate in Charleston on September 18, 1858. Coleman, *Lincoln and Coles County*, p. 177. During the course of that debate, Lincoln was faced with allegations that, while a congressman, he had voted against providing supplies for American troops during the Mexican War. Lincoln responded in what one newspaper remarked was "an entirely original, but it must be conceded, very effective manner." *Chicago Democrat* (September 22, 1858), quoted in Edwin Earle Sparks, *The Lincoln-Douglas Debates of 1858*, Collections of the Illinois State Historical Library 1 (Springfield: Illinois State Historical Society, 1908), p. 317. After explaining that he merely had taken the orthodox Whig position on the war itself, Lincoln "turned to Hon. O. B. Ficklin who was sitting upon the stand, and seizing him by the collar dragged him by main force before the audience, saying 'now, Mr. Ficklin, you sat by my side the whole time I was in Congress, and know very well every speech and vote given by me. Now, sir, I want you to tell this audience, the whole truth of the matter.'" Ibid. Ficklin responded that he could say only that he considered both Lincoln and Douglas "good personal friends" and that as best he could recall, Lincoln had voted for a Whig resolution "that the Mexican War was unconstitutional and unconstitutionally commenced by the President." Quoted in Coleman, *Lincoln and Coles County*, pp. 182–83.

45. *History of Coles County*, p. 520; *Historical Encyclopedia of Illinois*, I, p. 164.

46. Orlando B. Ficklin to William H. Herndon (June 25, 1865), Wilson and Davis, *Herndon's Informants*, p. 58.

47. Orlando B. Ficklin to [?] (December 7, 1862), Orlando R. Ficklin MSS Collection, ALPL.

48. Ibid.

49. Ibid.

50. Moses, *Illinois: Historical and Statistical*, pp. 687–88; Coleman and Spence, "The Charleston Riot," p. 4.

51. Coleman, *Lincoln and Coles County*, p. 227.

52. See Orlando B. Ficklin to Lincoln (July 22, 1864), The Abraham Lincoln Papers at the Library of Congress, Series 1, General Correspondence, 1833–1916, American Memory, found at memory.loc.gov (May 19, 2003). It is not clear whether or not Ficklin and Lincoln ever met face to face to discuss the issue. Ficklin asked Lincoln's friend Thomas A. Marshall to write to the president on the prisoners' behalf. Marshall did so. See Orlando B. Ficklin to Lincoln (September 10, 1864), The Abraham Lincoln Papers at The Library of Congress, Series 1, General Correspondence, 1833–1916, American Memory, found at memory.loc.gov (May 20, 2003). Marshall's letter refers to the request by "[o]ur old friend Ficklin," and pragmatically argues that "[m]ost of [the prisoners] are

poor miserable devils" who should be turned over to the civil authorities because "none of them are of sufficient consequence to be made state prisoners of." Thomas A. Marshall to Lincoln (August 23, 1864), The Abraham Lincoln Papers at the Library of Congress, Series 1, General Correspondence, 1833–1916, American Memory, found at memory.loc .gov (May 19, 2003).

53. Order Concerning Prisoners from Coles County, Illinois (November 4, 1864), *Lincoln Collected Works*, VIII, p. 90.

54. Bateman, Selby, and Curry, *Historical Encyclopedia of Illinois*, I, p. 164.

55. Quoted in Hendrick, *Rutherford*, p. 142. According to the *St. Louis Globe-Democrat* (March 8, 1886), "excursions were run on the railroad" to Ficklin's funeral "and a very large attendance was present."

56. Brattleboro (Vermont) *Weekly Eagle* (December 8, 1851).

57. Whitney, *Riding the Circuit*, p. 180.

58. Quoted in Lusk, *Eighty Years of Illinois Politics*, p. 416.

59. Ibid.

60. Ibid.

61. Ibid., p. 417.

62. Quoted in King, *David Davis*, p. 83. Unchastened, Linder reportedly replied to the judge, who weighed over three hundred pounds: "And I must give your Honor some advice and [in the flattest term] eliminate more or you will bust." Ibid.

63. Coleman, *Lincoln and Coles County*, p. 120.

64. See p. 100 supra.

65. E. B. Linder and D. W. Linder to Jesse Weik (September 3, 1895), Herndon-Weik Papers, LOC, Manuscript Division.

66. Linder, *Reminiscences*, p. 223.

67. Usher F. Linder to Lincoln (March 26, 1864), The Abraham Lincoln Papers at the Library of Congress, Series 1, General Correspondence, 1833–1916, American Memory, found at memory.loc.gov (May 19, 2003).

68. Ibid.

69. Palmer, *The Bench and Bar of Illinois*, p. 658.

70. *Chicago Times* (April 19, 1865), ALPL.

71. Linder, *Reminiscences*, p. 397.

72. James G. Randall, ed., *The Diary of Orville Hickman Browning*, 2 vols. (Springfield: Illinois State Historical Library, 1933), II, p. 381 (April 23, 1874).

73. Duff, *A. Lincoln: Prairie Lawyer*, p. 132.

74. Linder, *Reminiscences*, p. 371.

75. Ibid.

76. Ibid., p. 104.

77. Ibid., p. 396. Apparently, Linder had forgotten about the innocent man he sent to prison when he was Illinois attorney general. See p. 51 supra.

INDEX